The Learning Powered School

Pioneering 21st Century Education

Guy Claxton
Maryl Chambers
Graham Powell
Bill Lucas

TLO Limited,
Bristol

First published in Great Britain in 2011,
by TLO Limited, Bristol.

Reprinted 2013.

ISBN 978-1-901219-54-8

Foreword

It is a strange irony that in the face of substantial international evidence that schooling is out of step with the needs of society, there are so few signs of real change. Despite this powerful evidence, education systems around the world are proving deeply resistant to change, change that is needed, as this book makes abundantly clear, if young people are to be prepared adequately to live happily and productively in the twenty-first century. Young people need to be helped to build up the mental, emotional and social resources to enjoy challenge and cope well with uncertainty and complexity. And learning, so the research tells us, is one of human beings' deepest sources of happiness and satisfaction. Yet in the UK, as the authors of *The Learning Powered School* point out, over 200,000 persistent truants regularly miss a day a week of school. More than a quarter of pupils in Years 9, 10 and 11 actively dislike school. What has gone wrong? And more importantly, how on earth can we put it right? *The Learning Powered School* provides much needed answers to these urgent questions.

First, the book shows us the science, and clarifies the vision of twenty-first century education that the new sciences of learning are helping to underpin. No engineer would dream of attempting to design a bridge without due regard to the relevant design principles. So, quite rightly, *The Learning Powered School* starts from first principles. Contrary to the pervasive but erroneous idea that an individual's ability is fixed, we now know, for example, that the brain is like a muscle, in that its intelligence grows with exercise. Selling this idea to learners and their teachers could, in itself, cause a major shift in the prevailing educational axis. How much more learning of all kinds, how much more enthusiasm for engaging with the potential delights of learning, would be generated if all young people understood that learning is learnable; that their horizons are not fixed? The authors quote the work of Professor John Hattie whose comprehensive review of research has shown that helping pupils become more independent, more reflective, and better able to plan and evaluate their own learning, turns out to be a better way of boosting their attainment than drilling them in the subject-matter.

Research also shows that the language we use to talk about education and learning deeply affects how individuals see themselves as learners. Even something as simple as changing 'is' to 'could' or talking in the classroom about 'learning' rather than 'work' can make a difference. The Building Learning Power (BLP) approach which the book describes offers teachers and pupils alike a rich vocabulary for thinking and talking about what learners actually do, and this in itself enables them to expand their capacity and appetite for learning.

Having laid the scientific foundations, *The Learning Powered School* quickly gets down to the job of outlining a plausible and practical way forward. Mercifully, the solutions offered do not depend on convincing politicians or waiting for high-level policy changes. Nor does the BLP approach depend, to get going, on the availability of expensive resources. The great strength of BLP is that any teacher who is convinced by the evidence so powerfully presented in this book will be able to get started immediately. Indeed, the book's main focus is on a wealth of tried and tested strategies that teachers and school leaders can introduce today to begin to transform the learning experience of their pupils.

The experiences of the schools that have been using BLP principles and practices over recent years, clearly documented here, show that this is not a high risk strategy as far as results are concerned. In giving pupils a language with which to think about the process of learning; in giving teachers strategies to encourage their pupils to become more engaged and more effective in their learning, BLP provides a 'both / and' solution with which it would be hard for anyone to disagree. Teachers boost the development of students' confidence, capacity and appetite for learning itself, as well as helping young people to achieve as well as they can in terms of more conventional syllabus content. Students get a better preparation for life and improved examination performance—a seductive package indeed.

I challenge anyone to read this book and not find themselves convinced that the world of education is at a cross-roads. The choice is not whether to teach students Shakespeare or furnish them with skills for life; it is whether to join the growing army of teachers and educationists who are developing the 'both / and' approach, or not. One road perpetuates the sterile debate between 'traditionalists' and 'progressives' that is still largely characterised by nineteenth century attitudes and prejudices. The other road is shaped by science. It is a road that is built on the substantial evidence now emerging about what learning is and how it can best be fostered. It is a road out of the cul-de-sac of assessment-driven schools and a performance culture that produces 'teaching to the test' and dependent, passive learners—high and low-achievers alike—who frequently lack resilience and real-world intelligence.

The Learning Powered School is a unique book. It speaks in a voice that is at once authoritative, visionary, engaging and accessible. Its message is passionate and urgent, its intellectual underpinnings are beyond reproach, and its multitude of suggestions for action are imaginative, practical and tested by real teachers in real schools. In a globalised world characterised by rapid change and technological innovation, in which young people have few certainties about their futures; in which most people will have several careers; in which we are faced with some of the gravest international challenges ever to face mankind, it is vital that our young people are equipped with the values, the insights and the skills they will need to navigate their way through the jungle of opportunities and threats. The authors of *The Learning Powered School* are true pioneers; leaders of a growing band of innovators who have shown that an alternative is not only possible, it can be realised now.

Professor Patricia Broadfoot CBE

Acknowledgments

There are many people we would like to thank for making this book possible.

Dr Ian Millward. Ian was until April 2010 Principal Educational Psychologist for the London Borough of Newham and is now an Honorary Research Fellow at the University of Winchester, attached to the Centre for Real-World Learning. An enormously experienced and respected psychologist, Ian visited the majority of the schools, helped to design the research questionnaires and the semi-structured interview protocols as well undertaking the bulk of the data analysis.

Dr Ellen Hodgkinson. Ellen has recently completed her PhD at the University of Warwick Business School. Ellen is currently a Researcher at the Centre for Real-World Learning, working on research projects exploring studio learning, practical learning and the assessment of creativity in schools. Ellen visited schools whose headteachers had been amongst our longest-standing colleagues.

Judith Mortell, from the Borough of Kingston-upon-Thames, for her help in developing the LPQ as part of research for her doctorate in educational psychology dissertation at the Tavistock Institute in London.

All the BLP schools who took part in our research survey for this book:

Bay House School, Gosport
Dr Challoner's Grammar School, Amersham
George Pindar Community Sports College, Scarborough
Landau Forte College, Derby
Park High School, Harrow
Park View Community School, Chester-le-Street
St Paul's Catholic High School, Milton Keynes
Walthamstow School for Girls
Westcliff High School for Girls

Bransgore C of E Primary School, Dorset
Bushfield School, Milton Keynes
Eastway Primary School, Wirral
Mosborough Primary School, Sheffield
Nayland Primary School, Suffolk
Princeville Primary School, Bradford
St Mary's CE Primary School, Swanley, Kent
Simpson School, Milton Keynes

And the staff and students at the many other schools who have taken part in the work described in the book.

Thanks finally to Brian Davies for design and desk-top publishing of this book and for working through innumerable drafts in challenging circumstances.

About the Authors

Guy Claxton is Co-Director of the Centre for Real-World Learning (CrL) and Professor of the Learning Sciences at the University of Winchester. He previously held the latter title at the University of Bristol Graduate School of Education. He is a Fellow of the British Psychological Society and the Royal Society of Arts, and an Academician of the Academy of the Social Sciences. Guy is the originator of the Building Learning Power programme.

Maryl Chambers has spearheaded practical development of the Building Learning Power programme for TLO Limited, helping to bring Guy Claxton's ground-breaking ideas to schools and teachers. Maryl is one of the founders of TLO, where she has applied her wide experience of designing learning-focused training to creating the innovative programmes for which the company is renowned. She is editor-in chief of all, and co-author of many, of TLO's publications.

Graham Powell has been a Principal Consultant with TLO since 2000. He previously held posts of responsibility at all levels within comprehensive schools, including as headteacher of a large secondary school in Wiltshire, and was senior secondary inspector with Gloucestershire LEA. In recent years, he has established a widespread reputation for his work on coaching and the ways in which this essential leadership quality can radically improve schools at all levels.

Bill Lucas is Co-Director of the Centre for Real-World Learning and Professor of Learning at the University of Winchester. He has been a school leader, the founding director of Learning through Landscapes, and CEO of the UK's Campaign for Learning. Bill is a prolific author whose recent titles include: *rEvolution* (which won the Innovation category in CMI Management Book of the Year) and *New Kinds of Smart* (with Guy Claxton).

Contents

Introduction

Introducing *The Learning Powered School*

In this chapter we:

- introduce Building Learning Power
- explain its core beliefs and research roots
- give an overview of BLP's reach and practice
- outline the structure of the following chapters

What is Building Learning Power?

Building Learning Power is an approach to helping young people to become better learners, both in school and out. It is about creating a culture in classrooms—and in the school more widely—that systematically cultivates habits and attitudes that enable young people to face difficulty and uncertainty calmly, confidently, and creatively. Students who are more confident of their own learning ability learn faster and learn better. They concentrate more, think harder, and find learning more enjoyable. They do better in their tests and external examinations. And they are easier and more satisfying to teach.

Building Learning Power—BLP for short—is an attempt to refocus schools on preparing youngsters better for an uncertain future. Today's schools need to be educating not just for exam results but for lifelong learning. To thrive in the twenty-first century, it is not enough to leave school with a clutch of examination certificates. Pupils need to have learnt how to be tenacious and resourceful, imaginative and logical, self disciplined and self-aware, collaborative and inquisitive.[1]

Five core beliefs for a big ambition

There are five core beliefs that underpin this focus.

The tests of life

The **first** is that the core purpose of education is to prepare young people for life after school; to get them ready, as Art Costa, an American educator with similar views, says, 'not just for a life of tests, but for the tests of life'. We think this means helping them build up the mental, emotional, and social resources to enjoy challenge and cope well with uncertainty and complexity. If you strip away political dogma, the evidence is overwhelming that this aim is not currently being achieved for very many students. Of course, this has to be done in a way that also develops literacy and numeracy, and gets young people the best test results possible. That is the challenge that BLP schools and teachers are willing to take up.

A spirit of resourcefulness and resilience

Second, we believe that this is a goal that is valuable for all young people. Not all youngsters are going to do well in exams; that is a statistical certainty. So there has to be another outcome that is useful and relevant to those who are going to flip burgers and clean offices, fix cars and cut hair, as well as those who are going to plead cases in court or prescribe medications. We think this involves helping young people discover the things that they'd really love to be great at, and to strengthen the will and the skill to pursue them. BLP schools aim to build that spirit of resilience and resourcefulness in all their students.

Third, we think this aim is particularly relevant in societies, like ours, that are full of change, complexity, risk, opportunity, and individual responsibility for making your own way in life. In our grandparents' day, many youngsters knew pretty clearly what their role and station in life was destined to be—miner, housewife, priest, primary school teacher. Not any more. In the swirling currents of today's world, many youngsters are at sea. And that makes them anxious, angry, confused, and vulnerable. That is the lack that BLP aims to put right.

Confident in a changing world

Fourth, we believe that 99% of all young people are capable of developing this confidence, capability, and passion. We think that our society's notion of 'ability' has been too closely tied to academic achievement, and to the assumption that some youngsters have got a lot of that sort of ability, and some not very much. We think that real-world intelligence is broader than that, and that it is not fixed at birth, but something that people can be helped to build up. The aim of BLP is to generate and broadcast practical ideas about how to expand real-world intelligence more and more effectively.

Intelligence is learnable

And **fifth**, we don't think that this challenge has been anywhere near met yet. There has been a lot of talk globally about lifelong learning and the 'wider skills' or 'key competencies' for life. But much of it has been at the level of wishful thinking and vague exhortation, or simplistic 'hints and tips' that don't get close to doing the job that needs to be done. We think what's needed has to be seen as a gradual, sometimes difficult, but hugely worthwhile process of culture change by schools and habit change by teachers.

BLP is vital, difficult and do-able

The depth and challenge of what is involved, if we are genuinely to deliver on this big ambition, has been widely underestimated. BLP schools have been pioneering ways of taking this ambition really seriously. We think it is time to move from vision statements and soundbites to sustainability and precision.

Achieving the ambition: vital, difficult and do-able

This book shares with you the fruits of these endeavours so far. A good deal has been learned over the last decade about how to do this well—and about how not to do it! We know from what schools tell us that the ambition is achievable. As well as stories of success we have gathered cautionary tales, because the latter can be helpful and instructive. And a great deal more remains to be discovered. BLP is a journey of exploration, not a neat glossy package. It is a set of practical ideas, frameworks, and resources generated by schools and teachers willing to take these aims seriously and try them out.

We have been privileged to work, over those ten-plus years, with some superb teachers and headteachers, schools and local authorities, some of whose journeys you will read about in the pages that follow. They have generated and trialled all kinds of ideas, and have helped us to pull them together and present them in ways that other hard-working teachers will, we hope, find practical and inspiring. But it has to be said that those schools, adventurous and pioneering though they are, will always be the first to admit that they are still achieving only a fraction of what they now believe is possible. The journey deepens and becomes more exciting as you go along.

A journey of exploration

BLP is definitely not for those who want a quick fix. It demands of schools exactly the same kinds of resilience and resourcefulness that they are aiming to strengthen in their students. They have to be willing to keep going even though some teachers—and indeed some students—may not like it or 'get it' to begin with. There may well be rational scepticism, or even reflex cynicism, to be overcome. Is BLP, as someone put it, 'just another bloody initiative'? There are legitimate worries about whether the exam results might be put at risk, whether parents will appreciate what is going on, or whether the local authority or Ofsted (or similar regulators across the world) might disapprove. Leaders have to know their school communities well, in order to judge best how to challenge and reassure in the right measure: where they can push and take a few risks, and where they will have to be patient and prepare the ground more slowly. All of these issues, and many more, will be aired in the pages that follow.

Taking it up: doing it right

So far, thousands of schools and classrooms around the planet have experimented with BLP. Some of them, like Red Beach School in New Zealand or Park View Community School in County Durham, have really 'got the bug' and deeply embedded the principles of BLP in every aspect of school life. In such schools, you can find the spirit and language of BLP in the way reports are written, the way teachers talk to each other and plan their lessons, the kinds of work that is displayed on the walls, and the way the pupils ask questions, face difficulty, and work together. Some have had more of a 'dabble', and adopted some techniques that are still rather on the surface. Others have assimilated ideas from BLP into different frameworks—'personal learning and thinking skills', 'social and emotional aspects of learning' or 'key competencies', for example—or into the general ethos of the school, in a way that takes up some of the spirit of BLP but no longer calls it that. All of this we think is fine, and there are stories of all three kinds here.

Some have dabbled

Some have 'got the bug'

Whole-school experiences

Sometimes BLP gets taken up by enthusiastic individuals or groups of teachers in places that have not taken it on as a whole-school or college-wide project. This was more likely in the early days. Now we work mostly with schools where there is a collective will—or at least the senior leadership team wants there to be—to adopt the aims and principles of BLP across the whole community. It is these whole-school experiences that we are concentrating on in this book, so one of its main audiences, we hope, will be school leaders who are interested to know what the BLP journey might look like, what are the benefits and outcomes, and what are some of the pot-holes in the road that they could usefully avoid.

A collective will

Classroom culture

BLP is about culture change in schools. By a 'culture' we mean all the little habits and practices that implicitly convey 'what we believe and value round here'. The fact that Art occupies a fraction of the time devoted to Maths, or the emphasis on 'target grades' in school reports, tell you more, we think, about the culture of a school than does its Vision Statement. The medium of a school is its most powerful message. And the most important messages are conveyed to students in classrooms. Classrooms are the places where, hour after hour, students experience the values and practices that are embodied in the school, rather than just the ones that are espoused. We have learned that you can't make young people into powerful, proactive, independent learners by pinning up a few posters, or by delivering a stand-alone course on 'learning to learn' in Year 7. Unless you can actually see and hear the commitment to the development of students' learning capacities in the middle of a routine Year 9 lesson on simultaneous equations, or a Year 4 project on the Vikings, we don't think that the teachers have really 'got BLP' yet.

Culture change

So the heart of BLP concerns the details of the micro-climate that teachers create in their classrooms. What they do and say, what they notice and commend and what they don't, what kind of role model of a learner they offer: all these are of the essence. And especially what matters is how they design and present activities so that, over the course of a term or a year, their students are cumulatively getting a really good all-round mental work-out. All the learning bits of their brains are being stretched and strengthened, one by one and all together. As you will see, BLP teachers tend to get quite specific about what the elements that go to make up a 'powerful learner' actually are, and how they can best be exercised. We want this book to be of as much interest to classroom teachers as to school leaders.

All-round mental work-outs

5

Involving everyone

Anyone can be a role
model of learning

But BLP really takes root in a school when the whole community supports the vision and finds ways of helping to make it real. We have found that teaching assistants of all kinds can play a vital role. So do the administrative staff in the school. People who type letters or look after the buildings can be powerful role models of learning. Support from governors really helps to reassure heads and their staff that these ideas, though some of them might be a little strange at first, are worth trying out. Parents obviously play a vital role in supporting the school, and also in directly encouraging their children to persist in the face of difficulty, and to realise for themselves when they need help and when they don't. We have a growing body of knowledge about how schools can work with parents to forge stronger partnerships. And where schools feel they also have the sympathetic support of local authorities, they may feel free to be more adventurous, and so progress a bit quicker on their journey. Thus we hope this book will also be read by support staff, governors, parents, and local authority officers.

Convincing others

Finally, we would like national educational bodies to take more note of the things we are finding out. In England, that would mean Ofsted, the Department for Education, civil servants and government ministers, and the headteacher and teacher unions. Many of these bodies retain an overriding concern with 'standards', traditionally defined. They still measure the success of education largely in terms of literacy scores and examination grades—though many of them also bemoan the fact that there is too much 'spoon-feeding', or worry about the many bright students who struggle when they get to university because they have never learned how to manage their own learning.

An interim survey
of evidence

If these bodies could be convinced that there were smart practical things that schools could do that both increased the test scores and helped students develop positive attitudes towards learning more widely, how could they possibly not approve? Though we don't yet have a large-scale evaluation of BLP, we have sufficient evidence from schools to persuade us that this 'both/and' philosophy is an achievable reality. *The Learning Powered School* is an interim survey of that evidence, and we hope that these national organisations will indeed find enough here to make them take note.

The roots of BLP

BLP has three major root systems that nurture and stabilise it.

A vision of education

The first, which we have already identified, is a well-articulated vision of twenty-first century education. This vision (which we will explore in more detail in Chapter 1) grows out of the real demands, risks, and opportunities of the twenty-first century. It is appealing and accessible to all young people, not just the academically 'able' or inclined. It values, in reality as well as in rhetoric, more kinds of outcomes than literacy, numeracy, and examination grades.

Practitioner research

Secondly, BLP is grounded in the reality of schools and classrooms: in what busy teachers find it possible, practical, and interesting to try out. We strongly encourage teachers to see themselves as research partners with us, and where possible to record and write up their experiments as small action research projects, recording answers to the questions, 'What was I trying to achieve?', 'What was the status quo I was trying to improve upon?', 'What did I actually do?', 'What effects did I observe?', and 'What did I learn that I can take forward and try to develop even further?'. We have worked with a range of local authorities, including Cardiff, Oxfordshire and Milton Keynes, to enable groups of teachers to explore and record their BLP experiments in this way, as well as with a large number of individual schools and teachers. These teacher-researcher projects produce what David Hargreaves has called 'research with a small r'. This kind of research often has more effect on changing the practice of other teachers than more formal evaluative kinds of research, published in peer-reviewed education journals, which we might call 'research with a middle-sized r'. Hargreaves argues that both are needed, and we agree. However, it is only now that BLP practice is becoming mature, wide-spread and clearly-specified enough to submit to more comprehensive evaluation, and we are only just beginning this phase of the journey.

Teacher research projects

Fundamental scientific research into the nature of learning

Scientific Research

The third root system that underpins BLP is the more fundamental scientific Research with a capital R. It is only in the last ten years or so that a number of disciplines have come together under the banner of 'the learning sciences'. Geneticists such as Robert Plomin are now helping us move beyond the sterile 'nature versus nurture' debate and find out how heredity and experience work together to develop ability. Work in psychology by people like Carol Dweck and David Perkins is also focusing on the learnability of

intelligence, and showing how cognitive abilities, personality, and belief systems all weave together to shape the development of a person's intelligence. Developmental psychologists such as Howard Gardner have opened up our understanding of different types of intelligence, showing that academic ability is only one kind of 'smart', and, in real life, not always the most relevant kind. Neuroscientists like Chris Frith and Jean Decety have been using neuro-imaging techniques to investigate (among many other things) the way brains pick up mental and emotional habits from each other, and making us think about the important role teachers have in modelling learning to their students. Sociocultural researchers like Jean Lave and Barbara Rogoff have revealed how people work together to share and enhance each others' learning capability. Even academic philosophers like Daniel Dennett and Andy Clark are giving us food for thought, in Clark's case by showing how important tools are for learning, and how people can learn to amplify their own learning ability by hooking up with all kinds of smart devices—and by no means only digital ones. All of this and much more is shaping a new image of the malleability of young minds, and BLP tries to make as much use of these ideas as possible.

Taken together, we think these three root systems provide BLP with a strong and stable foundation. BLP has a well-articulated and defensible vision, a philosophy of education for the twenty-first century. It takes a clear stand on what schools ought to be doing. And it has a strong basis in different kinds of scientific research with a small and a large R. This book focuses on the practitioner evidence base and the practical suggestions for school improvement to which it has led. If you would like to read more about the roots of BLP, the vision and philosophy have been laid out in Guy Claxton's *What's the Point of School?* [2] and the scientific foundations are explored in Guy Claxton's *Wise Up*,[3] and Bill Lucas and Guy Claxton's *New Kinds of Smart*.[4]

BLP so far

Types of schools

In the eight years or so since *Building Learning Power* was published, with the enthusiastic participation of an ever-growing number of teachers, we have built up an array of resources to help schools implement BLP ideas, as well as a worldwide network of schools who are sharing ideas and helping to produce further resources. To date, we know of schools using BLP principles and frameworks in New Zealand, Australia, Thailand, Singapore, Malaysia, Philippines, South Africa, Dubai, Abu Dhabi, Albania, Sweden, Argentina, Chile, Bermuda, and the USA. In the UK we are in touch with schools using BLP in all four of the constituent countries from Belfast to Suffolk, Selkirk to Cardiff, and the Isle of Man to the Isles of Scilly. This book contains many of their stories

Examples from schools

Encouragingly, schools are finding BLP practical and useful with all ages, subjects and 'abilities'. They include special schools, infant, primary and comprehensive schools, grammar schools, academies and independent schools, as well as schools with 'serious weaknesses' or in 'special measures'. You could see BLP at work in Dhoon Primary School, a tiny school on the Isle of Man; George Pindar Community Sports College in a seriously deprived area of Scarborough; Dr Challoner's Grammar School, a high-achieving grammar school in Amersham; Simpson School in Milton Keynes, where a good many of the children still live in construction workers' prefabs that were condemned twenty years ago; and The Scots College, an independent boys' school in Sydney, Australia.

Useful in all types of school

We have worked with departments and teachers of maths, science, English, history, PE, design technology, art, drama, music, ICT, modern foreign languages, and religious studies. There is growing interest from further education and sixth form colleges, who are discovering that it is never too late to start building students' learning power. We have helped a number of local authorities to spread BLP across their schools, including Milton Keynes, Solihull, and the London Boroughs of Barnet and Ealing. We are just helping to develop the first school-based initial teacher training course that uses BLP principles. And we are currently also working with the armed forces, the Football Association and with centres of outdoor education to see how they, in their more practical settings, can help young people develop the habits of mind of disciplined exploration more effectively.

Working in many settings

The BLP network

BLP brings together schools and teachers who like the vision, want to work it as deeply as they can into their schools and classrooms, and are keen to help develop the precision and practicality of it in a wide variety of different contexts. There is no formal membership; schools participate as much or as little as they choose.[5] At the hub of this network there is a small training and publishing company, TLO Limited, which coordinates the work of the network, and collects and distils all the various experiences into useful resources to feed back to existing and new members of the network.

The Learning
Organisation

These resources include a number of publications; DVDs of ideas for creating BLP classrooms; local networks in various parts of the world coordinated by designated 'hub schools'; a team of teachers who have considerable experience with the implementation of BLP and can act as advisers and consultants to schools; and perhaps most importantly a variety of courses, workshops and seminars which offer stimulus and support to schools at various stages of their journey.

A helping hand

BLP people

We find that people attracted to BLP tend to share a number of traits. They are:

- Reflective and honest about their own practice
- Enthusiastic but discerning consumers of new ideas
- Open-minded and willing to try something out and 'give it a go' if it makes sense
- Patient: they know they are on for the long haul and aren't interested in a quick fix or something merely to get a badge for, or brag about
- Resilient: they don't give up quickly in the face of setbacks, but 'try it another way'
- Inclined to be open with their students about what they are trying to do, and to involve them in reflecting on and customising the way teaching and learning happens in their classrooms
- Collaborative and generous with each other about their thoughts and ideas

Researching this book

For ten years we have been going into schools, sitting in lessons, talking to teachers, and watching students' reactions. But the preparation of this book has given us an opportunity to undertake more systematic evaluation of BLP in action. We asked twenty schools we had worked with—roughly half primary and half secondary—if they would allow a researcher to come in for a day and take stock of how BLP had influenced the practices and outcomes of their school. In almost every case, they had been working with the ideas for two years or more and the schools we selected span different parts of the country, rural, suburban and inner-city environments, different demographics and different levels of attainment.

On all of our research visits to the schools, we gathered as much documentary evidence as possible about the role of BLP in the school, and its effects on the pupils' behaviour and performance. Obviously, we were keen to know if there had been any improvements to students' levels of achievement, attendance, and engagement since they started using BLP. If there were, we asked to what extent the school attributed these changes to BLP, and tried to evaluate the evidence they were using to justify their answers. We interviewed those who had been most involved in the development of BLP about their experience, and especially about lessons they had learned along the way about how—and how not—to implement BLP well. We asked to observe a lesson or two to observe the ways in which BLP was being used. And we asked to talk to some students about how they saw BLP, and whether they felt it was helping them to become more confident and resourceful learners, both in school and, more importantly, outside. We also tried to talk to a few parents and governors to get their impressions.

As you will see, BLP has evolved into a longitudinal and multi-layered culture change process. We do not believe that anything more short-term, or more simplistic, can really change students' mental habits and attitudes towards learning. It is also very easy for quicker 'initiatives' to flare up and then fizzle out after the initial enthusiasm wears off, or when key personnel move on. We want BLP principles to get so deeply into the lifeblood of a school that it will be resistant to such factors.

The problem is that such long-term, multi-layered change is hard to evaluate. Many other factors are also changing in the life of a school over the same period. And if your 'intervention' involves changing a whole range of things at once, you cannot tell which of them, or what combination, is the cause of any effects you observe. Nevertheless, we think that, taken together, the information and the narratives which we present here add up to an irresistibly powerful endorsement of BLP and its effects on young people. BLP is not snake oil; it is not a remedy for all educational ills. Some young people are hard to reach whatever you do, and so are some teachers. Schools are complicated places, and histories and personalities always loom large. But we are convinced that we are well on the way towards discovering how to make the vision into a reality. We hope you will be too.

A powerful endorsement of the effects of BLP on young people

How the book is organised

BLP has many different layers. And like a piece of plywood, the layers need to be strongly glued together to create maximum strength. So with this metaphor in mind, here is the structure of the rest of the book. Each chapter explores one of these layers.

The first three layers represent the background conditions for developing a learning-powered school.

PART 1

1. Vision: deepening the sense of why teaching for learning power is so timely and important—economically, socially, and in terms of individual well-being. Without this underpinning of clear values, commitment in the school tends to be weaker and more vulnerable in the face of competing demands.

Timely and important

2. Science: understanding what learning power involves, and knowing the evidence that supports the idea that each element of learning power is important, and capable of being cultivated and developed. Without this foundation layer, other more familiar ways of thinking about young people and their potential can creep back and further undermine commitment.

Understanding the science

3. Beliefs and assumptions: facing and challenging common assumptions about school, learning, and young minds that can be quite engrained and pervasive, although contrary to current scientific understanding. Without the vigilance of this layer, it is easy to think that BLP is (a) pie in the sky, (b) jeopardising to existing levels of achievement, or (c) something we are doing perfectly well already.

PART 2

The next four layers describe the activities at the day-to-day heart of a learning-powered school, and the steps that teachers can take to make these a natural part of their practice.

A learning language

4. Talking—and walking—the talk: encouraging teachers to use a language to talk to and about young people which supports their development as powerful learners; and to exemplify the traits of an effective learner in their dealings with students. Without this unifying layer, new intentions can remain rhetorical or cosmetic, and not permeate the culture.

What teachers do differently

5. Teaching and the classroom: designing learning activities that deliberately stretch and exercise the full range of learning-oriented habits of mind; providing increasing opportunities for students to design and direct their own learning; and using the physical environment to reinforce positive messages about exploration and experimentation. Without changes to pedagogy, teaching—however good at getting the results—may routinely stimulate only a narrow subset of students' mental faculties. Without changes to student ownership they are deprived of opportunities to develop their own learning styles and interests. Without changes to the physical environment, it can easily give out retrograde messages about teaching and learning.

Future-based design

6. Curriculum design: organising the content of school—the syllabus, timetable, tests, and so on—so that a varied repertoire of stimulating learning is continuously available and attractive. (This does not mean that all learning has to be 'fun', of course.) Without structural change at this layer, students' engagement and commitment are likely to be weaker, and the development of their learning power correspondingly slower.

Keeping on track

7. Assessment and progression: designing explicit ways of tracking students' growth as confident and independent learners. Without some creative thought, commitment, and honesty at this layer, traditional forms of assessment and certification will continue to determine what counts as 'high stakes' learning and 'bottom line' success in school.

PART 3

The final three layers focus on some of the most important activities at whole-school level that help to support the introduction and embedding of the BLP approach.

8. Leadership: understanding the culture of the school, with its unique dynamic pattern of strengths, vulnerabilities, and sticking-points; understanding what is being asked of teachers, what difficulties and demands it will involve; sequencing and prioritising aspects of culture change astutely, what is and what is not negotiable; recruiting the governing body to understand and support the direction of growth of the school; keeping an eye on the vital signs of how the embedding of BLP is progressing and the impact this is having on staff and students. Without wisdom and support at this layer, headteachers may be unable to resist the pressure to slide back into prioritising more traditional and familiar goals.

Leading the change

9. Professional development in a community of inquiry: encouraging teachers' openness about and enthusiasm for their own learning, and strengthening a whole-school ethos of non-defensive, supportive, and collaborative inquiry. Without the development of this layer of professional intelligence, teachers are not seen to 'practise what they preach' and the process of culture change is slowed.

Changing professional habits

10. Engaging parents: involving parents and the local community in the vision and practice of the learning-powered school, and harnessing parents' ability to deepen their child's attitude to learning is a critically important layer. Without such involvement, the transfer of learning dispositions between the training-ground of school and the wider world of learning is restricted.

Bringing parents on board

The last two chapters in the book are slightly different. They do not relate directly to the process of school development, but provide some background information and conclusions about the overall approach.

Part 4

11. The impact of BLP: does it work? What effect does the introduction of BLP have on students: their achievement, their development as learners, and their attitudes towards learning? We present evidence from a variety of sources.

Does it work?

12. Taking stock and moving on: the final chapter reviews the main messages that have emerged from the individual chapters, and presents some reflections on learning so far and some thoughts about possible futures.

Where is it going?

Part 1
Background Conditions

In Part 1 we look at the layers of Learning Power culture change that are to do with beliefs and values. A school that wants to go down the BLP route needs to keep reminding itself why this direction is so important; otherwise, when routine demands crowd in, it is all too easy to lose focus and commitment. It also needs to keep developing the collective understanding of the science behind BLP—otherwise it is all too easy to be blown off course by the re-emergence of more familiar habits of thinking and planning.

It is also important that a school develops its own curiosity about the approach and the research that underlies it, and to feed that curiosity with reading and discussion. And it helps to prevent the developing BLP culture being derailed by scepticism, or even knee-jerk objections, if those reactions can be anticipated and countered in a well-informed and rational way. If BLP is to take root, it is highly desirable, we have found, to allow plenty of time for such questions and objections to be aired.

BLP asks teachers to change their habits, and they quite rightly need to be convinced that the change is going to be worth the effort—and that it will actually make a difference for the better. Taken together, these form the background conditions— the preparation of the soil, into which the seeds of BLP are going to be sown—which will help to maximise the likelihood of germination.

Chapter 1

Vision: Why schools have to change

In this chapter we explore the reasons for seeking
to change education, focusing on:

- creating economic prosperity
- wellbeing
- social trends
- increasing digitalisation
- the competitive educational environment
- the pressure of being successful
- disaffection among young people

The world is changing fast, and education systems around the planet are trying to keep pace. Some are responding by trying to squeeze more pupils through tests of literacy, numeracy and knowledge. Others, like Building Learning Power, think we need to go deeper, and ask hard questions about what schools in the twenty-first century are actually for. We think there are a number of compelling arguments that all seem to point in the same direction: schools need to get better at helping young people learn how to flourish in complex and demanding times. This chapter summarises some of these arguments, so that schools can understand and explain clearly *why* they are trying to change—as well as how to.

Creating economic prosperity

Education is often justified, by governments and others, as an investment in national competitiveness and prosperity. 'We' need, so the argument goes, a national workforce that is highly-skilled, creative, and adaptable, so as to be able to compete in global marketplaces. But how well are schools actually doing, in terms of producing large numbers of youngsters who possess these characteristics?

In 2009 Guy and Bill undertook a major review of the kinds of wider skills that economies around the world are trying to cultivate, precisely in order to make their citizens more innovative and, therefore, employable. 'We found that, wherever you go, from Singapore to Venezuela, New Zealand to Sweden, Brisbane to Birmingham, employers are crying out for people who can think for themselves, show initiative and collaborate effectively.'[1]

Effective Education and Employment: a global perspective

Also in 2009, Edexcel, the giant multinational educational provider, published the results of an international survey entitled *Effective Education and Employment: A global perspective.*[2] The research canvassed the views of a wide range of stakeholders, over 2,000 of them, in over 25 countries. Two findings screamed out of this report. First, from the employers' perspective there was an astonishing consensus about the desirable outcomes of education. Whether in Brazil, China, South Africa or the UK, employers are crying out for 'workers who have the right attitude, a willingness to learn, and an understanding of how to conduct themselves in the workplace'. And second, there was an equally clear international consensus that schools and colleges are not delivering the goods. The report concludes that:

> *'There is a significant disconnection between education systems and the needs of twenty-first century employers. People may or may not have the right clutch of certificates—but far too few of them have the attitudes that employers know are the more important foundations of that elusive 'world-class work-force'.*

Ross Hall, the Director of International at Edexcel who commissioned the report, was surprised by the common dissatisfactions being expressed in Mumbai, Sao Paulo, Beijing and Dubai, and the repeated calls for a curriculum which would be effective at cultivating a core set of 'generic skills and attributes'—pre-eminently, 'the ability to learn'. Amongst the qualities of mind that kept being mentioned as both widely desirable and widely lacking were problem-solving, creativity, initiative, responsibility, team-work, empathy and communication. 'One of the most striking findings across the whole of the research', wrote Hall, 'was the commonality of these transferable qualities'.

Go back thirty years and it is depressing to see how similar the criticisms being expressed were then. The Royal Society for the Encouragement of Arts, Manufactures and Commerce, the RSA, published a manifesto in 1980 called 'Education for Capability' signed by 140 leading figures of the day in the world of work.[3] It said:

> 'The country would benefit significantly in economic terms... if educators spent more time preparing people for life outside the education system. A well-balanced education should, of course, embrace analysis and the acquisition of knowledge. But it must also include the exercise of creative skills, the competence to undertake and complete tasks, and the ability to cope with everyday life; and also doing all these things in cooperation with others...In schools, too often, young people acquire knowledge of particular subjects, but are not equipped to use knowledge in ways which are relevant to the world outside the education system.'

In the words of Anthony Seldon, Master of Wellington College:

> 'The new world does not need container loads of young men and women whose knowledge is narrowly academic and subject-specific which they can regurgitate in splendid isolation in exams. It needs people who have genuine understanding not just in one but in several academic domains, and who comprehend how these different fields relate to each other. It needs people who can work collaboratively, with advanced interpersonal skills, as opposed to those who have been tested merely on their ability to write exam answers on their own. It needs problem solvers rather than those who just hold a large body of data in their memories. It needs employees who will have mature thinking skills, able to understand the complexity and the interaction of intricate systems, people who are able to think way beyond standard and formulaic patterns.'

A curriculum
to cultivate the
ability to learn

Voices from the past

Social wellbeing and cohesion

Mental Capital and Wellbeing: Making the Most of Ourselves in the 21st Century

Tomorrow's world will be, if anything, even more complex and fast-changing than today's. The UK Government's major Foresight project on Mental Capital and Wellbeing gathered a wide range of expert advice on foreseeable social and technological trends, and the personal and material resources that will be needed to meet the challenges, and capitalise on the opportunities, which those trends are likely to bring.[4]

These trends include:

- **Ageing:** people are living longer; the elderly will become a larger and more important group in society; state pension provision may well become less secure. So the disposition in the young towards long-term thinking and planning, coupled with both empathy and flexibility as parents begin to require more care, will be essential.

- **Health:** government scientists are beginning to get 'tougher' on the issue of 'lifestyle disorders' and people's responsibility for their own health, as obesity, alcohol consumption and sedentary lifestyles cause expensive conditions like heart disease and diabetes to rocket. So dispositions towards self-discipline and personal responsibility will become increasingly important.

- **Economy:** the rise of highly skilled workforces in China, India, Brazil and elsewhere mean that much 'brain-work' can be digitally outsourced, while the practical skills of making and fixing things cannot. A reversal of esteem for the trades and crafts that cannot be 'done down a wire' may well be on the way, with a corresponding reappraisal of practical problem-solving and hands-on intelligence.

- **Social change:** continuing shifts in social conditions and expectations will surely require flexible mindsets across the entire lifespan, and a positive attitude towards lifelong learning, whether self-chosen and welcome or imposed and unwelcome.

- **Public services:** the trend in recent years 'has been towards a model of public services based on greater levels of personal choice, active citizenship, personal responsibility, and "co-production". This is set to continue. To work most effectively, these models of service/client relationship require the greatest number of the public to be equipped with the mental capital and disposition to participate. This calls for a policy mindset that aims to foster mental capital and wellbeing across the whole population.'

- **Environmental issues:** increasing concern about climate change, and initiatives like '10–10', will require people to change habits throughout their lives. So—and here we mix our metaphors a bit—we have to sow the seeds, through education, of the willingness and ability of leopards to change their spots and old dogs to learn new tricks!

The Foresight report concludes that human wellbeing in a complex time will become increasingly dependent on the dispositions to be curious, inquisitive, experimental, reflective, and sociable—in short, to be lifelong and life-wide learners.

What it amounts to

The digital revolution

Schools are no longer the prime sources of knowledge, as they were in the nineteenth century and much of the twentieth. The digital revolution has opened up many more ways for young people to learn. Many children who seem dull and disengaged in school are bright as a button on their home computer. With good-enough literacy and the will to learn, most of us can now teach ourselves what we need to learn from the internet. Or if we can't, the internet will hook us up with a teacher of our own choosing who, like as not, will be happy to swap their time and expertise for something we can do that they would like to. Websites such as www.schoolofeverything.com will help you arrange such learning exchanges for yourself. Within minutes one of us found a singing teacher who would have been delighted to exchange some singing lessons for some help with their pond maintenance, for example. Most of the 'students' and 'teachers' in the School of Everything are children and young people.

www.schoolofeverything.com

Sugata Mitra's famous 'hole-in-the-wall computer' experiments in India dramatically demonstrate children's ability to learn in an entirely self-organised way. Mitra set a computer and a touch-pad in a wall in a slum in New Delhi and watched what happened. Within hours, children as young as six years old had taught themselves how to access the internet, and within weeks, these children who had no previous knowledge of English had taught themselves enough English words to communicate both with the computer and with each other. Within a month they were happily emailing and surfing away. Typically, says Mitra, you will find one kid on the computer, three or four close advisers watching and advising her,[5] and a dozen or more other onlookers who are also watching intently and chipping in. If you test them, the entire group show substantial learning from each session. Take away the school, the teachers, the books, and the exams, and children, even from very impoverished backgrounds, will organize and teach themselves in highly efficient and successful ways.[6]

Children teaching themselves

The lesson seems to be: schools, watch out. If we do not find things to teach children in school that cannot be learned from a machine, we should not be surprised if they come to treat their schooling as a series of irritating interruptions to their education. A cautionary tale from nearly a century ago would do well to ring in our ears as we plan our lessons:

Greeting his pupils, the teacher asked:

> *'What would you learn of me?*
> *And the reply came:*
> *How shall we care for our bodies?*
> *How shall we rear our children?*
> *How shall we live and work together?*
> *How shall we play?*
> *For what ends shall we live?*
> *And the teacher pondered these words,*
> *And sorrow was in his heart,*
> *For his own learning touched not these things.'* [7]

Another way of winning at school

Judged by exam results

It is very hard to break the hypnotic spell of 'standards', as defined by examination success. Despite an increasing barrage of fine words and good intentions, it is the examination results by which schools' and students' performance are ubiquitously judged—by politicians, and by the media. Politicians like to look effective, so they have to show they are having an impact on 'hard data'—and examination grades are conveniently countable and statistically manipulable. Hence the ritual annual fanfare about 'best ever results' (1% more A grades; hooray!), and the equally predictable counterpoint of 'dumbed down tests'.

It is much harder to find ways of showing whether 16-year-olds are more inquisitive, determined, imaginative, and convivial than they were a year ago, so politicians tend not to try. But unless such indicators are developed, GCSE and A-level results will continue to be the tail that wags the dog of education.

Measuring what we value

As someone once said, if we do not find ways of measuring what we value, we will end up just valuing what we can measure. And that distorts the process of schooling, and inhibits teachers from pursuing other aims that they know to be more important.

It is also obvious that, once a single indicator is selected to be the measure of success, people will find ways of manipulating that indicator to their advantage in ways contrary to the original spirit of what 'success' was supposed to mean. In economics this is called 'Goodhart's Law': 'once an indicator becomes a target—especially if funding depends up on it—it stops being a good indicator'.[8] Only someone with a complete lack of insight into human nature could be surprised by the fact that, if 'number of operations performed' becomes a target, hospitals will start doing more of the quick and easy operations (like cataracts), and fewer of the harder and longer ones (like heart surgery). Or headteachers will discourage low-achieving pupils from attempting difficult subjects, connive at their absence on the days of the critical test, and enter more pupils for courses with assessments that are known to be easier.[9]

Examinations are competitive. Not everyone can be a winner. Your son's four A's at A-level only have value (for university entrance, say), because someone else's daughter didn't get them. This is an inconvenient truth that politicians tend constantly to fudge.[10] Less than half of all 16-year-olds will achieve the UK government's own benchmark of a 'good enough' education—five GCSEs, two of which must be English and Maths, at C-grade or better. Many fewer will achieve the 'English Baccalaureate'. So what do the others come away with, if not a sense of relative failure?

An inconvenient truth

From an assessment and certification point of view, there has to be another 'way of winning' at school that is valued by young people themselves. The word they often use is 'confidence', which is the opposite of 'insecurity', 'anxiety', and 'self-doubt'. In other words, young people themselves, so the surveys show, want those wider skills just as much as their potential employers do.

Disaffection

Very many young people don't find value in what they are doing at school, and either muck about or bunk off. Over 67,000 play truant every day, and the rate is rising—despite nearly 10,000 parents of truants in 2008–9 being prosecuted in an attempt to 'crack down' on absenteeism. There are over 200,000 persistent truants, those who regularly miss a day a week of school or more. According to a 2009 piece of research for the Department of Children, Schools and Families, more than a quarter in Years 9, 10 and 11 actively dislike school. They are at risk of dropping out or, if they stay, of disrupting the education of others. Only a third of 14- and 15-year-olds 'were highly engaged with school and aspired to continue with full-time education to degree level'.[11]

Why are so many young people disengaged? Some people blame the parents, or bullying, or 'trendy teaching methods'—as if good old-fashioned chalk-and-talk and 'firm discipline' were as unquestionably valid in twenty-first century London or Belfast comprehensives as they were in nineteenth century grammar and public schools. Some blame low levels of literacy, and urge that young people who are not good at reading and writing, and have learned to dislike it, should be made to do more and more of it—as if it were a mere technical difficulty totally divorced from youngsters' more general attitudes and feelings towards school.

Why disengaged?

Professor William Richardson of the University of Exeter has suggested that a major difference between those who stay engaged with school beyond the age of 14, and those who don't, is not that one group is 'brighter' or 'better behaved' than the other. It may be, in large measure, that those who stay engaged are simply more willing to remain in the role of 'pupil'—are better able to sit still and listen, or are just more interested in the subject-matter and procedures of school—while others are more impatient to take on the roles and responsibilities of adulthood. The route that seems to offer them this faster-track entry into adulthood is the vocational one, so their interests may develop in a way that allows them this escape. Richardson says:

Why some young people want to leave school

'It was always the case that large numbers of young people wanted to leave school at the earliest opportunity. They hated the uniform. They felt infantilised. They wanted to be adults... They were aware of the world "out there" and wanted to join it, and school felt like it was holding them back. So it is not just a matter of their interests or mentality; the vocational route is the one that seems to respond to that urgency. The majority of this group who want to leave school early have huge capacities and potential, but ... they [tend to] get shunted into a low-status, low-prospects route and then feel trapped and let down. Their potential could have come alive had the pedagogical environment been much richer. You see people thrive quickly when the setting changes.'[12]

BLP aims directly to develop that richer pedagogical environment. In BLP, the traditional concern with subject-matter is balanced fairly and squarely with an equal emphasis on the development of a broad repertoire of useful, transferable qualities of mind. It is these mindsets that all young people want and need. Some of them can stretch and strengthen them by studying physics or Spanish; others can get equivalent mental exercise in the context of learning to colour hair, fix engines or care for people with learning difficulties. It is, to use a fancy phrase, the epistemic exercise regime that matters most deeply, not whether you can solve simultaneous equations or analyse the causes of the First World War.

A richer pedagogical environment

'When I was at school and college, I would pride myself on being able to pass doing nothing. It was cooler not to study and pass than to study and pass—do you know what I mean? And I think that's totally wrong now... I'm ashamed of it. I think [writing the scripts for] The Office taught me that the struggle is the best bit... I liked learning the struggle. I've really tried to get good at writing. The pleasure is the journey, looking back and seeing how hard it was... The pure joy of learning is a revelation at forty-something!'

Ricky Gervais[13]

The pressure of being successful

In terms of 'life skills', key competencies', or 'essential qualities'—call them what you will—schools are failing high-achieving, as well as low-achieving, students. There is good evidence that high-achievers—especially, but not exclusively, girls—often develop an anxious attitude towards their own performance that makes them go to pieces in the face of unexpected difficulty, and avoid new kinds of challenges in case they 'look stupid'. They know how to get good marks in school's terms, but lack resilience and adventurousness in a wider sense. They know how to succeed, but they have not learned how to fail, or how to struggle.[14]

This failure to develop resilience, curiosity and independence at school stores up trouble for those bright young people later on. In 2009–10, around 1,500 students sought out the Cambridge University Student Counselling Service. Between 15 and 20% of Cambridge undergraduates will seek counselling at some point during their studies. Mark Phippen, head of the service, says the pressures on them are severe and getting worse. More and more intense spoon-feeding at school renders them less and less capable of coping with these pressures when they arrive. Many of them fear that they are impostors—significantly less capable than they have been helped to appear.

Fear they are impostors

It is the same at Oxford. Alan Percy, clinical director of the Oxford Counselling Service, has charted yearly increases in referrals for debilitating stress and anxiety. If these high-achieving young people cannot achieve quick success, they flounder. As their school courses have become more modularised and packaged, Percy says, so students have been deprived of the opportunity to learn how to grapple over time with genuinely difficult things. Percy notes a paradoxical trend which he calls 'pseudo-maturity': young men and women who seem much more confident and worldly-wise than their more gauche equivalents of 20 or 30 years ago—but who, below the surface, have fewer resources with which to meet difficulty.[15]

Being happy

Unless they are protected from change by living in highly remote places, or within closed societies that deliberately insulate themselves from the complex currents of globalisation, young people find growing up in the twenty-first century hard. From an increasingly young age, they are exposed to multiple pressures and uncertainties concerning such deep issues as livelihood, sustainability, sexuality, loyalty and identity. They have to select and craft for themselves answers to questions such as 'What matters?', 'What shall I become?', 'What am I ready for?', 'Where is my "place", both geographically and socially?' and 'Who is "Us" and who is "Them"?'

In Over Our Heads: The Mental Demands of Modern Life.
Robert Kegan

In his seminal book *In Over Our Heads,* Harvard psychologist Robert Kegan charts the ways in which young people are now growing up in 'stick-shift' rather than 'automatic' cultures. In an 'automatic' culture, as in an automatic car, much of the decision-making is built into the workings of the culture itself. You have neither the responsibility nor the opportunity to think about these deep questions: your path is largely mapped out by the way the culture itself functions. It is pretty clear when to get married and what it means to be a 'husband' or 'wife', for example.[16]

But in a stick-shift (or what in the UK we would call a 'manual') culture, much more is up for grabs. You, the driver, have to decide when to change gear. Different value systems collide daily on our television screens, as we are exposed to an endless fashion parade of learned academics, ardent environmentalists, narcissistic supermodels, gentle gardeners, insouciant fat cats, and misogynistic rappers. If young people are not to be swept away on this torrent of imagery, they have to learn how to think for themselves. And this is both exciting and liberating, and stressful and demanding. Whether young people flourish or flounder depends on the resources they have at their disposal. To swim rather than sink demands a level of mental and emotional development (as well as a good deal of stable and sensible external support) that those who live in more predictable times simply do not need.

The evidence is that a great many young people around the world are indeed struggling to cope. An authoritative comparison of teenagers' mental health between 1974, 1986 and 1999 documented a 'sharp decline' in a range of indicators of well-being. More recent surveys show that these trends are not just continuing but becoming worse. It is not just a few kids at the margins who are skewing the stats, nor is it merely a matter of increased frequency of reporting. Across a wide range of countries and backgrounds, youngsters are struggling to cope.

One of the most reliable sources of happiness turns out to be learning. People report feeling happy with themselves when, like Ricky Gervais quoted earlier, they are engaged in struggling with something difficult but worthwhile; when they feel in charge, and are not being chivvied or criticised by others; and when they are able to become so engrossed in what they are doing that all self-consciousness and self-awareness drops away.[17]

What is happiness?

So when parents say—as they often do—'I just want my child to be happy', here is one of the best pieces of advice. Help them, and get their schools to help them, to discover what it is that they would love to be great at. Help them discover the 'joy of the struggle': the happiness that comes from being rapt in the process, and the quiet pride that comes from making progress on something that matters. And help them to understand and develop the craft of worthwhile learning—how to make best use of imagination, reasoning, concentration, collaboration, and so on. **That is what BLP aims to do.**

A radical rethink for education

Taken together, we (along with many others) believe the arguments for a radical rethink of the priorities and practices of education are overwhelming. And so is the direction in which all these arguments are pointing. If you want that world-class flexible workforce, coach young people in the pleasures and skills of learning. If you want to help young people prepare for the stresses and uncertainties of twenty-first century life, help them to be more resilient. If you want them to be able to join the world of self-organising, resourceful learners, like those young computer whizzes in the slums of New Delhi, give them the confidence to experiment and collaborate.

If you believe that there has to be 'another way of winning' in schools, parallel to the examination competition, focus as well on developing the broader qualities and skills young people actually need in the real world. If you are worried about the thousands of young people bored and disengaged by the traditional school offerings, providing a more genuinely problem or enquiry-based approach may just engage them again. If you are worried about the brittleness and conservatism of some of the apparent successes of our system—articulate people with firsts from well-known universities but little resilience or initiative—then we can start them earlier on building those vital dispositions. If you just want to give children the best chance of being happy and fulfilled human beings, you can't do better than give them the passion, the confidence, and the capability to become the best whatever-it-is—hairdresser, dental hygienist, poet, animator, chef—they can possibly be.

For all these reasons, we believe that approaches like Building Learning Power are at the very heart of the work of designing schools that will be fit for the twenty-first century. And it is teachers and school leaders who really 'get it' who are making it a reality. The kinds of arguments in this chapter fuel their own conviction, and also give them the ammunition they might need to convince parents, students, and their own colleagues that the journey is vital.

What do we need to do?

Focus on developing qualities and skills for the real world

Chapter 2

Science: The underpinnings of BLP

In this chapter we explore:

- the key scientific ideas behind Building Learning Power
- other important educational research
- the thinking behind the language of BLP
- the core BLP frameworks

I n 2002 we published *Building Learning Power: Helping Young People Become Better Learners.*[1] This book was a direct attempt to distil the practical lessons for teachers that emerged from Guy's earlier book, published in 1999, called *Wise Up: The Challenge of Lifelong Learning.*[2] *Wise Up* first introduced the concept of 'learning power' as an interwoven set of habits and qualities of mind that together help us face challenges and uncertainties with confidence and capability.[3] Learning power does not claim to be a newly discovered faculty of mind. It is an umbrella term for a variety of familiar traits that, individually and collectively, affect how people go about learning.

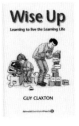

Wise Up reviewed a wide range of research into the psychological factors that underpin learning power, as well as evidence that these qualities are themselves learnable. For more detail on the experimental literature, we would refer you back to *Wise Up*. Here, we thought it might be useful just to review briefly some of the research giants on whose shoulders BLP stands

Major influences on BLP

Carol Dweck: the growth mindset

In a major programme of research extending over the last thirty years, Carol Dweck, Professor of Psychology at Stanford University, has demonstrated repeatedly that people's beliefs about intelligence have a marked influence on how they go about learning. Put simply, if you believe that 'intelligence' is fixed—that is, people are just born with a certain amount of 'ability' which is incapable of expansion—whether you are conscious of it or not, that belief undermines your resilience in the face of difficulty or frustration. It's as if people say to themselves, 'Well, if I haven't got what it takes, I'd be a mug to put in the effort, wouldn't I?' Conversely, if people believe they can 'get smarter', they are much more likely to see difficulty as an opportunity to do just that. Dweck teaches us to focus on the expandability of young people's minds rather than their fixedness; and this realisation—that what we do affects how children think and learn, as well as what they know—is the springboard that makes the very idea of 'building young people's learning power' credible.[4, 5]

Learning muscles

Dweck often makes use of an analogy between mental and physical activity, which we too find very helpful. When youngsters are taught to think of their brains as being like a muscle, capable of being strengthened and expanded through exercise, they mobilise the resources they have more effectively, they try harder, and their achievement goes up. That is why, particularly with younger children, we often talk about learning power as being composed of a set of 'learning muscles' that are capable of being stretched and strengthened. Like Dweck, we see the classroom as being like a 'mind gym', with each lesson making use of the content and activities to create a pleasurably taxing mental 'workout'.

Following Dweck's lead, the whole language of BLP is designed to reinforce the idea that learning is learnable, and ability is something that can always expand.

Howard Gardner: multiple intelligences

The two founders of Harvard's Project Zero—Professor Howard Gardner and Professor David Perkins—have both influenced the development of BLP significantly. Howard Gardner has had a huge effect on education worldwide over the last 20 years, and BLP is no exception. His theory of multiple intelligences helped us—like many others—to see human intelligence not as some kind of monolithic faculty, separate from the rest of our psychological processes, but as an umbrella idea, covering a variety of constituent abilities. The 'intelligence' traditionally valued and regularly exercised by school is overwhelmingly linguistic, mathematical and rational; but this is only a fraction of a much more comprehensive approach to intelligence, in Gardner's system, that also includes our relationships with others, our self-awareness and our imagination.

Multiple intelligences

Gardner always saw multiple intelligences as a psychological theory, and has been wary of drawing any educational implications—though this has not prevented a good many others from doing so. Perhaps that is why he has always been somewhat ambiguous about how learnable each of his intelligences is. He says, for example, that, 'all normal human beings develop at least these seven forms of intelligence to a greater or lesser extent', suggesting that they are 'nurtured' as much as they are 'natured'.[6] But he has not gone on to develop any educational model of how different cultures influence that nurturing process, which is at the heart of the BLP approach.

John Hattie: effect sizes and achievement

John Hattie is Professor of Education at Auckland University. His highly influential book *Visible Learning*, published in 2009, has really encouraged us to believe that focusing on building learning dispositions is not at odds with the traditional school concerns of literacy, numeracy and the mastery of examinable bodies of knowledge. On the contrary, Hattie's meticulous review of research reveals that *'the biggest effects on student learning occur when teachers become learners of their own teaching, and when students become their own teachers.'* Helping pupils become more independent, more reflective, and better able to plan and evaluate their own learning, turns out to be a better way of boosting their attainment than drilling them in the subject-matter.[7]

VISIBLE LEARNING
A SYNTHESIS OF OVER 800 META-ANALYSES
RELATING TO ACHIEVEMENT

"towards teaching's Holy Grail"
The Times Educational Supplement

JOHN HATTIE

Hattie has come to a view that is very similar to BLP. We should be aiming *first* to strengthen young people's sense of themselves as learners, and to help them learn how to learn, and *then* to assist them in mastering useful and important bodies of knowledge and skill. Unfortunately we have all too often put the cart of knowledge before the horse of learning. What makes John Hattie such a powerful 'godfather' to BLP is that he has arrived at this position not as a matter of belief, but through a detailed examination of the research evidence.

Ellen Langer: the power of language

BLP has been much influenced by the work of Harvard Psychology Professor, Ellen Langer. In a wide range of studies, Langer has shown that small shifts in a teacher's language can induce a marked change in the learning habits that students are bringing to bear on their work. Specifically, if you say definitively that something *is* the case, students take it literally and try to remember it. But if you say, of the same thing, that it *could be* the case, they become more engaged, more thoughtful, more imaginative, and more critical. That 'could be' invites students to become more active, inquisitive members of the knowledge-checking, knowledge-developing community, rather than to see themselves as merely doing their best to understand and remember something that is already cut and dried.

BLP recognises that there may be many ways in which subtle changes to the way we speak with (and talk and write about) young people can impact on their development as learners.

Jean Lave and Etienne Wenger: communities of practice

If it is to be successful, building learning power involves a process of deep culture change in a school that takes time, patience and commitment. The work of Jean Lave and Etienne Wenger on 'communities of practice' has helped us to think about school as a kind of 'epistemic apprenticeship'—a culture where young people pick up all kinds of attitudes and habits towards knowing and learning. Lave and Wenger describe how groups with particular trades or interests, such as Liberian tailors or American supermarket butchers, induct their apprentices into their characteristic ways of thinking and working. Newcomers move from being low-status apprentices to eventually becoming acknowledged skilled practitioners.

We think you can look at schools in the same way, except their trade is 'learning' itself—traditionally with an emphasis on the kinds of learning called 'scholarship'. As well as teaching numeracy, literacy and 'subjects', schools socialise their pupils into ways of thinking about learning: how to go about learning, which kinds of learning are most esteemed, and how to think of themselves as learners. In all kinds of subtle (and not so subtle) ways, schools imply answers to these questions that seep into young people's minds and shape their attitudes towards learning. For example, the traditional image of a 'master learner', conveyed by such means as end-of-year celebrations and 'honours boards', is someone who wins a scholarship to Oxford. As most youngsters are obviously going to fail in those terms, we think there ought to be a wider conception of what a real-world master-learner might look like, and greater precision about how schools are cultivating the relevant traits in all their students.

David Perkins: learnable intelligence and the transfer of learning

David Perkins's writing has inspired us to think carefully about what is possible and what is problematic in achieving the goals of BLP. His book *Outsmarting IQ* (1995) encouraged us by showing just how much of our so-called 'intelligence' is in fact learned—and therefore capable of being helped to grow in timely and productive ways. *Making Learning Whole* (2009) has more recently pointed up the discontinuities between the kinds of learning that are traditionally required in schools, and the kinds that get you places you want to go in the 'real world'. Perkins has therefore helped us think about the difficulties of getting what is learned in school—even what is learned about learning—to transfer out of the school gates, so that it becomes a genuine, spontaneous asset beyond the cloistered world of education. His work explains why we insist on talking about habits of mind and dispositions rather than skills (of which more in a moment).[8, 9]

Perkins's thinking has spawned its own practical spin-offs, most notably the project on Visible Thinking (not to be confused with John Hattie's 'visible learning') led by one of Perkins's graduate students and now collaborators, Ron Ritchhart. Visible Thinking is the regular use of a range of 'thinking routines'—such as 'Think–Pair–Share' or 'Predict–Observe–Explain'— that get students into the habit of attending more closely to evidence, reasoning more carefully, and discussing with others more skilfully. We have adopted (and adapted) some of these routines as a very useful way of getting teachers to embed a concern with the learning capacities into their teaching. Because of our overarching concern with real-world learning rather than disciplined thinking, however, BLP covers a wider range of habits of mind—including things like absorption and perseverance—than are usually given prominence in Visible Thinking.

Visible Thinking Routines website:

http://tinyurl. com/2udonw6

Other educational research

Several other strands of research have strongly influenced the development of BLP. In this section we note just a few of them.

Flow

Professor Mihalyi Csikszentmihalyi has significantly advanced our understanding of creativity and creative learning. His concept of flow, a state of focused attention in which one is wholly engaged in learning and which, he has demonstrated, has a hugely positive impact on learner well-being, has been important in developing aspects of BLP.

Leadership

Michael Fullan, Emeritus Professor at the University of Toronto's Institute for Studies in Education, has undertaken extensive research into educational leadership and change. He has demonstrated the central importance of creating cultures of learning which engage teachers collaboratively and has been consistently realistic about the persistence required by schools wanting to change their practices.

Real-world learning

Lauren Resnick is Professor of Psychology at Pittsburg University and one of the most eminent American psychologists of the last fifty years. Her thinking about real-world learning and how it is different from school learning is central to BLP. She has been a pioneer in advocating the central importance of habits of mind as the core component of what it is to be intelligent.

Creativity

Sir Ken Robinson has been a dominant force in shaping policy and practice, especially in the US and UK, with regard to creativity and learning. He has championed schools which put learners at the centre of their curriculum and do their utmost to unearth every young person's 'element', the aspects of their own talents which matter most to them and which will engage them throughout their lives.

Learned helplessness

Professor Martin Seligman is the director of the Positive Psychology Center at the University of Pennsylvania. His work on positive psychology and specifically his concept of 'learned helplessness' has done much to shape our understanding of what it is to be resilient and resourceful in learning.

Intelligence

Professor Robert Sternberg is Provost at Oklahoma State University and acknowledged as a world authority on intelligence. His thinking about the degree to which intelligence is both experiential and practical, and especially the degree to which it is part of real-world learning, is central to BLP.

Conception of learning and achievement

Chris Watkins is Reader in Education at the London Institute of Education. For several decades his tireless work with the International Centre for School Improvement has explicitly made the link between students who have more advanced conceptions of learning and higher levels of attainment.

Dylan Wiliam is Emeritus Professor of Educational Assessment at the London Institute of Education. His groundbreaking work on Assessment for Learning was an important stepping stone on the way to shifting teacher understanding of the role of formative assessment and the broader importance of a more scientific approach to helping learners become better learners.

Assessment for Learning

BLP's American cousin: Habits of Mind

Unfortunately, we didn't become aware of American educator **Art Costa's** work on 'habits of mind' (HoM) until around 2004, after we had developed our own framework. Costa had been developing an approach that is probably the closest cousin to BLP, offering advice to teachers about structuring their teaching around a list of 16 'habits of mind'.[10] These overlap considerably with BLP's 17 learning capacities. The common features include curiosity and questioning, noticing and observation, perseverance, questioning, exploring possibilities through imagination, clear thinking and reasoning, checking and improving, distilling principles and applying lessons for the future, meta-learning or metacognition, interdependence with others, and listening and empathy. Included in Costa's list, but which may appear to be missing from BLP, are

Similarities and differences

- managing impulsivity (thinking before you act)
- taking responsible risks (living on the edge of your competence)
- finding humour (looking for the whimsical and incongruous)

Put simply, we tend to think that:

- 'Managing impulsivity' falls within BLP's managing distractions—whether the impulse is a response to an external, distracting, event, or an apparently spontaneous self-distraction.

- 'Taking responsible risks' is often mentioned by teachers as being part and parcel of being a good learner; with hindsight, this could have been given higher visibility in the BLP framework — while 'responsible' is covered by aspects of Reflectiveness and Resourcefulness, the core 'Will I or won't I [start doing this]?' seems to relate quite closely to the 'Will I or won't I [carry on doing this]?' of perseverance. A fairly minor broadening of the scope of our concepts might be the answer here.

- 'Finding humour' could be included within BLP's notions of imagination and playfulness of mind—though we wonder whether humour, per se, really belongs in the core list of learning dispositions.

The BLP learning muscles that do not seem to overlap strongly with Costa's habits of mind are

- absorption (the tendency to get lost in one's learning)

35

- imitation (openness to picking up other people's ways of thinking and behaving).

We think these are interesting differences that are worth debating. But clearly the overlaps and synergies greatly outweigh the differences, and, as BLP has developed, we have learned a good deal from HoM about what these capacities mean, and how to develop them.

Learning to talk about learning

The Project for Enhancing Effective Learning (PEEL) began in a Melbourne high school in 1985, and has since produced a stream of publications that are both practical and well-researched. PEEL brought together a group of innovative teachers and a group of education academics based at Monash University. Still going strong more than 25 years later, PEEL was the first project to explore the use of 'metacognition'—getting students to think about their own thinking—in classrooms. PEEL has generated empirical evidence for the effect of these interventions on students' engagement, achievement, and the development of positive dispositions towards learning in general. These included what we would call in BLP questioning, persevering, planning, reasoning, revising, making links, distilling and collaborating, as well, of course, as meta-learning. With its concern for conjoining detailed practical techniques with sound theory from cognitive science, and rigorous evaluation, PEEL was a vital influence on the development of BLP.[11]

From skills to dispositions

'Dispositions to learning should be key performance indicators of the outcomes of schooling. Many teachers believe that, if achievement is enhanced, there is a ripple effect to these dispositions. However, such a belief is not defensible. Such dispositions need planned interventions.'

John Hattie, *Visible Learning*

Beyond skills

Many people who are interested in learning talk as if it were a set of skills. But in BLP we seldom use the word 'skill' now; we talk instead about learning habits, dispositions and attitudes, or sometimes the 'qualities of mind' of the powerful learner; and about 'capacities' in a particular sense outlined later. This shift in terminology reflects the influence of a particular strand of research that has emphasized the difference between skills and dispositions.

David Perkins and others have shown that people often appear less capable than they are, not because they don't possess the skill they need, but because they don't realise that now is the right moment to call that skill to mind and make use of it. They lack what Perkins calls 'sensitivity to occasion'. People frequently do not think as well as they might, for example, not because they can't, but because the situation did not activate the thinking capacity which they actually have. To put it crudely, we have to be *able* to think and learn, but we also have to be *ready* and *willing* to do so.

Thus there is no point in training young people in 'thinking skills' if, the moment they leave the classroom, those skills curl up in a dark corner of their minds and go to sleep. If we want young people to be enthusiastic in pursuit of their interests, and robust in their response to life's challenges, then skills and techniques are not enough. They must not only possess the requisite capabilities; they must be ready, willing and able to deploy them when the time is right.

And that means we have to help the skills turn into dispositions. Our job is not finished until using the 'learning muscles' has become second nature: a spontaneous part of the way our pupils look at the world. And this implies that we have to think about how to help learning power become flexible and pleasurable, as well as skilful. We need to move from thinking about learning as a set of techniques and skills that can be 'trained', to a set of dispositions, interests and values that need to be 'cultivated'.

From training to cultivation

> 'The starting point—the new idea—is that everyone can develop learning power. In the past children were coming in with a certain 'intelligence' level and we were topping it up, filling the brain with knowledge. But in fact all children can learn; it's just tuning in to different dispositions.'
>
> Primary teacher, Bristol

Learning versus performance cultures

Several recent research papers[12] have found, paradoxically, that pupils do better on their tests when they and their teachers focus on learning rather than on performance and achievement. These add considerable weight to BLP's working assumption that there are ways to get better results at the same time as helping students strengthen their learning power more generally.

Building students' confidence in their own capacity to learn turns out (not surprisingly) to boost their examination performance. On the other hand, several studies have found that narrow pressure for results—'achievement pressure' in the jargon of the trade—is not an effective way of raising results. Pressure to raise children's levels of reading has very little effect on their ability to read, and does significant damage to their enjoyment of reading[13].

For example, in a very well conducted study by Cheryl Flink and her colleagues, two groups of teachers of 10-year-olds were told either that 'your job is to help pupils learn', or 'your job is to ensure that pupils perform well'. The latter group felt under greater pressure, and were thus more likely to 'screw down' the classroom, being more directive, giving the students less choice, and passing on their pressure to the students. When this happened, students' achievement went down. It did so because the students were learning less resiliently and resourcefully; they were trying to perform rather than to learn. As a result, the authors found that 'the effects of a performance orientation include greater helplessness, reduced help-seeking, less strategy use, more maladaptive strategies, and a greater focus on grade feedback'.[14]

A second finding is that helping students learn how to be better learners is one of the most effective ways of raising their achievement (never mind its role in preparing them for life). The more curious, adventurous, resilient and independent they become, the better are their grades. When students are encouraged to help each other learn, for example, there is a substantial effect on their achievement, and the size of the effect increases the more control and responsibility they are allowed to take.[15] When they are encouraged to keep a diary recording their experiences of and reflections on their own learning, secondary science students, for example, show dramatic improvements on a number of indicators. The authors of this study report that 'the learning journals helped students to develop more sophisticated conceptions of learning, showing an understanding of the purpose and processes of learning'.[16] And, as Chris Watkins notes, we have known for more than 25 years that 'students with more elaborated conceptions of learning perform better in public examinations at age 16.'

The languages of learning power

In general our attitude is that any list of learning dispositions—ours, Costa's, Richhart's—serves the very useful purpose of getting teachers into the right territory—we all share a general sense of what 'right' means. Many schools are not used to focusing on the habits and processes of learning itself. Teachers are used to thinking about their lessons in terms of two dimensions: the subject-matter they are trying to get across (the 'syllabus') and the effectiveness with which they have done so ('assessment'). How to teach *Macbeth* or Atomic Weight, for example, and how to check students' understanding, are familiar issues, and teachers think and talk fluently about these aspects of what they do. But there is a third dimension which is at the core of learning power: the learning habits and attitudes which are being exercised *by the way those subjects are being presented, taught and assessed.* You can teach *Macbeth*, and get good exam results, in a way that stretches students' abilities to imagine, collaborate, and question. And you can also teach *Macbeth*, and get good results, in a way that makes students more passive, docile, and dependent. For BLP, it is this difference that is crucial.

The third dimension of teaching

Traditionally, teachers have been less articulate about this dimension. But if students are to be helped to build those 'elaborated conceptions of learning', we need to have, and to make regular use of, a vocabulary that captures this richness. Teachers need to become fluent in a language of learning power. It is surprisingly helpful for both teachers and students to have understood concepts such as 'noticing', 'collaboration', or 'managing distractions', and to have learned to use such words and phrases routinely. It is only when we name such things explicitly that students (and their parents) know what it is we are noticing and valuing.

Noticing what we value

Naming these ideas also enables teachers to notice which habits of mind they *do* routinely require or encourage pupils to use in lessons and other activities—and then to think more carefully about whether there might be other learning muscles they might be calling on instead—and other ways in which to stretch and strengthen them. They begin to think, 'How is learning happening, and what qualities of mind are we cultivating in young people by the way we are designing and delivering the curriculum?' Many schools discover, when they start to think this way, how much they are doing to build their students' learning power already—but they just haven't pulled that aspect of their work together so clearly. And they may also begin to see where some of the 'holes' might be in the 'epistemic apprenticeship' which they are providing for their pupils, and how they might be able to provide a more 'broad and balanced' set of mental workouts for them.

How is learning happening?

A working vocabulary

One way we could go from here, as researchers, is to try to make our list, our vocabulary, ever more comprehensive. We could create a fuller list of learning-related dispositions and capacities by integrating the frameworks of BLP and HoM, for example. But, as people who first and foremost want to support the practical development of a certain kind of education, there are a number of other considerations that hold the quest for the Holy Grail of the definitive list in check.

First, we have found that it is important to get schools to treat these vocabularies as open to questioning. We want them not just to accept and use BLP (or any other terminology), but to be thoughtful, critical, and creative in the development of a language that they can truly understand and own. When staff and students are involved in developing their ideas of the Learning Qualities they want to strengthen, they are much more likely to be meaningful. So we want the BLP model to 'stick' and be good enough to get that process of conversation and customisation going; to help schools to see what talking about the How and Who of learning actually sounds like—and then to continue the discussion for themselves.

Discuss and customise

In practice, developing and using vocabularies requires a delicate balance, one that we find we have not always got right. On the one hand we want

Think critically and creatively about the framework

to be 'directive' enough to encourage schools to really understand what can be an unfamiliar perspective. At the beginning, we encourage them to understand and use the vocabulary of BLP quite explicitly. But we aim always to remind them of the spirit that underlies the letter of BLP, so they can think critically and creatively about the framework as soon as they are able. The research we have done with schools shows that sometimes BLP can come across as too prescriptive—we have not been good enough at balancing the direction with the discussion. And sometimes it is almost as if schools want only to be given the Definitive List, and so don't take us as seriously as we would like when we say: 'Now go away and make it your own'.

A usable vocabulary

Second, the vocabulary of learning power has to be usable, and that means not making it either too long or too short. If you merely give teachers two or three categories (like Visual, Auditory or Kinaesthetic, or Bright, Average or Below-Average levels of intelligence), there is not enough detail to help them think about how they might develop their own practice. The repercussions tend to be rather superficial. We have found this, to some extent, with our language of the Four R's. Schools that just latch on to the broad organising concepts of Resilience, Resourcefulness, Reflection and Reciprocity, and don't burrow down into the detail, tend to find that initial enthusiasm can dry up as people don't know what to do next, once they have used the high level lingo. On the other hand, if you allow lists to expand to include 16 (Habits of Mind) or 17 (BLP learning capacities) elements, it can be daunting for a newcomer—whether teacher, child or parent—to get to grips with.

4 domains of learning
17 learning capacities

Our solution has been to structure the BLP learning language at two levels, across four domains of learning. At the first level, Learning Power breaks down into the Four R's; and then, at the second level, each of those are subdivided into four or five finer-grain learning capacities. Each of the R dispositions covers a broad domain of learning,

Building emotional engagement

Resilience covers aspects of the learner's **emotional** and experiential engagement with the subject matter of learning. It includes concentration and the ability to resist distractions; close attention and fascination; and tolerating the emotional ups and downs of learning, and bouncing back from frustration or failure.

Building a wide range of cognitive approaches

Resourcefulness embraces the main **cognitive** skills and dispositions of learning: scepticism and curious questioning; making links and connections within your mind; balancing reason and imagination; and the ability to create a good 'learning niche' for oneself by collecting and capitalising on tools and resources.

The Supple Learning Mind

Reflectiveness

- Planning: working learning out in advance
- Revising: monitoring and adapting along the way
- Distilling: drawing out the lessons from experience
- Meta-learning: understanding learning, and yourself as a learner

Reciprocity

- Interdependence: balancing self-reliance and sociability
- Collaboration: the skills of learning with others
- Listening/Empathy: getting inside others' minds
- Imitation: picking up others' habits and values

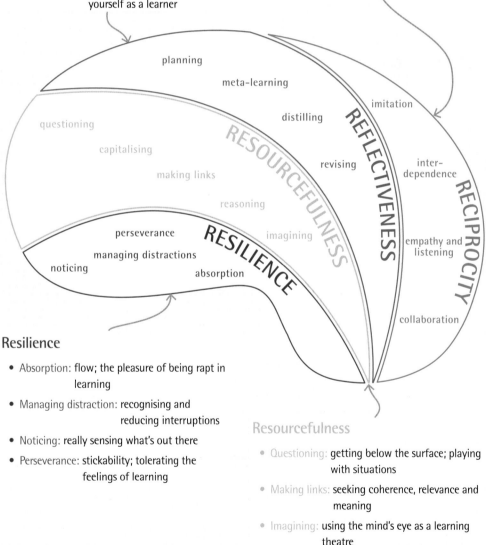

Resilience

- Absorption: flow; the pleasure of being rapt in learning
- Managing distraction: recognising and reducing interruptions
- Noticing: really sensing what's out there
- Perseverance: stickability; tolerating the feelings of learning

Resourcefulness

- Questioning: getting below the surface; playing with situations
- Making links: seeking coherence, relevance and meaning
- Imagining: using the mind's eye as a learning theatre
- Reasoning: thinking rigorously and methodically
- Capitalising: making good use of resources

Building
interpersonal
interaction

Reciprocity covers the **social** and interpersonal side of learning: being able both to argue your corner and keep an open mind in discussion; listening carefully and seeing other sides to the question; being a collaborative team member and team-leader; and being open to positive skills and attitudes that are being modelled by those around you.

Reflectiveness covers the **strategic** and **self-managing** sides of learning. It includes planning and anticipating needs and obstacles; taking stock and flexibly revising your approach as you go along; distilling out lessons and applications for the future; and honest self-appraisal of yourself as a learner.

Building
responsibilty
for learning

On page 41 you can see the vocabulary we used to capture these complementary aspects of what we called 'the supple learning mind'.

Many schools clearly like this way of giving structure and meaning to the dispositions. Others, however, can either get stuck at the 'coarse grain' level, or dive down into the 'fine grain' level too fast, and get confused.

An accessible
language

Third, if the language of learning is to have the pragmatic function we want—if it is to become part of the everyday lingo of a school—we think that it must be couched in terms that are accessible to students and their parents, as well as to teachers. This has meant resisting the temptation, all too strong in educational circles, to use language that is designed to look academic or abstruse. We have already mentioned 'reflectiveness', for example, which is an important facet of powerful learning. But the concept can perfectly well be brought to life through everyday phrases such as 'thinking about what you are doing', 'standing back and taking stock', or 'checking your approach'. We have almost had to become bilingual, using one kind of language to convince officials or academic colleagues of the legitimacy of the BLP approach, and another to get the ideas across to students, parents and teachers.

Optimising the
positive

The need for accessibility also means looking for ways of designing and presenting ideas to schools that are attractive and appealing. We don't see any merit in perpetuating the idea that if something is to be taken seriously, it has to look dull. In our view, such an attitude is merely self-defeating. This is not a matter of 'dumbing down' the concepts, nor of 'being patronising' (both accusations have been levelled at BLP, mostly by academics). It is a matter of trying to optimise the positive impact of what we are doing, and what we care about.

Since 2002, schools have helped us learn a lot about getting the language right—though the feedback has not always been what we would have expected. Take the word 'reciprocity', for example. When we were putting the framework together, we were looking for a fourth word beginning with R to cover the social side of being a powerful learner.

'Relationships' or 'relating' were obvious contenders, but we rejected them on the grounds that were not quite the same kinds of abstract nouns as the other three R's—so we went with the rather fancier notion of reciprocity. Some schools have told us that they have had trouble with 'reciprocity', some joking that it's even hard to say. However, many have reported a different experience: children even as young as four love words like 'reciprocity', precisely because they are difficult, and they feel grown-up being able to say them and use them correctly. Our attitude to such questioning would usually be: look behind the words to the meaning they are trying to convey, discuss it with your staff and pupils, and choose the words that have the strongest resonance and 'stickiness' for them, but which hold true to the original concept. Ownership is more important than linguistic nicety; the letter is always subordinate to the spirit!

Can you say reciprocity?

The frameworks of BLP

BLP has a clear social, moral and philosophical rationale. It puts at the heart of education the development of psychological characteristics that are judged to be of the highest value to young people growing up in a turbulent and demanding world. It has a robust scientific rationale for suggesting what some of these characteristics are, and for the guiding assumption that these characteristics are indeed capable of being systematically developed. With this in mind, what are the 'tools for thought' that are at the heart of BLP? What does BLP offer schools and teachers who resonate with its vision to help them implement it?

'Tools for thought'

Essentially, BLP provides two frameworks.

- The first is a coherent picture of what the powerful learner is like—a working language for talking about young people *as learners*.
- The second is a route map of how regular schools can build the constituent dispositions of the powerful learner.

These two frameworks give teachers and students a 'big picture' to hang on to, the picture on the box, as it were, to provide a context whilst they are working on one small corner of the learning power jigsaw puzzle.

The first framework, which we called the Supple Learning Mind, is a pragmatic tool that illustrates the ingredients of learning power and provides a basis for discussion. It reminds everyone that they don't have to work on exercising all the learning muscles at once (just as you don't try to do your stretches while you are on the running machine). We can zoom in on 'managing distractions' knowing that, in due course, the big picture will remind us to work on building up 'empathy' or 'reasoning' as well.

The Supple Learning Mind

This first framework is essential, we believe, if teachers are going to think precisely and creatively about how they can become more effective learning

The Teachers' Palette

Commentating

- drawing individual students' attention towards their own learning
- responding to students' comments and questions in ways that encourage learning-to-learn
- commenting on difficulties and achievements in learning-positive ways
- recording the development of students' learning power

Orchestrating

- choosing activities that develop the learning habits
- clarifying the learning intentions behind specific activities
- helping students set and monitor their own learning power targets
- making use of displays and physical arrangements to encourage independence

COMMENTATING

nudging
replying
evaluating
tracking

ORCHESTRATING

selecting
arranging
target-setting
framing

EXPLAINING

informing
reminding
discussing
training

MODELLING

reacting
learning aloud
demonstrating
sharing

Explaining

- making clear the overall purpose of the classroom
- offering ongoing reminders and prompts about learning power
- inviting students' own ideas and opinions about learning
- giving direct information and practice in learning: tips and techniques

Modelling

- responding to unforeseen events, questions, etc. in ways that model good learning
- externalising the thinking, feeling and decision making of a learner-in-action
- having learning projects that are visible in the classroom
- talking about their own learning careers and histories

power coaches. We often use the analogy of a fitness coach in a gym. Such coaches are able to construct broad, balanced and effective exercise regimes that will help people get fitter, because they have a model of what the different ingredients are that go to make up 'fitness'. There's suppleness, strength, stamina, speed of cardiovascular recovery from exercise, body-mass index, and so on. They can get us to work on all those things, and gradually, in concert, they add up to improved fitness.

'Learning power' is the same kind of idea. BLP assumes that a working model of learning power helps us design targeted, effective activities that, over time, add up to greater confidence and capacity in facing all kinds of uncertainties and challenges. Just as fitness is a basic springboard for the acquisition of all kinds of more specific physical skills, so learning power is a springboard for all kinds of more specific learning activities—both in school and out. The first framework provides a design template for that springboard which schools can then develop in their own ways.

The second framework, which we called the Teachers' Palette, maps the aspects of a school and classroom culture that help to cultivate those habits of mind. If we want young people to become better at concentrating, say, what does that suggest about the way we structure our lessons? If we want them to become more willing to take risks in their learning, and more tolerant of making mistakes, how should we alter the way we mark their work, or the choices we make about what to display on the walls of the classrooms and corridors? If we want youngsters to become better at giving supportive feedback to each other, and at learning how to take such feedback without getting defensive, what does that suggest about how we might let them see more of us, the teachers, engaging in peer observation and discussion? And so on.

The Teachers' Palette

Just as learning power itself is made up of a number of different interwoven capacities, so is the school culture that cultivates learning power. We have good reason to think that the way teachers talk is important, as is the visibility of their own learning habits. We think the design of activities, the structuring of space, the accessibility of resources, and the messages of the visual environment are all important too. And it is not just teachers who embody the principles of learning power: so do learning support assistants, midday-supervisors, administrative staff, governors, and parents. A learning powered school helps everyone to know how to add to the nutrient medium—the culture—in which its pupils are immersed.

The Teachers' Palette provides a complementary overview of all the different aspects of their work which teachers can use to build learning muscles: how they explain learning and invite debate about the practice of learning; how they orchestrate activities to develop learning habits; how they commentate on learning to nudge progression; and how they model being a learner. There are many layers, we have discovered, through which a school can build up a culture that nurtures the development of inquisitiveness, responsibility, and independence. The Teachers' Palette provides a basis for long-term planning and change. Some of the layers may be relatively easy for a teacher or a school to work on straightaway. With others it will take a bit of thought to see how to be ready to take the necessary steps.

In this chapter we have summarised the intellectual foundations of learning power, explained why we talk as we do and use the metaphors that we do, and shown the distinctions that we make and how these map onto the two original frameworks of BLP. We think it is important for a school to understand these footings of BLP thoroughly, to ensure their efforts to change don't unwittingly slide back into more familiar grooves that are 'not quite it'.

Chapter 3

Beliefs and assumptions: Barriers to whole-hearted buy-in

In this chapter we explore a variety of doubts, anxieties, challenges, and misapprehensions about BLP through a series of frequently asked questions, including:

- risking examination results

- affording the time for BLP

- fear of Ofsted

- 'It's what we have always done'

- 'Does it work for gifted and talented?'

- 'Parents will be suspicious'

- 'Pupils like to be spoon-fed'

Some teachers and school leaders are keen to get going with BLP; they like the ideas, and all they want to know is how to put BLP ideas into practice in their own situations. But over the years we have encountered a variety of doubts, anxieties, challenges and misapprehensions about what BLP means for a school, and what its likely effects might be. Some teachers are more cautious, and may have quite legitimate questions they need answering before they are willing to try out some of the ideas whole-heartedly. Perhaps they have seen educational fads and fashions come and go, and are naturally a little sceptical of what might turn out to be, as one teacher called it, a JABI—'just another blooming initiative' (or words to similar effect).

These questions are of many different kinds. Some are to do with beliefs and values. 'Does this fit with my own identity as a teacher?' Some want to know the rationale: 'How solid are the foundations?' (These two we have tried to answer in the previous two chapters). Some questions are requests for evidence. Some concern the specifics of implementation. Some reflect more-or-less conscious, more-or-less deep-seated beliefs about teaching and learning—even about the natures and capacities of young minds. In this chapter, we try to articulate some of these FAQs, and sketch our answers to them. (The rest of the book provides much more detailed answers to some of these questions.) We hope that this overview will be useful to individuals, as they figure out whether BLP is something for them, and seek to understand just what is being asked of them.

We also hope this chapter will be helpful to senior leadership teams, as they travel the inevitably rocky road to culture change in their schools. It is obviously essential to allow these questions to surface, and to treat them with respect. Most of them are not born out of knee-jerk cynicism or entrenchment. They deserve time and attention. The research of Michael Fullan and others shows that time allowed for discussion, argument and the expression of misgivings is almost always time well spent. Where dissent and challenge are suppressed, polarisation and even subversion are much more likely to emerge.

Here are some of the common 'Yes, Buts'—or even just plain 'Buts'.

'It sounds interesting, but we just can't risk the examination results.'

When pupils are helped to become more confident and independent as learners, and more articulate about the process of learning itself, their results go up, not down. Under test conditions, they are less likely to 'go to pieces'; they are more resilient in the face of difficulty—they don't give up so easily; they are more resourceful—if it doesn't work one way, they are better at finding other strategies or avenues to try. And so they do better. BLP depends on this 'AND' philosophy: better preparation for life AND better examination performance.

'AND' philosophy

However, some people seem to want to keep surreptitiously replacing that AND with an OR. It's as if they can't quite let themselves believe that AND is a real possibility. But the evidence says it is. The real choice is not between 'results' and some risky, new-fangled stuff called 'key competencies' or 'character capabilities'; it is between results achieved through cramming and spoon-feeding, and results achieved through the development of initiative and self-reliance. This EITHER / OR mindset can be countered through reading and discussion of what the research actually says—a discussion in which parents and governors (as well as students themselves) can fruitfully be involved.

> 'There might well be a wobble in the results while we are getting used to new ways of working—for which we might be clobbered.'

This concern is a perfectly reasonable variation of the previous one. It is not the worry that there is a deep incompatibility between the two goals; it is more that the implementation of BLP might destabilise the pupils' learning (for a while), and the results might go down in the short term, before they go up in the longer term. The worry is that the 'powers that be'—the local authority, Ofsted—might not have the patience or the faith to wait for the recovery, and penalise the school in the meantime.

The extent to which this is a real risk depends on circumstances. Some schools have to work with local authorities that are in highly draconian mode, demanding short-term improvements in test scores at any cost. The moment might indeed not be right to take on a new approach. And results do wobble even at the best of times, without the attempt to install a learning-to-learn culture. It would be much more supportive and intelligent if schools were judged on a rolling three- or five-year average of their results, say, not solely year by year. The extent of these wobbles can be seen in the 'multiple baseline' graph on the next page. (The bulk of our data is presented in Chapter 11.) This graph charts the GCSE performance of our group of BLP secondary research schools from two years before they introduced BLP, until the present. This gives us some idea about the variability in GCSE results from year to year before and after BLP was introduced. As you can see, the 'wobbles' occur just as much on both sides of the BLP start year.

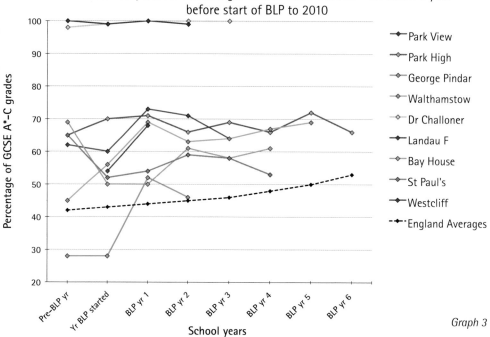

Graph 3

Perhaps the most reassuring thing to remember here is that BLP involves not a quick revolution but a gradual evolution. It offers a clear direction of travel for a school, and then a whole variety of ways in which progress in that direction can be made in small steps. Every teacher can start to make small adjustments to the way they plan lessons, or talk to students, that do not threaten or overwhelm anyone. Every school can experiment with small changes to the way they write reports or organise assemblies that won't jeopardise hard-won league table positions. Many of the changes that BLP involves are quite small-scale, and are not destabilising in the least. Yet these small shifts very often seem to make a tangible difference to levels of curiosity and engagement in all concerned. BLP's 'slow and steady' approach minimises the risk that there will be any sudden shocks to the system of a school which might impact adversely on results.

'It's all very well, but we just can't afford all the time it would take.'

Yes, BLP takes time to embed in a school, and effort by individual teachers before it becomes second nature. It isn't a quick fix or a glossy veneer, and we make no apology for that. But, as we have just said, the gradual, long-haul nature of BLP means you can take it slowly and by degrees. The guiding principles translate into a smorgasbord of small suggestions and possibilities, each one of which is not too demanding, and which build cumulatively into a significant shift in atmosphere and focus.

Take it slowly

> 'Something hit me very hard once, thinking about what one little man could do. Think of the Queen Mary—the whole ship goes by and then comes the rudder. And there's a tiny thing at the edge of the rudder called a trim tab. It's a miniature rudder. Just moving the little trim tab builds a low pressure that pulls the rudder around. Takes almost no effort at all. So I said that the little individual can be a trim tab. Society thinks it's going right by you, that it's left you altogether. But if you're doing dynamic things mentally, the fact is that you can just put your foot out like that and the whole big ship of state is going to go. So I said, call me Trim Tab.'
>
> Buckminster Fuller

BLP is not a whole new initiative or technology at all; it doesn't require mastery of a complex set of procedures, and there isn't a fat manual to be memorised. It is a set of small adjustments to 'the way we do things round here' that set the big, complicated entity that is a school off on a different course. Buckminster Fuller used the idea of a trim tab—the tiny 'rudder within a rudder' that makes it easier for a big ship to change course— as a metaphor for the effect that one individual can have on his or her society. BLP is constantly on the look-out for small changes that can have big effects in schools. BLP is more about trim tabs than grand revolutions.

Small changes, big levers.

'Ofsted won't like it. We've got an inspection coming up, so we will need to 'revert to type' when the inspectors come in.'

Again, the risk of such judgements is real, but we have found it to be much smaller than many schools fear. Though the inspection framework does not explicitly value the development of students' independent learning habits, overwhelmingly we find that inspectors love it when they see it. From the reports we have gathered from inspections of BLP schools, their overwhelming reaction is to congratulate schools where they find the pupils are self-aware and articulate about their learning, happy to take responsibility for their own learning, good at collaborating, and so on. And if the results in high-performing schools hold up, and those in lower-performing schools increase...what's not to like?

Actually, we have found that reverting to type, when the inspectors come to call, can be counter-productive. One academy nearly lost its 'outstanding' assessment, because the teachers tried to 'play it safe', and it was the pupils themselves who saved the day—as the Principal explains:

A cautionary tale

53

' *[The children]spoke about learning in a way that could not have been shaped by the lessons the inspectors were seeing. The inspectors said, "Hang on a minute: there's a mismatch here. We're seeing predominantly quite defensive lessons, not much risk-taking. But your children are talking a completely different game! The teaching we are seeing can't be representative of what the children are getting!" And that got them [the inspectors] looking more deeply at the culture of the school as a whole.*'

'I suspect that BLP is just "good teaching" wrapped up in fancy words. It is what good teachers have always done.'

Well, that depends on your definition of 'good teaching', and the outcomes by which you judge it. There is plenty of evidence that some schools and teachers consistently get good exam results, but they do it by spoon-feeding, and their students do not develop high levels of emotional resilience, cognitive resourcefulness, sociability, and self-awareness along the way. If you don't notice, or don't care, that a good many of them become anxious and lost during their first year at university—if you don't think it is any of your business—then you could call what you do 'good teaching'—but we don't.

What learning habits do we want to develop?

There are many schools and teachers that adopt an in-between position. 'We make our students think and stretch their minds', they say, and they do. But it is a rare school that, without the benefit of BLP (or similar approaches such as Habits of Mind) has thought through exactly what learning habits they are trying to develop, and how, systematically, they are going about it. 'Today, class, we are going to learn about electromagnetism, AND we are going to stretch our ability to use visualisation productively in a scientific context', is not something you hear as often as 'Explain carefully your reasons for thinking that'. In other words, many schools do aim to train students' powers of reasoning and argument—but they often miss out many of the other elements that go to make up a powerful learner, and they leave learners in the dark about what's going on in their learning.

A new rigour for 'training of the mind'

BLP brings a new degree of rigour and precision to the venerable view of education as a 'training of the mind'. It broadens and makes more explicit what that intention involves. So, yes, BLP is about 'good teaching', but it is a rare school, when it realises what BLP actually involves, that can honestly say 'We are doing all this already'. Usually, on closer inspection, what they are doing is somewhat patchy and partial. In our experience, it is the schools that have taken BLP most seriously, and made the most innovative uses of it, that are always the first to say, 'And we are still only doing a fraction of what we now see is possible'.

'OK, but it's still my job to help students get the right answers.'

Yes it is. They will need to get 'right answers' if they are to pass their exams. But the critical thing is how you help them. Do you help them in a way that means they have to remember what it is that you did, or which merely gives them a technique that is triggered by a particular problem? If so, they may not really understand what it is they are doing—and that means they may be completely thrown by an apparently trivial change in the way the problem is worded. David Perkins describes a class of students who complained bitterly that they had been taught how to calculate the time it took for an object to fall from a twenty metre tower, but that the exam had asked them about a rock falling down a twenty metre hole— and they couldn't do it.[1] In the rush to help them 'do it', you may not be helping them to do it for themselves, or to do it in a way that is flexible and thoughtful. Nudging, coaxing and encouraging may have better long-term impact than explaining and drilling.

Professor Jo Boaler of Sussex University has found that girls in top maths sets often struggle for a very particular reason. Teachers have high expectations of top sets, so they tend to rattle through the material at a speed that enables students to learn techniques and procedures, but not to really 'get their heads round' what is going on. Boys, Boaler discovered, are more willing to settle for this instrumental kind of understanding than girls. The girls tend to worry more that they don't really understand what they are doing, and this leads not only to greater anxiety but also to underachievement. Boaler concludes:

> 'Maladaptive patterns will be countered when students are exposed to environments in which they are encouraged to try things out, to get things wrong as they do so and to have the time and space in which to develop their understanding... Only when these conditions are realised will students feel happy about facing challenges on which they may not succeed.'

'BLP sounds like warmed-up 1970s romantic liberalism to me. It didn't work then, and there's no reason to suppose that it will work now.'

Apart from the evidence that it does work—in the sense of producing more confident young people who do better on their tests—this fear (or criticism) is misguided. Yes, BLP encourages students gradually to take more responsibility for their own learning; but this is very far from being merely 'child centred' or worse, 'laisser-faire'. BLP does not suppose that a hands-off approach will result in every little spirit being able to flourish in its own way. We know that, for example, an absence of adult direction results in as many children who flounder as who flourish. BLP owes nothing to the romantic conception of Rousseau's *Emile*, and everything to a cold, hard appraisal of the psychological and social qualities today's young people are going to need as adults.

BLP suggests we look for ways to give pupils more and more responsibility for organising and evaluating their own learning, not because telling them what to do and how well they did it damages their development, but because—pretty obviously—you learn to be independent and self-disciplined by being given opportunities to exercise independence and self-discipline! Within weeks, four-year-olds can, given the chance, strengthen their ability to choose and manage aspects of their own learning. And the BLP teacher is constantly on the look-out for opportunities, not to abandon children to their own devices, but to stretch their ability to 'do it for themselves'.

Learn to be independent by practising being independent

'We've got a stand-alone Learning to Learn course in Year 7 already; we don't need another initiative, thank you.'

The trouble with stand-alone courses in Thinking Skills or Learning to Learn is that they don't have much impact beyond the particular setting in which they happen. Evaluations of such courses tend to find, disappointingly, that any benefits don't last, and they don't generalise to other contexts.[2] Transferable benefits are much more likely to result from an 'infusion' approach, in which the cultivation of thinking and learning habits is addressed and promoted across the curriculum and beyond. As David Perkins's work has shown, skills that are taught or trained directly, in only one kind of situation, tend to remain tied to the content, context and purposes that obtained in that situation. If the skills are to turn into flexible, generalisable habits of mind, they have to be used in a range of contexts, especially those where their use is not explicitly prompted.

The problem of transfer

'We've done learning to learn, thinking skills and so on. We've moved on to much more cutting edge developments such as X, Y or Z.'

Following on from the previous question, schools and teachers have to help that process of generalisation to occur, and that won't happen just in a lesson or two a week of playing with logical puzzles, or sitting in a circle discussing philosophical chestnuts. If there is an infused culture of learning in a school already, then we find that some time explicitly talking about the learning habits can help students deepen their grasp of them. But if that broad culture is missing, then lessons on thinking or learning by themselves are unlikely to lead to any benefits that last and spread. That is why BLP, as it has evolved, has expanded its focus from the design of lessons to include the background culture of the classroom, and, beyond the classroom, to include many different aspects of the ethos and fabric of the school as a whole.

Schools that see BLP as a time-limited initiative that you 'do', and then you have 'done it', simply haven't understood it. BLP is a creative journey, not a quick fix. It is not a package that you implement; it is an ever-deepening exploration of how to build a culture that breeds confident, intelligent, powerful lifelong learners. Andrea Curtis, Head of Bushfield School in Milton Keynes, says, *'When I first came across BLP, what I didn't realise was the depth of it. I didn't realise how challenging it was going to be.'* Bushfield has been working with BLP for three years, and has made huge strides. It is one of the most innovative and successful BLP primary schools. And yet at one point they felt the need to apologise for achieving less than they now know they could achieve. Not all schools are ready to think as deeply and explore as creatively as Bushfield have done. But it is important to understand that changing a culture is not a quick and easy thing to do.

A creative journey

'We think BLP looks OK for the more able students, but what about the less able?'

Our review shows that there is a degree of truth in this concern, but that it is far from being the whole picture. It is true that students who are already confident learners can catch on to the BLP language more readily than those whose learning confidence and capacity have been limited or stunted. Students who have more or less given up on learning may be harder to enthuse with the idea that, with effort, they can build their confidence and capacity back up. But it is not impossible. You may have to start at a lower level than you hoped, and cajole them more persistently, but lower-achieving students soon latch on to BLP and find it useful.

Take George Pindar Community Sports College, which serves a very deprived area of Scarborough, and with many low-achieving students. As in many schools in similarly demanding areas, we have found that currently lower-achieving students thrive on learning experiences that stretch their learning muscles. For example, a group of lower ability Year 9 students at George Pindar were challenged to investigate a painting. Given pieces of the picture bit by bit, they were required to pose questions, make links, reason and imagine. As one student said to her teacher, *'You're making my brain hurt—in a good way; I want to work this out for myself.'* Although these students had little experience away from their Scarborough council estate, their perceptions became increasingly astute and their capacity to develop greater collaboration, and to keep an open mind to new ideas, was impressive. Even when they had assembled the whole picture, the students, egged on by their teacher, were still full of questions, and sought out internet resources that would enable them to check and refine their ideas still further.

In the thousands of hours that we collectively have spent in lessons, we have noticed that lower attaining students are often given experiences that are well within their capabilities. They are not challenged by what they are given to do, and do not yet know how to make it more challenging, and therefore interesting, for themselves. But when provided with an intriguing and well-orchestrated learning stretch, and encouraged to take more control of their learning, such students very often show greater engagement, and surprise both their teachers and themselves. At Simpson School in Milton Keynes, for example, Charlie, a seven-year-old tearaway, describes his changing experience of school very clearly:

> *'Until I got my learning muscles, I used to kick off; but now I know that I've got a good imagination, and my teacher helps me use it, I don't kick off no more.'*

'We think BLP looks OK for our less able students— but what about the high achievers and the gifted and talented?'

This is the exact reverse of the previous worry. Some schools think that, while the low-achievers can use a bit of help, their 'high-fliers' are fine as they are. They must already be powerful learners, right, or they wouldn't be high-achievers? However, BLP draws a sharp distinction between students who have mastered a narrow set of learning techniques that they have found to deliver examination success, and students who have developed a broader, deeper capacity for learning in all its forms, in school and out. We sometimes ask teachers: 'Do you think it is possible to be a successful student, and not a very powerful learner?' After a few seconds thought, the vast majority say 'Yes'. They can easily think of students who do well on tests, but who are anxious and conservative in their approach to learning more generally. They also agree with the converse: that it is possible to be a powerful learner, and not a very successful student.

So BLP can indeed be of value to high-achieving students and high-achieving schools. Take Dr Challoner's Grammar School, a very high-achieving secondary school in the leafy Home Counties town of Amersham, for example. In Mark Sturgeon's A2 geography class, as in many other lessons, the students had got used to their teachers providing them with prescribed ways of answering examination questions. They had become rather passive and 'instrumental' in their approach to learning—and Mark wanted to do something about it. He wanted his 18-year-olds to pose more questions for themselves, to explore issues from a variety of angles, and to venture their own ideas and solutions. So in a unit on the developing world, he reversed his normal teaching strategy, and asked them to raise their own questions about agriculture, trade and international relations before showing them a video about Tanzania. He wanted them to be prepped with their own interests, so that, when they watched the film, they would do so with greater curiosity and discernment. Nor did he simply let the film run its course: he constantly stopped the film, quizzing the students about how their ideas and questions were developing, and getting them to pool their thoughts on mini-whiteboards. After a few weeks of such teaching, Mark's students have moved from being passive recipients to active interrogators of information and ideas. Such a shift is hardly revolutionary, and it is certainly not unique to BLP. But it does illustrate how a small change in a teacher's habits can quickly produce a concomitant change in the learning habits of his or her students—even the high-achievers. And no prizes for guessing whether the A-level results went up or down as a result.

'By the time we get them, it is really too late to try to shift their attitudes to learning.'

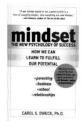

This is a concern that is sometimes expressed by sixth forms, sixth form colleges or further education colleges. And yes, as with many other traits, as people get older, so their beliefs and attitudes towards learning may become more fixed and resistant to change. But all is not lost. Carol Dweck, in her book *Mindset*, describes research with teenagers, undergraduates and working adults, which shows, as Dweck puts it, that 'it is never too late to develop a growth mindset'. Many high school students changed their attitudes towards learning after even a relatively brief intervention.

Luton Sixth Form College

Luton Sixth Form College had been using the BLP framework for some years. In 2008 they commissioned a project, funded by the National Association for Gifted and Talented Youth and carried out by the Villiers Park Educational Trust, to explore students' experience of the use of the BLP capacities in their lessons. The project was planned jointly with a group of students, who decided to focus on a subset of the capacities:

- absorption, managing distractions
- questioning, making links, capitalising
- planning, revising, distilling
- collaboration, empathy and listening

Students kept logs of the frequency and utility of these capacities in about 50 lessons in eight subjects over a period of four weeks. All the capacities were used with empathy and listening topping the list. The scoring scales indicated that all the capacities were felt to be useful and effective overall. Variations between students' judgements indicate the significant differences that they bring to bear on their learning. High-achieving A-level students found it both plausible and useful to think about their approaches to and methods of learning.

Overall, we are encouraged by such examples to believe that older students can indeed benefit from the explicitness of the BLP approach.

'We've tried it and the pupils don't like it. They want to be spoon-fed.'

There is an old Polish proverb which says, *'One who sleeps on the floor need not fear falling out of bed'*, and there are indeed some students like that. They prefer to be passive passengers rather than active 'crew' as far as their education is concerned, because that way they do not have to take any risks or be held responsible. And the more we tow them through the curriculum, rather than making them learn how to use their own muscles to swim, the more likely they are to develop that passive attitude. We should not be surprised—and certainly not defeated—if at first some of them resist our efforts to get them to think for themselves. But we have found that, for the vast majority of pupils, this is just a habit that, with a bit of persistence and persuasion, they can get over; and when they do, they discover that school is more engaging and more rewarding. They become more keen to be proactive and independent.

Start small
Be persistent

The Golden Rules, when you start to push students towards taking more responsibility for their own learning, are:

- start small: make just one or two small shifts to 'the way we do things round here'
- but be persistent and consistent in reminding pupils what your expectations are, and in noticing and commenting approvingly when they meet those expectations.

Don't try to get them to run before they can walk, and don't back down in the face of any resistance. Remember: BLP is not laisser-faire. You are coaching and training your students in a positive attitude towards learning.

'What about the parents? They may be suspicious, and many of them mainly want their children to 'make the grades', and will get upset if it looks like we are going to jeopardise that.'

BLP does focus on an aspect of education that many parents will find unfamiliar. Some may take a while to grasp what it is you are up to, and some may indeed be sceptical. They may well think that school is mostly about examination results (and 'good behaviour'), because that is what they experienced when they were at school. If they did badly, in those

Another game
afoot—another
way of winning

terms, they may have decided that 'school isn't for people like us', and tacitly collude in their child's passivity or disengagement. If they themselves enjoyed what school had to offer, and did well at it, they are more likely to be pushing their child to succeed in the same ways. Either way, they may take some persuading that there is another game afoot—another way of 'winning' at school, regardless of the exam results.

And they may take some reassuring that this other game, the game of building their child's confidence and capacity for real-life learning, will boost rather than risk their examination performance. As we will see in Chapter 10, explaining and demonstrating to parents what BLP means for their child, so that they will support your efforts, is an important layer of the culture change process that schools need to attend to. It may take a year or two of gentle persuasion before the bulk of them are on board; or it may happen sooner. We have found that, if school leaders and teachers take the time to discuss what they are doing, and why, the vast majority of parents understand it, support it, and want to know how they can help.

'What can you do with our local kids? It's their background that determines their attitudes to learning. That's just how they are, and there's no point trying to change it. '

The final two concerns are cries of fatalism. The first one suggests there is no point in trying to develop students' capacity as learners because their home background—usually presumed to be one of disaffection with education—will overwhelm any attempts to do so. It is fair to say that this objection is much less common now than it was ten years ago. We now know that young people's attitudes are not fixed by their early experience, but remain quite malleable. Some youngsters may be very hard to change, but the majority, our schools tell us, respond well to the idea that their minds can get fitter, stronger and more supple—just as their bodies can.

Attitudes remain malleable

Learning habits are amenable to coaching. If your pupils are not very good at listening to each other, or justifying their opinions, or concentrating in the face of distractions—set up a training programme and coach it. Over the course of a term (or even just a few weeks) these habits of mind can be developed. Scatty children can become more able to concentrate. Dreamy children can learn to think more carefully. Solitary children can learn to collaborate effectively with other children who they may not know, or even like. Dependent children can learn to enjoy evaluating and improving their own work. Children with brittle self-esteem can discover the pleasure to be had in choosing and struggling with difficult things. That is the BLP teacher's mindset: 'If you want it, coach it!'

'If you want it, coach it!'

'It's all very well, but at the end of the day it's mostly down to a child's ability—and there's not much you can do about that. '

The second kind of fatalism is the one that attributes most of a child's success or failure to their 'ability' or 'intelligence', which is seen as fixed, and therefore beyond the teachers' power to influence. This can be quite a 'sticky' idea in some teachers' minds, but we saw in the last chapter that it is false. It is not a child's 'ability' that sets a ceiling on what they can do, it is their (and their teachers') *belief* in their ability that is much more potent. And these beliefs can be changed. As Henry Ford is reputed to have said, 'The person who believes they can, and the one who believes they can't, are both right.' The evidence is overwhelming, in BLP schools as well as in the research literature, that small, smart practical shifts in the way teachers talk and act can either unleash, or dam up, students' learning power.

It is belief in ability that counts

_____

As part of its journey, a school may have to address some or all of these Frequently Asked Questions for discussion. It will probably take more than these short paragraphs to convince a sceptical colleague or parent; but this chapter should at least help to get the conversation going. The rest of the book provides much more detailed advice about how to implement the BLP philosophy successfully.

Part 2
The Classroom Experience

In Part 2 we turn to the question, What exactly is it that teachers are being asked to do differently? The chapters explore four key aspects of this change that impinge directly on students.

Chapter 4 looks at teachers' demeanour: at the way teachers talk about learning, and the attitudes towards learning that they model in the classroom. Both of these influence how students engage with what is going on in their lessons, and the attitudes toward learning which they themselves develop.[1]

Chapter 5 focuses on pedagogy—the way teachers design and deliver lessons—and discusses ways in which the learning-power habits can be cultivated, both implicitly and explicitly, through the activities that are on offer, and the way the classroom environment is constructed.

Chapter 6 looks beyond the individual lesson at the broad design of the curriculum—the way the timetable is constructed, or how enrichment activities are used to broaden learning power.

Finally, Chapter 7 discusses assessment and progression: practical ways in which teachers can check whether BLP is actually making a difference—both so that individual students can be supported and encouraged in their developing learning habits, and so that teachers can know how well their own hopes and aspirations are being achieved.

'Every word and action can send a message. It tells children or students how to think about themselves. It can be a fixed-mindset message that says: "You have permanent traits and I am judging them." Or it can be a growth-mindset message that says: "You are a developing person and I am interested in your development." It is remarkable how sensitive children are to these messages.'

Carol Dweck, *Mindset*

Chapter 4

Teachers: Walking the talk

In this chapter we explore:

- the importance of teacher language
- power of teachers as role models
- examples of BLP talk
- examples of BLP 'walk'

There is much evidence that classroom cultures are hugely shaped by teachers, both through the language they use and in the way that they act under the watchful eyes and listening ears of their students. Indeed the kind of learning culture created in classrooms depends a good deal on the way teachers talk about learning (and the attitudes to knowledge and life that such talk shows). Learning cultures also emerge in the way that teachers talk about their students. So, it is possible for them to talk to young people in ways that suggest their students are powerful learners and potential learning coaches—young teachers even—or in ways that infantilise or depreciate them.

Equally important are the learning attitudes and habits that teachers themselves model. Are teachers themselves resourceful when things do not go to plan? Do they see it as useful to offer glimpses of their own learning lives, for example, letting their class see that teachers find some learning difficult and have to really persist at such things?

Talking the walk

By the way they express themselves, teachers create a potent linguistic milieu that teaches young people what kinds of learning are valued 'round here', what their role is with respect to knowledge, and what aspects of learning are worth paying attention to. In this chapter, we explain a number of practical shifts that teachers have been making in the language they use and the example they set, that encourage an inquisitive, resilient, and imaginative attitude in students. This shift in their demeanour forms a vital backdrop to the more visible and concrete changes that we describe in the other chapters of Part 2.

Play versus work

The power and subtlety of this milieu has been demonstrated in research studies. For example, Harvard psychologists Ellen Langer and Sophia Snow have shown that merely changing one word in the way an activity is described can have a significant effect on people's levels of enjoyment and engagement.

Two groups of volunteers were asked to rewrite the captions to Gary Larson cartoons (*The Far Side*) so as to change their meaning. For one group this activity was referred to as 'play' while for the other it was referred to as 'work'. Not only did the 'play' group find the activity more pleasurable than the 'work' group, they also reported being much more locked on to it, their minds wandered much less, they were more imaginative, and they learned more from the activity.

Could-Be language

On page 32 we met Ellen Langer's work on the importance of using 'Could-Be' language and how this encourages more genuine engagement with what is being taught; how students will question and solve problems more readily if knowledge is presented to them as being provisional. Langer's studies document the effect of shifting the tone in which knowledge is presented on students' learning.[2]

What we might call 'Is language' is full of certainty. It sets clear boundaries, and it often looks as though it is complete and definitive. 'Could-Be language', on the other hand, is more tentative and provisional: it leaves open the possibility that things might not be cut-and-dried, and that the reader or listener might be able to spot a flaw or an improvement. When Langer presented these different versions to two matched groups of students, she found no difference in their factual comprehension. 'Could-Be language' had not interfered with their grasp of the material. But when she probed their understanding with more creative or open-ended questions, she found that the 'Could-Be students' far out-performed their peers in the 'Is' group.

The reason for the difference is not hard to see. 'Is language' positions students as knowledge-consumers. Their job is to try to understand and remember. But 'Could-Be language' immediately invites students to be more thoughtful, critical, or imaginative about what they are reading.

If we want young people to grow up to be inquisitive about what they are told, and imaginative in their responses to it, it would seem to be patently self-defeating to talk to them in a linguistic register that prevents them from bringing those learning dispositions to bear. 'Is language' invites—or almost requires—students to use learning muscles like 'verbatim remembering' and 'accurate transcription'. There is nothing wrong with these; they are indeed useful in the real world. But they are not the be-all and end-all of learning. Nor, many would argue, are they the most useful habits of mind with which to meet a complex and contested world. 'Could-Be language' invites critical thinking, imagination and resourcefulness, as well as helping students to develop a richer set of transferable skills.

Encouraging critics and makers of knowledge

A central belief of BLP is that, to breed powerful and enthusiastic young learners, we need to engage them not just as consumers of knowledge, but as critics and makers of knowledge. We need to talk to them as if the subject-matter we are discussing is provisional and contestable, not as if it is cut and dried. Of course, much of the knowledge and theory in the curriculum has stood the test of time very well. But in order to turn out thinkers rather than hoarders and regurgitators, we need to find and emphasise its unravelled edges, and help them discover how to function intelligently in this zone of contest and uncertainty. BLP schools know that it is in this zone that much real learning happens, and that this is where they have to learn how to be comfortable and effective. As a consequence, BLP teachers observe that not only the words they use change, but also the tone they adopt shifts.

'I used to ask leading questions which structured their thinking towards the "right" answer that I wanted, but that was too much scaffolding. So now I use an inquisitive tone and nudge them to work things out for themselves. It's always surprising what students can find out for themselves when you let them.'

Secondary Teacher

The illustration opposite shows an example of how textbook knowledge, which is often presented in cut-and-dried, brook-no-questions language, can be softened and made more conditional, tentative, or open in a variety of simple ways.

Never and always

Some words can be especially challenging. So, for example, Martin Seligman has shown that toxic words like 'never' and 'always' can be damaging to learners in certain circumstances. If a student says 'I can never understand what my teacher is going on about', or 'Maths is always too hard for me', they betray a view of learning which is pessimistic and unlikely to cultivate the kind of persistence that more optimistic accounts of events might bring. Their 'explanatory style'—Seligman's phrase for the way they account for things that happen to them—lacks resilience, so that something which may be a one-off occurrence assumes the status of something that is permanent and unalterable. If 'always' or 'never' become sentences to fail for ever then they breed a kind of learned helplessness. BLP teachers will be keen to help students to reframe such perceptions. So the two examples above might become:

'I am finding it really hard to understand this today; maybe I should look back at what I did last time.'

'I know I can get stressed when I have to calculate angles, so I'll look at my checklist to remind me how I get started.'

Learning versus work

Another interesting way in which teachers can betray their attitudes very easily is over their choice of vocabulary when talking about learning itself. Teachers have traditionally talked much more about 'work' than they have about 'learning'. Indeed, 'traditional' classrooms may ring to the sound of 'Get on with your work', 'Have you finished your work?', 'How's your work coming on?' and so on. One study carried out in London schools in 2002

IS language (dogmatic)

Municipal bonds
are issued by states,
territories and
possessions of the
United States, as well
as other political
subdivisions. Such
political subdivisions
would include counties,
cities, special districts for
schools, waterworks and
sewers. Public agencies
such as authorities and
commissions also issue
municipal bonds...

For local jurisdictions
such as cities, the most
common taxing power
is on property. An *ad
valorem* tax on the
assessed value of real
estate is the source
of funds the local
government uses to
support its expenses.
School taxes are also
charged at the local level.

COULD-BE language (provisional)

In **most cases**, municipal
bonds are issued by
states, territories
and possessions of
the United States, as
well as other political
subdivisions. Such
political subdivisions
may include counties,
cities, special districts
for schools, waterworks,
sewers and many other
bodies. Public agencies
such as authorities and
commissions **may on
occasion** issue municipal
bonds for a **wide variety**
of public projects...

For local jurisdictions,
which **could be** counties
and cities, the most
common taxing power
may be on property.
An *ad valorem* tax on
the assessed value of
real estate is **probably**
the source of funds the
local government uses
most often to support
its expenses. Of course
there are other ways
a local jurisdiction can
obtain money, **one of
which** is through school
taxes.

Invites students to be more thoughtful, critical, or imaginative

Looks clear and definitive

More tentative and provisional

Leaves open the possibility that things might not be cut and dry

A reader might be able to spot a flaw or an improvement

Positions students as knowledge consumers – to remember and understand

71

compared the frequency of use of these two words, and found that 'work' was used 98% of the time, and 'learning' only 2%

Now there is nothing wrong with the word 'work': it is a useful noun that means, roughly, 'a more-or-less disagreeable activity carried out to achieve an end'—whether that end be a pay-packet or a grade. But it doesn't invite you to get interested in the activity itself. A good many teachers have come back to us and expressed pleasant surprise at the effect on their students of talking less about 'work' and more about the process of learning itself.

In this chapter we invite teachers to reflect on some of the more subtle— but no less powerful—messages that are conveyed by what they say and the way in which they say it. Linguistic habits are contagious, and we have found that these changes can quickly rub off on, for example, the way students talk to each other. Both research and experience suggest that some small shifts in both talking and modelling can have surprisingly significant effects.

The language of Building Learning Power

Of course, Building Learning Power has its own language through which to understand and discuss the learning process. The language framework was described in Chapter 2 and its learning dispositions and capacities are shown in more detail opposite.

Having this language enables teachers to do a number of things. They can plan lessons that deliberately stretch these 'learning muscles' one or two at a time. We will cover this aspect in more detail in the next chapter. They can make use of questionnaires that deliberately try to gauge students' self-perceptions in terms of these concepts, and then use the results to stimulate reflective conversations and learning power target setting. ('I could really do to build up my concentration muscles over the next half-term.') We explore this more in Chapter 7.

The choice of the word 'muscle' is not accidental, of course. Words, as this chapter points out, matter. For muscles, like minds, are expandable. And muscles get stronger by exercising, just as minds get stronger by practising and continually challenging themselves.

Some teachers find the BLP language strange at first.

> ' When we started it was a bit clunky, a bit formulaic. And for some teachers that was good—they felt reassured that they knew what "the right thing to do" was. But others—me included—wanted to get more into the spirit of BLP, and not so much the particular words. A child saying "I need to be more resilient" doesn't make them more resilient: we need to be cultivating that spirit more across the board.

Talk less about work and more about learning

Using the BLP language

The Language of Learning Power

Resilience is being ready, willing, and able to lock onto learning—knowing how to work through difficulties when the pressure mounts or the going gets tough. Your resilience is made up of...

Absorption	Managing distractions	Noticing	Perseverance
Being able to lose yourself in learning — becoming absorbed in what you are doing; rapt and attentive; in a state of 'flow'.	Recognising and reducing distractions; knowing when to walk away and refresh yourself; creating your own best environment for learning	Perceiving subtle nuances, patterns, and details in experience.	Keeping going in the face of difficulties; channelling the energy of frustration productively; knowing what a slow and uncertain process learning often is.

Resourcefulness is being ready, willing, and able to learn in different ways—using both internal and external resources effectively, calling on different ways of learning as appropriate. Your resourcefulness is made up of...

Questioning	Making links	Imagining	Reasoning	Capitalising
Asking questions of yourself and others; being curious and playful with ideas; delving beneath the surface of things.	Seeing connections between disparate events and experiences; building patterns; weaving a web of understanding.	Using your imagination and intuition to put yourself through new experiences or to explore possibilities; wondering 'what if...?'	Calling up your logical and rational skills to work things out methodically and rigorously; constructing good arguments, and spotting the flaws in others.	Drawing on the full range of resources from the wider world—other people, books, the Internet, past experience, future opportunities ...

Reflectiveness is being ready, willing, and able to become more strategic about learning—taking a longer-term view by planning, taking stock, and drawing out your experiences as a learner to get the best out of yourself. Your reflectiveness is made up of...

Planning	Revising	Distilling	Meta-learning
Thinking about where you are going, the action you are going to take, the time and resources you will need, and the obstacles you may encounter.	Being flexible; changing your plans in the light of different circumstances; monitoring and reviewing how things are going; seeing new opportunities.	Looking at what is being learned; pulling out the essential features; carrying them forward to aid further learning; being your own learning coach.	Knowing yourself as a learner — how you learn best; how to talk about the learning process.

Reciprocity in learning is being ready, willing, and able to learn alone or with other people—using a sense of independent judgement together with skills in communication and empathy. Your reciprocity is made up of...

Interdependence	Collaboration	Empathy & listening	Imitation
Knowing when it's appropriate to learn on your own or with others; being able to stand your ground in debate.	Knowing how to manage yourself in the give-and-take of a collaborative venture; respecting and recognising other view points; adding to and drawing from the strength of teams.	Contributing to others' experiences by listening to them to understand what they are really saying, and putting yourself in their shoes.	Constructively adopting methods, habits or values from other people whom you observe.

Teacher prompts to nudge tendencies or learning dispositions

Crafting:
'What do you need to practise a bit more?'
'What would you need to do to improve that?'
'What could you tinker with?'

Nudging Adventurousness:
'Just give it a try'
'How could you make that more interesting / exciting / risky?'
'Choose a topic that is going to stretch you'

Transferring:
'Where else could you make use of that?'
'Where could you apply what you've just learned?'

Nudging Self-Awareness:
'Does this way of working play to your strengths?'
'How could you organise things to help you learn better?'
'What "qualities of mind" would it help you to strengthen?'

Capitalising:
'What could you use to help with that?'
'What could you use as a tool to help you?'
'What are you going to need?'

Nudging Connecting:
'What does that remind you of?',
'What do you know that might help?',
'What would be a good analogy for that?'

Nudging Leading:
'How could you help the group work better?'
'What would you suggest if you were in charge?'
'If you were to take the initiative, what would you do?'

Nudging Self-Evaluation:
'Tell me about that'
'What are you not so pleased with?'
'What do you like best about that?'
'How would you do it differently next time?'
'What would "even better" look like?'

Inquisitiveness:
'That's curious'
'What's odd about that?'
'What does that make you wonder?'
'What do you want to find out?'
'How else could you do that?'

Customised vocabulary: Drayton Manor High School and Twyford CofE High School, Ealing

So it's a hard one: the more prescriptive phase was good for some people, and for others it felt a bit too clunky and simplistic. '

Wren Academy

Most report that, while any new terms are unfamiliar at first, the fact that BLP language is different is useful, focusing attention as it does on the fact that these muscles are really 'attributes', 'dispositions', 'capabilities', and so on. Indeed, teachers who have been using the approach for a while often remark on how, while it may seem strange to begin with, very rapidly they realize that there is a shift in what they are noticing about students and that this is helpful.

What do you notice about students?

'I often used to just tell students to make more effort, and got blank stares back. But when I started using BLP language I realised I could be much more specific about "making more effort." I could turn my prompts and nudges into really useful statements. So now I watch students carefully through the BLP lens and say things like "how could you use your imagination to...?", Or, "what questions might be helpful to take you further with this?". I've started defining the sort of effort I want them to make'.

Secondary Teacher

Defining the effort

The language can help teachers to think about how they might talk in a way that helps to cultivate each of the learning muscles and help students to gain a better personalised understanding of content.

Schools that have adopted BLP approaches tend to:

Adapting the language

- customise the BLP language: play about with the words and create their own versions.
- create versions for younger children
- extend the vocabulary
- add more capacities
- blend it with other lists of habits

The panel opposite shows how some teachers in schools, such as Drayton Manor High School and Twyford Church of England High School in the London Borough of Ealing, have customised the vocabulary, and turned each of the learning habits into a set of casual prompts or nudges that teachers can focus on as they chat to students in the class or comment on their progress.

'Do you speak Learnish?'

Through such questions students are being encouraged to:

slow down, notice, and appraise strategies and steps

stop skipping quickly on to 'the right answer'

become more reflective and thoughtful

look for alternative ways of proceeding

develop the habit of thinking for themselves

become more interested in difficulty itself

bring a flexible intelligence to bear

think how they might regulate the difficulty of tasks for themselves

1. How did you do that?

2. How else could you have done that?

3. Who did that a different way?

4. Which are the tricky bits? What's tricky about them?

5. What could you do when you are stuck on that?

6. What would have made that easier for you?

7. What else do you know that might help?

8. How could you help someone else do that?

9. How could I have taught that better?

10. Where else could you use that?

11. How could you make that harder for yourself?

12. ...

Talking about the process and experience of learning

Teachers who have become confident with BLP almost always find that the kind of language they use is different from what it was before. Their classroom talk is all focused on the process and the experience of learning itself. During an activity, as teachers go around helping students and checking on their progress, they quite easily start using more of the kinds of prompts and questions that are shown overleaf. They have, in effect, started to speak 'Learnish'!

Commentating on learning

The questions in the panel opposite illustrate the kinds of things that teachers can encourage students to pay attention to. Instead of skipping quickly on to 'the right answer', they are asked to slow down and notice and appraise the strategies and steps they are using along the way. This helps students to become more reflective and thoughtful about their own learning. They are being encouraged to explore and compare different strategies for making progress. This helps them become more flexible and resourceful in the face of difficulty, and to get into the habit of looking for alternative ways of proceeding if their first tack turns out not to work. They are being encouraged to develop the habit of thinking for themselves about what helpful knowledge or strategies they might already possess that could help them out in this situation, and thus to become more independent and resourceful.

Becoming reflective and thoughtful about learning

Although students may at first find such questions unfamiliar, and may not have much to say, teachers have found that over time, and with a little gentle persistence, they can nudge students towards greater awareness of what is going on as they learn things, and they grow the ability to articulate that awareness. With this encouragement, students start to show this kind of talking and thinking in their conversations with each other, and as this becomes more habitual, so they need less and less explicit coaxing or prompting to do so.

Note that the last 'suggestion' is blank, to symbolise that the list is by no means definitive or exhaustive, and that each teacher (preferably along with her or his students) is being encouraged to think of other, even better, prompts to encourage the growth of independent, intelligent learning.

What would your suggestion be?

77

Examples of positive commentaries used in BLP schools[3]

Describing the effort

'What did you do to do so well on that test? You read the material over several times. You underlined the key points. You picked out the hard parts and focused on those. You wrote summaries to help you remember. And it really worked!'

Recognising flexibility

'I like the way you tried all kinds of strategies to help you crack that maths problem. You kept on finding alternative things to try and in the end you did it: well done.'

Praising concentration, being absorbed and managing distractions.

'That home-learning project was so long and demanding—I really admire the way you kept at it and managed to keep concentrating despite all the distractions there must have been.'

Probing creativity

'That essay was very imaginative—can you tell me about what you did to come up with so many creative ideas?'

Being honest about effort. Recognising stretch.

'I know school used to be easy for you and you used to feel like the smart kid all the time. But you weren't really stretching your brain very much. I'm really excited about how you are pushing yourself now—choosing hard things and really sticking at them.'

Learning together

'I liked the effort you put in, but let's work together some more and try to figure out what it is that is making this hard for you to learn, and what might help you get the hang of it.'

The language of success and failure

Earlier, on page 30, we touched on Carol Dweck's seminal findings on the importance of seeking to develop growth mindsets in learners and how words can so easily transmit unintended messages.

> ' Every word and action can send a message. It tells children or students how to think about themselves. It can be a fixed-mindset message that says: You have permanent traits and I am judging them. Or it can be a growth-mindset message that says: You are a developing person and I am interested in your development. It is remarkable how sensitive children are to these messages. '
>
> Carol Dweck

Messages about learning

A chapter on walking the talk would be incomplete without a little more about these important ideas. When students have done something well or poorly, or when they have learned something easily or with difficulty, it is all too easy to fall into the trap of overemphasizing the role of ability—'you must be really talented to do so well' or 'I don't think you are really cut out for this kind of thing'.

By contrast, BLP teachers are looking to highlight effort as the main cause—'You must have tried really hard' against. 'I don't think you can have really tried your best'. Or they can focus on the developing habits of mind—'You were really using those questioning muscles there' or 'I wonder if you would have found it easier of you had stretched your imagination muscles a bit more'.

Highlighting effort

If we want young people to turn out to be robust and confident learners, we have to talk to them in terms of a growth mindset. When they have done something well or poorly, or when they have learned something easily or with difficulty, parents and teachers tend to offer back to them 'attributional stories' that purport to offer an explanation of why they did as they did.

According to Carol Dweck's extensive body of research, if we feed student's ability attributions, they are very likely to develop a fixed mindset. They will come to think of themselves not just as having done well or badly, but as 'smart' or 'stupid' people, and one of the results of this is that they will start to chose only easy things to do, and will stop trying so hard when they do encounter difficulty. In other words, they will become more conservative and less resilient. As one of Dweck's students said, reflecting back over her own life:

'Smart' or 'Stupid' people

> ' If we want young people to turn out to be robust and confident learners, we have to talk to them in terms of a growth mindset.'

79

Mental and emotional fitness

In a fitness centre we don't write people off the minute they find something hard. Exactly the same applies in classrooms, except we are focusing on the development of their mental and emotional, rather than their physical, fitness. That means in classrooms we need to be using comments that focus on effort, habit, and disposition. Teachers using BLP almost inevitably begin to use language that focuses students on how they get better at learning that kind of thing, not on carving the world into things they are 'good at' or 'not good at'. They are encouraging them to look for ways to try harder or differently, and to learn smarter.

Too much praise for effort?

It is just worth noting, however, that there can be a problem with praising people too much for effort, as there is with praising them for ability. If a pupil has already picked up the fixed-mindset bug, they can easily hear praise for effort as a confirmation of their lack of ability. 'You did well because you tried hard' can sound like 'You only did well because you compensated so assiduously for your untalentedness'. The safest thing is for teachers to develop the habit of interesting their students in the learnable skills and strategies that underpinned their performance, and to be continually looking for ways to expand and strengthen those learning muscles. Page 78 shows some of the ways that teachers can talk to students in this vein.

It may be that we have come to treat young people too much with kid gloves, as if the slightest failure might be a body-blow to their self-esteem, so we have to keep reassuring them, praising them, or even protecting them from difficulty. But this can just exacerbate the problem and diminish their spirit of adventure. Maybe—provided we strive to give them a growth mindset—they can bear more reality than we think.

Walking the talk

**The End of Education
Neil Postman**

In his book *The End of Education*, university teacher Neil Postman describes how he sets the scene with a new group of students at the beginning of the college year.[4] He says something like this:

> ' During this year I will be doing a good deal of talking. I will be explaining things, answering questions, and conducting discussions. Since I am an imperfect 'knower', and even more certainly a fallible human being, I will inevitably be making factual errors, drawing some unjustified conclusions, and perhaps passing off some of my opinions as facts. I should be very unhappy if you were to remain unaware of these mistakes. Your task in my classes is to make sure that none of my errors goes by unnoticed. At the beginning of each lesson I will, in fact, be asking you to tell me whatever errors you think slipped by in the preceding lesson. You must, of course, say why you think these are errors and, if possible, suggest a more accurate or less biased way of formulating what I said. Your assessment this

*year will be based partly on the rigour (and courtesy!) with which
you pursue my mistakes. And, to further ensure that you do not fall
into the passivity so common amongst students, I will, from time
to time, deliberately include some patently untrue statements and
attempt to smuggle past you some opinions disguised as facts. You
don't have to do this critical thinking on your own. Please talk to
each other and form your own study groups to review the things
I have said. I would be very pleased if some of you were to ask for
class time in which to present a revised or improved version of my
own presentations.'*

Clearly Postman is talking to university students who might be expected to
have developed the critical faculties and resilience to be able to deal with
the kind of challenge he makes.

But what if we were to adopt a similar approach to knowledge when talking
to younger people at primary and secondary schools? Some teachers seem
to feel that it is their job to be—or at least seem to be—omniscient and
infallible. They believe that if they say 'I don't know' that means they do
not know their stuff as well as they should, and risk losing the respect
of students and parents. Yet, assuming teachers are knowledgeable and
passionate about their subject(s), and assuming they are not *always*
saying 'I don't know', most teachers find that this is, in fact, a very positive
role model to offer pupils, provided they move on from their position of
uncertainty to a discussion with a learner about how they can find out
what it is that they are keen to learn.

Infallible teachers?

There are parts of the world, and groups of parents, who do not distinguish
between 'acknowledging genuine uncertainty' and 'being incompetent'.
If that is the situation in your school, then you have a job of work to
do, to help those parents learn to make that distinction. But wherever
possible, teachers have found that it is not only more honest, but also
more productive, to be a model of a fallible finder-outer than a brittle
know-all. If we want children to grow up to be capable of exploring and
experimenting, able to make mistakes and learn from them, then we should
be able to model those qualities ourselves as much as possible. BLP teachers
are not afraid to let students see them using their learning muscles: it
encourages them to use theirs. Where students see that teachers are non-
defensive and inquisitive, they are less likely to be ashamed of their own
ignorance.

**Modelling being
a learner**

Questions like Postman's are, in fact, exactly the kinds which BLP teachers
ponder when thinking how to be a powerful role model for their students.

In practice, this might mean:

- deliberately sharing new or contested findings and ideas in our subject with students
- cheerfully acknowledging when we don't know the answer to a question we are asked
- inviting students to throw tricky questions at us, so they can see how more expert people 'think on their feet' when faced with uncertainty
- being happy to share with students the task of finding things out
- pausing and thinking aloud when lessons do not go according to plan.

Modelling being a learner

BLP teachers act as role models by noticing and highlighting certain aspects of learning (as in the many examples earlier in this chapter). But they also tend to:

- talk about their own learning lives
- talk about people they admire who have particular learning strengths, and what they have learned from them.

The panel opposite shows just some of the ways in which BLP teachers choose to model the different aspects of learning power.

This small-scale research study illustrates what teachers have been finding out about modelling.

In a study by Trish Sangwine and Ann Janes at Bartlemas Nursery School in Oxford, adults modelled 'having a go, not succeeding and trying again, achieving after persisting, and verbalising feelings associated with risk-taking and persisting'. In addition, those children who were already showing positive learning dispositions were encouraged to verbalise their own feelings for the benefit of the others. As a result, a target group of four initially very timid and withdrawn children 'all gained in confidence and began to engage in more adventurous activities'. Trish and Ann also note how adults' language can inadvertently convey subtle messages that work against the development of resilience, for example, 'Hold on tight and you won't fall' implies 'You might fall', while 'Hold on tight and you can climb a little higher' carries the message 'you can climb'.

Teachers role modelling being a learner

Managing distractions

Sharing—at the end of the lesson—the distractions that you had to manage during the lesson & how you did this.

Noticing

Talking about what you have noticed about...

Coming to work to work that day

Absorption

Sometimes explaining that you intend to get stuck into a book of your own and asking the class to get on with their own reading without interruptions.

Planning

Sharing lesson plans—the intentions, the shape, the time it may take. Explaining what you took into consideration in working it out.

Revising

Sharing how you have revised the planned course of a lesson and what made you do that.

Perseverance

Talking about examples of things that you are finding difficult and sharing the strategies you are using to keep going.

Empathy

Responding to the feelings and ideas being expressed with sympathy and understanding.

Making links

Explicitly making links between something being learned in class and its use in your own life and in the lives of your pupils outside school.

Listening

'I think I have understood what you are saying. Let me try to summarise what you said.'

Imagining

Sharing how you are improving a skill (e.g. badminton) by practising it in your mind's eye.

Questioning

Actively enjoying not knowing the answers to some questions and creating a focus on questions to which no one in the class yet knows an answer.

83

Chapter 5

Teaching practice and the classroom environment

In this chapter we explore:

- the changing role of the teacher
- classrooms where the process of learning is made visible
- teaching through dual-focused objectives
- taking account of emotional intelligence
- the social aspects of learning
- designing activities which stretch learners
- the importance of reflection in learning

I n the preceding chapter we set the scene for a learning-powered classroom by focusing on some of the ways that BLP teachers adjust their demeanour in the classroom: the ways they talk, what they notice and encourage, and what they themselves model. In this chapter, we start to zoom in on what they do: how they design lessons and activities, and how they orchestrate the classroom environment, so that students stretch their learning muscles and cumulatively build their learning power.

The learning gym

It is this progressive mental development that matters most. BLP teachers think of their classrooms, and the activities which they provide, more like a 'learning gymnasium' than a place where knowledge simply gets handed on. The 'epistemic exercise' which students get, as they struggle with topics and problems in particular ways, comes to the fore. Teachers think of themselves as learning power *coaches*, helping students to help themselves in the development of their learning habits. Lessons are less likely to be talk-and chalk, and much more likely to contain challenges and activities that get students thinking and learning for themselves. Teachers tend to provoke students to explore a challenging question, problem or assertion and then become observers of their learning, only intervening as appropriate to refocus and stretch individuals and groups. The guiding question for teachers is likely to be: 'What's the *least* I can do to get productive learning happening (again)?'

A rich conception of learning

This general philosophy is not new, or course. There have long been many advocates for learning where students are more active and engaged. But because BLP teachers have a particularly rich conception of learning and the habits that underpin it, they are able to design nudges and activities that might target quite specific aspects of learning power. Students might be given cryptic drawings to pore over, thus stretching their 'noticing muscles'. They may be subject to a series of minor distractions, to help them build their powers of concentration. There are a host of such small, low-risk strategies and activities which teachers can use to make visible and salient to students the learning power aspects of what is going on in their classrooms.

Thinking differently about planning learning

For some teachers, this way of operating comes entirely naturally. For others, it means changing their own habits to some extent. Our experience with schools has taught us that it is really important that teachers are involved in shifting not just what they say but what they do. Talking to pupils about the learning habits, or writing a new learning-power intention on the board at the start of a lesson, may be a start, but it is only that. We have seen schools where the pupils have become very fluent in talking *about* their learning, but show little sign of having changed the way they actually learn. Being able to explain the concept of resilience is not the same thing as being resilient. And that means teachers have to think slightly differently about the way they plan and deliver lessons.

Designing and delivering learning powered lessons

This chapter is organised around six principles of learning which BLP teachers have found it useful to keep in mind as they are designing and delivering their lessons.

One: Visible learning

To get into the spirit of BLP, students need to be very clear about the learning habits and processes which they are using. Teachers seek to make every aspect of the learning process as visible as possible through the language they use and through the words and images they display on the walls.

Surfacing learning

Two: Split-screen teaching

Here we look more closely at the ways in which teachers have learned to design activities that combine the dual objectives of 'what' will be learned and 'how' it will be learned. Students know that the content they are studying is a way of giving their minds a useful workout.

Dual focus

Three: Emotional engagement

Here we look at smart ways in which teachers can design lessons that intrigue their students. Students will not put in the effort to stretch their learning muscles unless their energy and attention are captured by what they are doing. Emotional engagement is a prerequisite for learning that stretches and develops students' powers of learning.

Capturing attention

Four: Handling uncertainty

What is engaging tends to be what is challenging. If education is a preparation for a learning life, students have to be helped to learn how to handle increasing degrees of complexity and uncertainty. Here we explore how teachers are creating challenging tasks and stretching learning muscles.

Challenge

Five: Relationships

Learning is both a sociable and a solitary activity, and students need to learn how to move around in the social space of learning to best effect. Here we explore how teachers enable their students to become interdependent learners who know how to handle themselves in collaborative groups.

Working together

Six: Reflection and responsibility

Students learn how to manage and organise their learning by being given increasingly demanding opportunities to do so. Here we explore the way in which teachers have encouraged their students to take charge of their own learning, planning what they do, distilling meaning from it, and revising it accordingly.

Taking charge

One: Visible learning

John Hattie's book *Visible Learning*, you remember, distilled out of a huge amount of educational research one core principle: students learn most successfully when the processes and demands of learning are explicit. The more students are thinking about how they learn, and how they can make their own learning more and more effective, the better they do.[1] Before we try to describe systematically what this means, let us take a look at a classroom where learning itself—and not just its fruits—is highly visible.

What the principle looks like in practice

In Sara Radley's Year 1 classroom at Eastway Primary School the walls are covered with useful prompts about what pupils could do when they become stuck. They frequently look at these to remind themselves how they could be less dependent on their teacher to come and rescue them when they don't know what to do. Displays of pupils' work show many drafts and examples of work in progress—the walls celebrate the sketching and improving that goes on all the time in the classroom, not just the final outcome. Puppets that have 'taken on' the attributes of good learners—there is one called Distilling Dino, for example—are being taken around to groups of learners by learning assistants who offer prompts and steers to move the children's learning along. The whiteboard displays icons showing the learning muscles they are focusing on just now. Pride of place on the back wall is given to the Learning Wall which contains photographs, some taken by the children, that have captured themselves and their peers concentrating hard, imagining, watching each other carefully (to pick up good ideas from each other) or listening intently to each other. Some of the children are very proud of these images that show them achieving a 'personal best' in concentrating or collaborating.

Learning muscle icons

Collaborating

Imagining

Children move about freely, helping themselves to the resources they think will help them with their task. The dictionaries are kept on a low shelf so that the children can just go and make use of them without having to ask an adult. The room has different learning zones—places where pupils can go to think and imagine quietly, places where they can work together as a group, places where they sit and work on their own. In one corner of the room there's a stack of the children's 'learning journals' which they use every so often to illustrate and record the difficulties they have encountered and how they have been able to overcome them. Pupils are working on a range of tasks, some which they have chosen according to the learning stretch they want to manage just now, others to which they have been directed by the teacher and have a more specific outcome. Dexie is preparing to write a fantasy story by closing her eyes and practising letting her imagination muscles come up with images and ideas. Josh has asked Tamara if he can work with her, because he wants to get better at collaborating with girls. And somewhere in the busy classroom Sara is explaining to a group of pupils how she herself overcomes tricky problems of the kind they are struggling with.

What the principle means

This classroom is humming with the language and imagery of learning: the processes and activities of bold, intelligent learning are visible, audible and tangible. The natural process of learning has been unearthed and given high status. How we talk about, try out, recognise, celebrate, and get better at learning is what drives the subject syllabus in this classroom. The culture of the classroom is one that exposes, nurtures, respects, and honours the process of learning. The learning power purpose of the classroom has been made clear, both physically and culturally: it is to enable those young learners to be able to play with a full deck of learning cards; to knowingly use and develop a whole range of learning behaviours and become disposed to do so when necessary.

Playing with a full deck of learning cards

Shifting the routines

In Chapter 2 we mentioned the Visible Thinking Routines (VTRs) that have been developed at Harvard University. These are another excellent way of bringing to the fore the mental muscles that students are using in class. *Making Thinking Visible*, a recent book by Ron Ritchhart, Mark Church and Karin Morrison, describes a wide range of VTRs, and how to make use of them, in considerable detail.[2] VTRs are, as they say, simple routines that apply across a wide range of subjects and contexts, and which require students to think in a variety of different ways, that are used so regularly by teachers that they become woven into the fabric of the classroom culture and progressively hard-wired into the thinking practices of students. Through repeated use, students get into the frequent habit of working things out for themselves with the teacher being able to adopt the role of learning coach.

One common thinking routine is called 'See–Think–Wonder'. Students are asked to pay careful attention to a demonstration, a video clip, or an image, and then to 'do an STW with your learning partner'. Very quickly they learn that this means: share with your partner the details that you saw, the thoughts that those impressions suggested to you, and the further questions that these trains of thought made you wonder about. Another very simple routine is called 'Think–Pair–Share' which invites students first to spend a few seconds marshalling their own thoughts on a question they have been asked, then to discuss the issue with a partner, and finally to be ready to report back the fruits of that discussion to the whole class. A third routine, which prompts students to unearth and justify the reasoning that lies behind their observations, is called 'What's Happening Here? – What Makes You Say That?' which speaks for itself. Students may again be shown a puzzling scene—in a painting or a poem, for example—and then take turns to quiz each other using the two questions. Each of these routines helps to build learning power because they push students to be more explicit, more observant, more cautious or more thoughtful about what is going on than they might normally be—and over time, they build up more robust habits of better thinking and learning.

These small-scale enquiries offer further glimpses of what teachers have been doing to make the processes of learning more visible.

Using the environment flexibly

Carol Down at Glastonbury Thorn School in Milton Keynes was keen to get a breakthrough with the reluctant writers in her Year 1 class, The Elephants. Carol's brainwave was to enlist the children as co-researchers in a project to find out if *where* you were writing made a difference to *how* you wrote. The children had special 'Go Anywhere' writing books, and they explored writing in a wide variety of locations—and postures: writing in the dark, in their bedrooms, lying upside down, in the staffroom, in the local park (in the rain), on a nearby estate, on a coach, and so on. The children were very engaged in their 'experiments', sometimes just writing whatever came to mind and sometimes agreeing to focus on the same topic. The genius of Carol's strategy was to get the children interested in thinking about the process of writing indirectly—by getting them to notice whether the different locations influenced their minds in different ways. The Elephants became very excited about their discoveries—but did these experiments have the desired effect on their willingness to write? Carol's action research observations revealed that, over a term, all the children had made markedly more progress in their writing than expected, and the number of children confidently writing at level 1c had risen from 20% to 62%.

Changing the environment to stimulate learning habits

At Roath Park Primary School in Cardiff, Victoria Scale-Constantinous discovered that her Year 1 children had little conception of imagination as being an essential part of 'good learning'. They thought 'good learning' meant neat, correctly spelled and done on time, while imagination 'is when you think about stuff and see pictures in your head'—but they didn't get the connection. So Vicki decided to deliberately try to stretch their imagination muscles, and to show them what an important part of learning imagination could be.[3] She wanted to give the children the opportunity to 'incubate' their ideas, so she changed the 'home corner' into a 'Creativity Corner' by dint of making a dark tent with a black sheet, decked out with fairy lights and CDs of relaxing music. The children were told that they could use the tent if they wanted to consciously make use of their imaginations to help them with whatever they were doing. To get them going, Vicki held whole-class 'imagination sessions' where the children closed their eyes, listened to music, and then discussed the ideas that had bubbled up into their minds. The children decided they would record their ideas in special 'imagination books' and they made their own 'imagination badges' (along the lines of Native American 'dream-catchers') which they could wear whenever they thought they had made productive use of their imaginations.

After just a few weeks of this deliberate focus on imagination, the number of children who said that their imagination helped them to learn had shot up from 4 to 19, and many now go into the Creativity Corner if they are stuck or want to improve their work. They have learned to use imagination as a powerful learning tool.

Nayland Primary School, Suffolk

Practical ways to make learning visible

Learning characters

In the foundation stage at many primary schools, the children are introduced to the learning muscles through puppet characters who embody the different capacities. Ronnie Resilience is the one who never gives up. Ruby Reflection doesn't get upset but sits down quietly and thinks things over. And so on.

Learning Hero of the week

The learning capacities can be used as the basis for regular celebrations or rewards, as the example shows. There are many interesting and admirable things about Josh, as you can see—but, with a bit of skilful nudging, the teacher coaches the children to begin noticing each other's learning strengths, and to add those to their list of appreciation. Quite quickly they get used to congratulating each other for 'really good listening' or 'brilliant at putting yourself in someone else's shoes'.

5H Star of the Week...

JOSH!

☆ He's great at football, swimming and basket ball - a fast, fast runner!

☆ He's a good mate with wicked hair.

☆ He's weird but in a good way.

☆ He has good noticing skills.

☆ He's funny - a real cool dude.

☆ He is top banana and a cheeky monkey.

☆ He is getting better at managing his distractions.

☆ He's a good learner and we're glad to have him in our class!

Christ Church C of E Primary Folkestone

Examples from *Learning Power Heroes*[4]

Two: Split-screen teaching

The 'what' and the 'how'

Here we look more closely at the way in which teachers have learned to weave together the dual objectives of 'what' will be learned and 'how' it will be learned.

There are different ways of designing a lesson on the Tudors. With the same content—the nature of the Elizabethan court, say—one lesson could be designed to exercise students' skills of accurately transcribing notes and retaining information more-or-less verbatim; another lesson could stretch students' ability to appraise someone else's knowledge claims, and to put themselves in the shoes of people with very different worldviews from their own. Same content but a world apart in developing real-world learning habits

What the principle looks like in practice

Paul Arrowsmith from Park View Community School in Chester-le-Street puts dual-focus teaching at the heart of all his lessons. He routinely and skilfully blends different kinds of epistemic exercise with the content area he is covering. In the description of a typical lesson that follows, the different learning muscles that Paul is asking his students to use are indicated in italics.

One of Paul's Year 9 Geography lessons begins with an intriguing cartoon picture of a rabbit teaching a class of rabbits—pointing at a picture on a blackboard of two human beings in close proximity! Paul asks students to *imagine* the caption to go inside the bubble that is attached to the rabbit teacher's mouth. All offers are accepted—the more unlikely the better. He tells the class that the cartoon links to the topic that they are about to start: they need to work this out as the lesson proceeds by *making links* for themselves. Students then sit in pairs, back to back, with one facing the whiteboard and one facing away. The one who can see the board has to provide information that will enable the other to recreate the image on the screen. (The images are of different unlabelled three-line graphs, and the describing students are told they cannot use the words 'graph', 'vertical', 'horizontal' or 'axis'). Paul knows that he wants to develop the capacities of *attentive noticing* and clear *describing* on the part of the first student, and focused *listening* on the part of the second.

Once this task is completed, each pair joins with another pair in order to develop *collaboration* still further. The groups of four have to decide what their graphs might signify. Each quartet is then given three cards without comment. Each card has a statement: 'Rabbits in Australia', 'Elephants in India' and 'Humans on Earth'. Without being told to do so, the groups begin to *search for the link* between each graph to one of the three statements, and to figure out the relevance of the opening cartoon. Paul asks the class to *reflect* on: 'What are we learning today... What *questions* are you asking yourselves about the topic... How have you been learning today?'

What the principle means

Paul's lesson was clearly concerned with an investigation of issues concerning population growth and decline. But it was also designed to stretch some key learning habits that students will need not only in Geography but in other aspects of their lives. This class is already very familiar with the BLP way of doing things, so they do not need to have the specific learning muscles spelled out to them beforehand—though Paul does ask them to reflect on which they have been using in retrospect. Where both teachers and students are less familiar with the BLP approach, the lesson may well be designed to focus on just a single learning habit, and this is made very explicit to the students to begin with.

Whether we realise it or not, all lessons have a dual purpose, irrespective of the age and ability of young people or the subject area being taught. There is the content dimension, with some material to be mastered; and there is the 'epistemic dimension', with some learning skills and habits being exercised. The risk in conventional classrooms, where the teacher remains the focus of attention and the initiator of all activity, and where the epistemic dimension is not acknowledged or made explicit, is that students can be learning habits of compliance and dependence, rather than curiosity and self-reliance. Where teachers are making conscious choices about what habits they will introduce and stretch in the course of the lesson, we call that split-screen, or dual-focus, lesson design.

Split-screen or dual-focus lesson design

As we have said, BLP really takes off when these habits of split-screen teaching, and making learning visible, become second nature to all concerned. And this seems to take real commitment to the vision of BLP and determination to take its implications seriously. Habit change isn't easy, and it doesn't happen overnight. When a tennis coach suggests you experiment with a new grip, you often feel awkward, self-conscious or even 'false' to begin with. You have to work through that feeling, and soon the new way begins to feel quite natural. It is the same with BLP. Being asked to plan a split-screen lesson so that you are simultaneously 'doing the Tudors' and 'stretching their empathy muscles' can sound strange, and when they first teach such a lesson, many teachers feel that their teaching has become rather stilted or artificial. But such a period of awkwardness soon gives way to a more natural fluency in the language and habits of BLP. And as fluency and familiarity grow, so there is less need to be explicit or ponderous about 'which learning muscle we are stretching today'.

The difficulty of habit-change

Designing split-screen lessons

Designing a 'full blown' split-screen lesson involves a number of considerations, some of which may be a little unfamiliar to start with. Planning might start with the normal question: what do I want all / most / some of the pupils to know / understand / be skilful in by the end of the lesson? But then comes the learning power thinking:

Learning powered lesson design

- *How* do I want my students to be learning? What learning habits do I want them to stretch in this lesson?

- What sort of learning challenge [at the heart of the lesson] will extend or expand their learning in ways that will intrigue and challenge them?

- How competent are these students already in using this learning habit—do I need to warm up the relevant learning muscle at the beginning or during the lesson?

- How can I really stretch this muscle so that we build on past experience?

- When will I build in moments of reflection to evaluate how effectively they are or have been learning?

As teachers get used to asking '*What would this lesson on forces or poetry or positive and negative numbers look like if I coupled it with listening or imagining or noticing or capitalising?*', a whole new world of lesson design comes into view. Lessons on the same familiar content can be transformed when viewed as opportunities to stretch a wide variety of different learning capacities. Once the unfamiliarity wears off, we have found that this way of looking at classroom learning captures teachers' interest and renews their creativity. It has led to the creation of thousands of engaging, challenging and intriguing lessons that are growing students' ability to be confident, independent learners—at the same time as helping them to master the content and improve their grades.

A new world of lesson design

The panel opposite illustrates in a little more detail what a split-screen lesson might look like. Here students are given more control and independence by being required to make sense of pieces of information that arrive scrambled; some teachers will know this as 'cut up and rebuild'. The lesson unfolds in a way that requires students' active engagement and curiosity to make sense of what is happening. These design features can be applied readily to any subject area. For example: simultaneous equation proof in maths, any scientific process, rebuilding sentences or paragraphs in MFL, timelining events in history, flow diagrams in DT... and so on.

You will see from her plan that the teacher has a very clear sense of what the learning power intention is behind each part of the activity.

A split-screen focus plan

Resource: poem cut up into stanzas. Students in groups

	Capacity being stretched	Teacher action	Teacher talk	Learner action
Phase 1	noticing imagining	Each group given a random stanza from the poem	'Look at this closely' 'What could it be about?'	Discussing the concepts, making predictions, thinking possibilities, connecting with what they know
Phase 2	questioning reasoning making links	Offer each group another stanza	'What questions is this making you ask?' 'What do you think this is about?'	Focusing questions. Seeking further detail, rethinking possibilities
Phase 3	listening revising capitalising collaborating	Mixing groups	'Walk around, and talk with other people' 'Gather other people's views' 'How are your views changing?'	Comparing and contrasting ideas with others listening to others, gaining other points of view, re-considering their original ideas
Phase 4	revising distilling	Regroup in original groups	'Are you changing your views?' 'What do you think this is about?'	Discussing what they have found out from others, focusing their new ideas
Phase 5	planning revising reasoning	Give each group their remaining stanzas. Add-in technical reminders about construction devices	'Plan how you will come up with the right sequence.' 'What will help you here? (e.g. punctuation) Be ready to justify your answers and offer a title for the poem.'	Considering the most effective way of completing the poem, agreeing a plan of action, reconsidering the meaning of the poem, noticing their justification, sharing their ideas succinctly with others.

The teacher's interest

She is interested in the sorts of questions students pose, whether and how they notice details, how well they maximise working as a group, how efficiently they organise themselves to make a plan. The design of the task is only a start. The real work of the learning power coach is in nudging, prompting and recognising the learning muscles in action.

What is the effect of split-screen teaching?

Clair Faid at Green Park School wanted to know if 'split-screen teaching' would help to boost the confidence and the achievement of the seven- to nine-year-olds in her maths class. Clair designed lessons that focused on the individual learning habits within the general headings of resilience and resourcefulness (see the table on page 73). She took baseline measures of pupils' confidence as learners (using a simple self-report questionnaire which she devised) and their achievement (based on maths tests derived from appropriate SATs questions). She then taught the children in her traditional manner for four-weeks, and tested them again. Then she introduced the split-screen lessons for a further four weeks, being very explicit about helping the pupils to develop their ability to persevere in the face of difficulty, manage distractions, search their own minds for links, ask good questions, and so on. At the end of this period she tested the children's confidence and achievement again for a third time. Using this design, Clair was able to use the children as their own 'control group'.

Impact

At the third testing, 43% more children said they could 'always stick at solving a problem' than at the second. In terms of mathematical achievement, after the first four-week period of 'traditional good teaching', the only child to show improvement had progressed by one sub-level. After the further four weeks of BLP-style teaching, three more children had made a one sub-level improvement, but *five had progressed by two sub-levels*. This major spurt in achievement by almost half the group (of 18) during the split-screen lessons, compared with the previous four weeks, seems to offer fairly strong evidence for the effectiveness of this approach.

Clair's study corroborates others of our action research studies which have shown that focusing on the generic habits of good learning has a much more powerful effect on mathematical achievement than 'booster classes' or extra tuition, specifically in maths.

Three: Emotional Engagement

Here we look at the way in which teachers recognise emotional engagement as being integral to learning and a key element in building resilience and reflectiveness.

What the principle looks like in practice

Ian Bacon's lower-ability Year 9 mathematics group consisted of several students who are on the autistic spectrum. He knows that teaching these students about spatial rotation and translation will be challenging and he will need to find a way to engage their interest through hands-on experience if they are to understand the concepts, and put the energy into stretching their learning habits.

Before the students arrive in the room, Ian has rearranged the furniture. When they arrive, some are clearly disoriented by the new configurations in the room. Calmly, Ian asks them 'What's the matter?' Some students tell him exactly what is wrong in no uncertain terms and start to move chairs and tables. He says: 'Before you do that, can we draw what the room usually looks like and what it looks like now?' This they do. 'What are you noticing?' he asks. Their responses are vocal and clear: 'That table should be there, it needs to be turned that way and these chairs should be over there...' They move the room back to normal and settled down. 'I did this on purpose, I want you to try and work out what we're learning this afternoon.'

He takes them outside into the schoolyard and asks them to organise themselves into a square. They shuffle themselves into place and make the best they can of their 17 bodies. Ian places a red cone on each corner. 'Let's suppose that this cone is nailed to the ground and the square can move around anchored in this corner. What do you think would happen?' The group begin to move around in a variety of directions and lose their shape. They soon recognise that it isn't working properly. Ian lets them try it out, get it wrong, and then begin to organise themselves in ways that work. They spin the square in a clockwise direction until he tells them to 'Stop and hold that position'. He places blue cones on the new three corners and says 'Let's go back inside'. He takes them upstairs so that they can look down from the staircase onto the yard. '*What are you noticing... How does this link to what we were doing in the classroom... What do you think we are finding out today?*' They continue the discussion back in the classroom and Ian shows them a video clip of shapes being stretched and transformed. He moves the discussion on to a consideration of times when people might need to experiment with shapes and formations in the world outside school.

Much of the students' motivation came from the way in which Ian orchestrated the pace and variety of experiences in the lesson. There were moments of urgency interspersed with time for reflection and rumination. As the lesson developed so he set fresh and surprising challenges that involved students moving around and engaging with different people.

What the principle means

BLP aims to develop a certain kind of emotional intelligence in young people—that which enables them to stick at things even when they are confusing or frustrating, and to find pleasure and satisfaction in overcoming obstacles and mastering difficulties. Athletes talk about 'mental toughness': the ability to bounce back from difficulties and keep seeking out new ways of doing things. In Carol Dweck's terms, we are trying to help young people develop a growth mindset.

Emotional Intelligence,
Daniel Goleman

As Daniel Goleman has said in his book *Emotional Intelligence,* emotional intelligence involves self-awareness and self-regulation. Such awareness allows us to stay flexible in the face of challenges and eager to capitalise on opportunities. The idea is not to 'manage feelings away'. For us, learning is always an emotional business, and often a passionate one. And emotional intelligence means finding ways to increase that sense of engagement, as often as it involves knowing how to calm ourselves down and cool off enough to be able to take stock and plan next steps. We think this kind of emotional learning is best done 'on the job', as it were, in the course of learning, rather than as a separate stand-alone activity. We don't think that confining learning about the social and emotional aspects of learning (SEAL) can properly be done in one or two special lessons a week.

A certain kind
of emotional
intelligence

We also see emotional engagement as a prerequisite for powerful learning, rather than an end in its own right. We don't think pupils who are busy and happy are necessarily stretching their learning muscles. You could spend hours in a gym busily doing things that are well within your capability, and enjoy doing so, and not get any fitter. Engagement is what gets you interested enough to be willing to put in the effort to get better. Building Learning Power tries to give both teachers and pupils the understanding and motivation to see that the value of learning lies in pushing yourself, so that your capacities are stretched and strengthened as a result. So it is not enough for teachers to design lessons in which pupils are merely making use of different learning muscles if they are not also giving those muscles a decent work-out. In the learning sphere, activity and exercise are not the same thing—just as they aren't in the physical sphere. However 'bright' their students are, BLP teachers are always trying to design activities that are challenging, and where being stuck and confused are regular and fruitful experiences.

Is it possible to build students' tolerance for frustration by giving them more responsibility for their learning?

Claire Richards teaches English at Bay House School in Gosport. She wanted to see if there was any effect on the resilience of a Year 7 class of being given opportunities to choose, organise, and evaluate their own learning, so she designed an action research project to find out. Before the pilot, her students displayed behaviours suggesting low self-esteem, such as pent-up frustration, and a fear of 'losing' in group activities and games-- even when the games were set up as non-competitive.

For one lesson a week for ten weeks, she gave her Year 7s a similar experience to one she had observed in a local primary school, giving students the opportunity to take responsibility for planning, monitoring, and reflecting on their work. They were able to choose a writing project and plan and evaluate it for themselves. She gave them before and after questionnaires to assess how they rated their own independence, and made systematic observations of students' activities over the course of the ten weeks.

Comparing her observations in the second and eighth weeks of the project, she found that the number of times students needed direction by an adult significantly reduced, as did the amount of inactive or off-task behaviour. Over the ten lessons, there was a progressive, positive shift in the learning behaviour of students. The group asked her far fewer questions than usual and they became increasingly engaged in finding the answers they wanted for themselves. They became more prepared to take risks and produced ideas that could be adapted and improved with far less worry about failure. There was also a dramatic increase in cooperation and collaboration between the students. Increasingly they felt able to invite praise and criticism from peers. Claire's report concluded: 'I have learnt that by involving students more in how they learn, they gain a greater sense of ownership and confidence about their voice in the classroom and in their own ability as a learner'. Giving students greater responsibility over their learning seems to be an effective way of increasing their engagement—and thus creating the conditions in which they are willing, even keen, to put in the effort and stretch themselves.

> Far less worry about failure

Four: Handling uncertainty

In the fourth principle we suggested that there is a strong relationship between engagement and challenge. Obviously this relationship is not linear: when things get too challenging they become threatening and disorientating, and 'fight and flight' take over from 'approach and investigate'. But things that are too easy are boring—unless you have become one of those characters that Carol Dweck has dubbed 'performance orientated': more concerned to look good than to try something new and risky.

What the principle looks like in practice

Science teacher Steph Palmer begins her Year 9 lesson with an intriguing question: 'How much air do you breath in a day?' Since her classes are used to such challenges, they know that she expects them to address the question without too much help from her.

They begin by talking with each other in this week's learning groups and tentatively sorting out their ideas using scribbled notes and then—more confidently—with spider diagrams. Over the term, their capacity to question, collaborate and use their imaginations has expanded the more they have been required to work in these ways. Steph gives them time and then takes their suggestions. All offers are accepted, provided they are backed by sound reasoning to justify the thinking.

Then she asks: 'So, how could we find out?' More learning group discussion ensues and a variety of suggestions are made to which Steph responds with interest, but never giving a sense of what might be the right answer or the prescribed experiment. As a BLP teacher she has trained herself not to give her students the impression that she wants them to 'guess what's in my head'; she wants them to find things out for themselves.

They set to work to design their own experiments to arrive at a reliable estimate of how much air people breathe in a day. She tells them that at the back of the lab there is some equipment that might help them. She has made a variety of household and scientific equipment available to each learning group, but it is up to them to decide how to use it. In order to make the challenge particularly effective, she has added some equipment that may not be useful to this experiment so that they learn to manage distractions and focus on the issue at hand.

What the principle means

BLP aims to prepare students for the complexities and confusions of real life, and this means progressively upping the amount of uncertainty they can tolerate, or even enjoy. In Chapter 11 we report on A-level biology students at Park View school who were not much fazed by being given an exam paper on topics they hadn't been taught. They used their gumption—and got good marks—while the students who had been drilled in examination answers to expected questions went to pieces.

For a teacher, this principle means resisting the temptation to rattle through the subject-matter in the most efficient way possible, and instead allowing the students to flounder a little. The recent trend towards greater modularisation and bite-sized learning is anti-educational, in the deeper sense that BLP is trying to get at, if it systematically deprives students of the opportunity to 'learn what to do when they don't know what to do'. BLP teachers like to stretch their students' learning behaviours by getting them stuck, and then ensuring that they enjoy the process of getting unstuck.

Resist rattling
through it

David Perkins has argued that the curriculum contains too many '*tame topics*' and not enough '*wild ones*'—where there is plenty of scope left in them to get lost and perplexed.[5] John Hattie makes a similar point in his book *Visible Learning: 'A teacher's job is to make work difficult. If you are not challenged, you do not make mistakes. If you do not make mistakes, feedback is useless.'* At the heart of a powerful learning opportunity lies a challenge where young people learn that to struggle with a problem is ultimately satisfying and brings its own rewards. So one of the early culture shifts in a BLP classroom is to encourage pupils to see being stuck as an interesting rather than a shameful place to be.

Designing a 'stuck challenge'

When teachers design what we might call 'stuck challenges'—ones that are designed to build their students' relish for difficulty—they tend to ask themselves the following questions:

- How can I orchestrate a problem-solving activity to enable students' understanding of *xyz* content without telling them?
- How can I intrigue them with something that is open to several interpretations?
- What could I say / do / show to stimulate their curiosity?
- How can I make this grab their attention...visually and aurally?
- How long shall I allow them to stay stuck before I ask them how they are thinking?
- If they are well and truly stuck, what can I offer as a nudge to get them thinking differently that doesn't give the answer away?

Putting the 'stuck'
into challenges

- Will I leave it as a problem hanging in the air to which we will return later?
- When will I ask them to make links between the challenge, and what and how we are learning in this lesson?

The challenge isn't about the inherent complexity of the subject matter but about how the content is orchestrated to encourage students to use their learning habits to resource their solution.

Getting used to stuck challenges

Mixed responses to challenge

As you might imagine, young people do not always respond with enthusiasm to stuck challenges—especially when they have come to expect to be spoon-fed and protected from genuine difficulty. Several schools and colleges have seen the start of Year 12 as an opportunity to try to realign students' thinking about what it means to be an effective learner. Old habits die hard, however, and sixth formers may have had many years' experience of being dependent on their teachers to do the hard stuff for them.

Nigel Appleyard at Goffs School in Cheshunt had been responsible for managing the considerable improvement in examination performance. His systematic approach had secured high standards of attainment and good judgements about the quality of teaching. However, he became concerned that these approaches were making students increasingly dependent on their teachers, less able to make decisions for themselves, and less likely to respond to the unexpected in their GCSE and A level examinations. Having been persuaded by the philosophy of BLP, Nigel planned scrupulously for its introduction at Goffs and determined to try out BLP approaches in his own History lessons in the sixth form. He explains what happened.

Winning students over

"I started to provide them with stimulus material that would get them stuck. I wanted them to generate their own questions and explore possibilities for themselves. I was determined to make them do the thinking. At first, I met with some resistance. One student in particular intimated that it was my job to teach the group and give them the answers that they could repeat in the exam and get the grades they needed. I explained to them that this wasn't going to prepare them properly for the demands of the exam or their future needs. I sensed that some of the group were not convinced. I didn't give in and gradually they began to expect to be challenged in lessons and to rise to it. They started to get disappointed if I didn't set them something intriguing and problematic. Things have moved on and they are now much more actively engaged and involved in the planning and delivery of lessons. They have now taken on responsibility for creating provocative, relevant, and stimulating starters to warm up their learning muscles, and they lead the

discussions that distil what we have learnt and what we need to learn. They have become a different group: they have transformed themselves into students who no longer depend on me to provide them with all the answers.'

A very satisfying outcome—but it took Nigel's determination to ride out the storm of their disapproval, to get there.

Practical ways to help learning stretch

Internet Search.

Establish a topic which the pupils could research on the Internet. Ask them to use search engines to find out what they need to know, without being precise about what the outcome should be. Find out which key words have been most successful in helping them to access useful information. In pairs, use these key words to construct good questions. Try typing those questions into a search engine to see if they produce different or more focused information. Discuss the different ways that questions might need to be structured in different contexts and for different audiences.

Is Your Question Important?

Identify a project which the class might investigate. Write a series of questions on separate pieces of cards and give each group a set of the cards. The group shuffle the cards and deal each student one card. They have to decide:

- the best order for the questions, to do the project well
- if they have to ask all the questions or whether some are irrelevant in the context
- whether there are any missing questions and if so, what they might be
- what they have learnt about questions from this.

Where on Earth is Mars?

From *Building Learning Power in Action*[6]

Five: Relationships

Learning is both a sociable and a solitary business. There is a huge amount that young people can be helped to learn about how to move around in the social space of learning—choosing the right moment to confide the germ of an idea; knowing when it is best to go off and have a quiet think by yourself—that goes way beyond the conventional understanding of 'group work'.

What the principle looks like in practice

In Stella Lightfoot's English class they are studying *Macbeth*. Students arrive at the lesson bringing artefacts that they could connect to themes in the play, which they put in the centre of the classroom. Stella gives them a few minutes by themselves to quietly prepare their thoughts for the whole-class discussion that is to follow. Having reminded themselves in a quick buzz with their neighbour of the conventions for Circle Time, they engage in a whole-class discussion that pursues well-honed and respected routines. One student nominates himself to initiate the discussion, and thereafter leadership passes maturely from person to person. Listening is attentive, and the students are keen to check that they have understood the previous speaker correctly. They ask questions of each other in a positive and supportive way. Stella functions as an equal participant in the group rather than the controller or initiator of ideas. She times her interventions subtly in order to nudge and probe without telling the class what to do. In many ways, she is modelling the social respect she wants to strengthen in her students, and she is coaching the class as whole.

After this discussion, the class work effectively in a variety of different sized groups and exhibit the same high levels of collaboration as they did when working as a group of thirty. They have a well-developed awareness of how groups work and understand the changing roles and responsibilities to be adopted. Occasionally one student in a group might stop to check the other members' perceptions of how well the group is working, or to see if quieter members would like an opportunity to speak. They gain ideas from others and show considerable empathy and respect whilst being prepared to challenge and disagree. They come to collective decisions about what they wish to explore, having learnt to adapt and compromise as necessary without abandoning their own opinions.

What the principle means

Remarkable social skills

Stella Lightfoot's class shows remarkable social skill and cohesion. Through the gentle coaching and modelling of Stella and her colleagues, the students have imbibed the social habits that will make group learning productive and enjoyable. This social expertise has been built up over time, not as a result of a few workshops and exhortations, but by virtue of a deliberately created set of social habits, practices, modelling and expectations. The necessary underpinning behaviours had been introduced and discussed; ground rules were created and agreed; actions were reflected on and distilled; improvements were noted and praised.

This process does not happen just because students are told to work in groups. The component skills need naming and coaching. Having students work in groups is part of every teachers' repertoire, but across hundreds of visits to lessons we have noticed many groups having difficulty completing the activities. This has not been due to any lack of cognitive ability but because the students were unaware of teamwork protocols or even basic social behaviours.

Learning complex social skills

This social expertise is multi-faceted. Students are being coached in how to listen carefully and take turns in conversation; how to give feedback to others in a way that makes it easy for them to hear, and how to accept feedback graciously; how to disagree respectfully, and who to choose as a sounding-board for what type of learning. Students learn to notice when a group is working well and when it isn't, and how to suggest a quick 'process check' without making anyone feel they are being criticised. We have seen groups of seven-year-olds from poor neighbourhoods exercising these skills and sensitivities, in ways that might not always be echoed in adult meetings, as a result of conscious shifts in their teachers' ways of organising and orchestrating lessons.

In some cases, teachers are nervous of allowing students to work in such ways since they fear a loss of control. They may be concerned that students will abuse the apparent freedom and lose focus and commitment. But in our experience, provided teachers introduce changes in ways that are gradual and cumulative, and do not create too much anxiety or disruption, their fears that students will abuse the responsibility they are being offered are rarely realised. On the contrary, we hear time and again from schools who took small steps in this direction, and were astonished by the levels of maturity and responsibility which their students showed—especially those who were lower achievers or who had histories of disaffection.

Why bother?

It is not very radical to point out that, in their future lives, students will be expected to work constructively with many different kinds of others and contribute purposefully to a common end. They will be ill-prepared for this if they have little practice at doing so in school.

Here is another example of this social coaching in action. In a PE lesson on trampolining at The City Academy Bristol, students are gathered around the equipment practising being coaches to each other as they attempt a progression of activities. The teacher makes her expectations clear: students are to notice details of each other's performance, distil the key features that were successful and identify one area for improvement. They are to give feedback constructively so that the recipients are helped to identify for themselves what they need to do to improve. One student who has recently arrived at the Academy from Somalia is extremely cautious and disinclined to climb onto the apparatus. Her peers use their learning language to coach the vulnerable newcomer to try some modest trials and experiments. After a few attempts and some time to reflect and gather her courage, she is able to bounce, sit, and stand up on the trampoline. The delight, sense of achievement and boost to self-esteem is apparent in her beaming face—and that of her classmates. These students and their teacher have worked with a collective sense of responsibility, patiently and sensitively coaching this fragile student to succeed. They have stretched their trampolining skills, but more importantly, they have stretched their ability to support, empathise, and couch feedback in ever more subtle and successful ways.

Students coaching partnerships

As students develop their reciprocal skills of empathy, listening, collaborating, and so on, some schools take coaching a stage further and develop students to act as their own coach and as coaches for each other. At North Oxfordshire Academy, and indeed elsewhere, students have been explicitly trained to understand what coaches do and apply that understanding to themselves. They develop ways of reflecting on their own performance that enables them to design their own 'exercise regimes'. Students use the familiar Skill: Will matrix—as Tom did in the diagram opposite—and note down how they respond to different aspects of their lives in school and beyond, judging separately their levels of accomplishment and motivation in each area.

Tom looks at one aspect of his school life (in this case maths) that he wants to shift from one quadrant to another. In the top right quadrant Tom captures areas of Maths which he considers he is **skilled** in and is **motivated** to do. In the bottom right he notes those aspects which he is **keen** on but needs more **assistance.** In the top left he notes those aspects which he is **skilled** in but **not interested** in. In the bottom left he records those aspects that he is really **challenged** by and **doesn't enjoy.** Another student coach may support him in seeing his grid objectively and identifying for himself small steps that are designed to create the desired movement. The skill-will matrix gives an insight into how varying levels of skill and motivation call for different coaching styles. Things in Tom's bottom left quadrant need a very different coaching style to those in the top right.

Student coaching using the Skill:Will matrix

Coaching style – Inspiring

- Aim to increase motivation
- Try to re-kindle interest
- Explore reasons for loss of interest
- Encourage short-term action
- Accentuate positives

Coaching style – Delegating

- Encourage freedom to experiment and make mistakes
- Offer further challenges but don't over-manage
- Maintain interest
- Encourage them to coach others

High Skill

Geometry
- Circle rules
- Pythagoras
- Shapes properties

Arithmetic
- working with numbers
- +/-/÷/x

Low Motivation

High Motivation

Algebra
- Quadratic equations
- Graph-work
- Formulae

Geometry
- Trigonometry
- Curves & waves

Knowing how to get a high grade

Probabilities

Low Skill

Coaching style – Directing

- Work towards increasing motivation and skill
- Set short-term goals
- Structure learning through short-term cumulative tasks
- Remain in close contact
- Monitor progress

Coaching style – Guiding

- Work towards raising skill levels
- Envision the future when skills are developed.
- Secure learning opportunities
- Provide reflective feedback.
- Let go as confidence grows

Skill ladders for collaboration

Step 1

Understanding and improving the individual groupwork behaviours

Stretching our learning muscles

Better 'self' collaboration

- I think carefully about the part I played in the group's success
- **I will step back to allow others to contribute**
- I involve quieter members of the group
- **I am patient with others who find it difficult**
- I am persistent when I think my point or idea is important
- **I listen to other people's ideas and offer my own in turn**
- I fulfil the role that the group needs
- **I take responsibility for my own contributions to the group's success**
- I dominate the group, wanting everyone to follow my ideas
- **I get impatient with others, take over and 'do' for others**
- I get impatient with others, and show my frustrations with words or body language
- **I do my own thing/ switch off when my bit of the task is done**

Step 2

Understanding and improving collective behaviours

Stretching our learning muscles

Better 'group' collaboration

- **We value each other's contributions**
- Work as a cohesive group (all work together)
- **We establish working rules**
- We are all committed to the common goal
- **We talk to other people, but not the whole group**
- We talk over each other
- **We cannot stick to the brief/ become distracted**

Step 3

Understanding and improving leadership behaviours

Stretching our learning muscles

Better leadership

- Praise members/ the whole group for working well
- **Step in if people are not fulfilling their roles**
- Direct people to complete their roles
- **Choose roles based on people's skills**
- Give group members roles and tasks
- **Decide on a plan from the ideas of others**
- Listen, but make clear you are leading the group
- **Listen to ideas from other group members**
- Try to please those who talk the loudest
- **Let others talk over you, make decisions for you**

So how do teachers go about deepening collaborative habits?

David Armstrong, Deputy Head at Simpson School in Milton Keynes undertook a classroom learning enquiry as part of a BLP Foundation Course. He wanted to discover whether it was possible to create a map of progression in collaborative skills, and use it to design a suitable set of activities that would enable his reluctant Year 6 students to get better at collaborating. This particular class had some fiercely individualistic children and there was a real need to develop their abilities to work together, to take individual responsibility in a group, and to take an active interest in the group's success as a whole.

David identified three students to observe who showed large differences in their responses to collaborative activities. He watched these students at both their best and their worst and recorded their range of behaviours. From this he was able to create Skill ladder 1 (see panel opposite) which mapped out a continuum from poor to good collaborative behaviours.

He talked with his class about what it meant to collaborate and shared with them his newly created skill ladder. Over the next four weeks he designed maths challenges which needed strong collaborative skills for success. The students were given lots of opportunities to reflect both privately and with a partner on how they behaved, or wanted to behave, during group-work. They wrote and talked about what was easy or difficult about collaborating and what the potential benefits were for the group and for themselves. (Skill ladder 2)

David chose to focus his observations on the impact of each individual on the performance of their team and he introduced the pupils to the notion of team spirit, with each team member playing different but complementary roles. He found he had to coach some of the more reluctant students in taking on leadership roles. Sarah, for example, was originally timid, allowing herself to be talked over, and would adopt the ideas of the pushiest group member. After coaching in how she might deal with different personalities Sarah's confidence grew. She was able to deal with different characters using a range of strategies, such as anticipating and pre-empting dissent, or giving potentially troublesome group members special tasks that played to their strengths (Skill ladder 3). David's records show that, over a period of four weeks, student behaviour and focus was transformed, and a couple of months later the maths SATs results far surpassed the expectations for that group.

Coaching
leadership skills

Practical ways to build relationships

Rights and Responsibilities

Work in pairs and small groups to suggest a charter of matching rights and responsibilities or ground rules for collaboration. If everyone has a right to have their voice heard, everyone also has a responsibility to listen attentively to others and wait until they have finished speaking. What else might be important and why?

Lesson starter to deepen the capacity to listen

Use the first three minutes of a film (in one case this was *Donnie Darko*) without showing the visuals. Ask the class to anticipate what they might see on the basis of the sound effects, sound track and dialogue. A boisterous and demanding class became rapt and attentive as they listened to details and sketched out—in pairs—what they thought they would see. The activity not only created intense engagement but also taught the class some useful lessons about the way 'listening' is actually a multimodal skill

The ICT routine

After the class has been told about the next activity, give them a minute to decide for themselves if they are going to choose to do it on their own, with a small group of other students, or in a group with the teacher. When this is used regularly, it becomes the Individual–Collaborative–Teacher (or ICT) routine. They might write a brief reflection in their Learning Journals about whether, in retrospect, they thought they had made the best choice. Over time, this builds their awareness of how different tasks might call for different kinds of social interaction, or none at all.

Six: Reflection and responsibility

Here we explore the way in which teachers have encouraged their students to take charge of their own learning, planning what they do, distilling meaning from it, and revising it accordingly.

What the principle looks like in practice

Barbara Imrie of Chosen Hill School in Gloucester knows that reflection on learning isn't just something that happens in the few minutes before students leave the room. Reflection is a formative part of the lesson and she makes sure her students practise it regularly to secure their understanding, review progress, and plot changes of direction. With her Year 10 English class, Barbara regularly takes the opportunity to pause and help her students reflect on how they are progressing. She prompts them to check their understanding: 'What do you know now that you didn't know before?'. She encourages them to generate their own questions for enquiry: 'So what questions are you asking yourself about his character and motivation?'. And she nudges them to attend to *how* they are learning and the ways they might need to hone the learning habits that are in use: 'Do you think we need to stretch our link-making habits at this point?'. A quick link-making workout (some 'spot the connection' games) could fine-tune her students' ability to delve deeper into the text. Barbara also encourages them to take time to reflect more deeply on their learning. When a student stumbles over an explanation she says: 'Do you need time to think about it... I'll come back to you later'. A little later, it is the student himself who says: 'I'm ready to come back to that point now, Miss.'

What the principle means

Lessons where reflection and responsibility go hand in hand give students more say in the process of selecting, planning, organising, adjusting, and evaluating their learning than is normal in the traditional teacher-centred school. This is a common theme in innovative schools these days: we hear a lot about 'student voice' and 'co-construction of the curriculum'. BLP tends to potentiate these kinds of innovation by giving the students a richer language in which to couch their reflective thinking. And it also helps to keep both students' and teachers' eyes on the underlying purpose behind giving students greater control over their learning: to build habits of mind that will stand them in good stead in a wide variety of real-world situations after they have left school (or indeed university).

Winning
students over

A central idea in this context is the concept of 'work in progress'. Drafting, prototyping, experimenting, and trial-and-error are the hallmarks of this. Students are encouraged to bring their reflection to bear on the process of crafting an increasingly satisfying product—whether that be a poem, a mathematical proof, the design of an experiment, an essay, a gymnastic move, or a dance performance. BLP teachers know that the process of revising and improving work is at the heart of successful and satisfying learning.

Cycles of reflection

In commenting on these cycles of reflection, self-evaluation, improvement, teachers ask the prompting questions similar to those we discussed in Chapter 4—questions such as:

- Are you using the best method here?
- Which bits of this are you most / least satisfied with?
- Where could you go for ideas about how to improve this?

Prompting questions

- Who might be able to give you good advice?
- What can you learn from this mistake?
- Would it help to do some quick sketches of possibilities at this point?

In such lessons students are likely also to be asking questions like these of each other, acting as learning coaches. BLP classrooms sometimes come to resemble communal workshops or studios, where everyone is helping each other to craft their individual products, rather than the traditional teacher-focused schoolroom.

Although reflective thinking runs through the activities in a BLP classroom, learning-powered plenaries at the lesson's close can be helpful in prompting reflection on how students have been as learners, as well as what they have learnt. Moreover, such reflection provides a springboard for deciding where the learning will go next. These end-of-lesson plenaries needn't be formulaic (as they sometimes tend to be). Our schools have come up with many creative ideas to keep plenaries fresh and interesting. For example:

- Pupils can be asked to think back over their learning as if it were like panning for gold. In the first sift they might throw away irrelevant material. The last sift leaves only the shining nuggets—the really important things they have learned which they will take forward and use again. Get the students to discuss what they have left behind, and what they can take forward from what they have learned that might be of real value to them in the future.

- At the end of a week of linked lessons, have a 'Desert Island Disc' session where students choose four aspects of what they have learned to take with them. These can be skills / techniques/ approaches / formulae that they think would be useful to them in a strange environment—as well as specific bits of knowledge and understanding.

Is it natural?

Being able to reflect on what they are doing before, during, and after its occurrence does not come naturally to many young people. They may be keen to dive in and get started, respond to things that emerge as they go along, and come to a conclusion as soon as possible before moving on to something else. Teachers can find it hard to persuade students to slow the process down in order to encourage forethought, planning, review, and improvement. This is how one primary school teacher tackled the issue.

Elaine Wade is a Year 2 teacher at Simpson School. She wants her pupils to understand the meaning and importance of being a good planner. As part of their work in DT pupils have to make a vehicle using several parts. Elaine keeps the components safe and pupils have to 'order' the parts they need. They are given a shopping list which itemises the vehicle parts, and have to indicate what and how many of each they require. The ordered items are carefully counted out by Elaine and put into a special shopping bag. So far so good. However, on unpacking their shopping bag, many of the pupils, realise that they do not have enough or, in some cases, the right parts. This provides a strongly-motivated opportunity for the children to discuss the need to plan carefully, after which the pupils thankfully accept missing parts. When the activity is used again in another context later in the year, missing parts of their order are not restored and the pupils are expected to make the best they can with what they have ordered.

Reflection has become widely seen as part and parcel of good learning. Strategic approaches such as 'Plan Do and Review' have been with us for many years and form the basis of a good deal of learning in Early Years. More recently 'Assessment for Learning' has emphasised the role of reflection in improving learning and achievement. Students are now much more familiar with such techniques. And yet, reflection is still used by many schools for summative evaluation of a piece of work, rather than being woven formatively throughout the learning and production process. Dylan Wiliam, one of the main architects of Assessment for Learning, uses the example of being a pilot. You don't wait till you have landed till you review the course you have taken; you keep making small checks and revisions all the time as you go along. But to achieve this, as we have seen, pupils need to be coached to develop that reflective, self-evaluative frame of mind. BLP teachers keep encouraging their pupils to see under the skin of learning, helping them to understand that good learners constantly have choices about how they go about their learning. They prompt pupils to notice and comment on their own learning, and to offer each other advice as to how they might approach tasks or improve a specific piece of learning.

Reflecting on learning isn't new

Paula Birch teaches Art in a reflective way. She gives her students a Learning Journal in which to chart their experiments and progress, showing ideas, influences, and materials. Given a starting point and a clear sense of direction, students know that they are the explorers who will be piloting themselves to a destination that is flexible and constantly under review. Her students are good at talking about how and what they are learning; they like to show where their thinking has taken them, what trials they have attempted, and what choices they have made. Although this is axiomatic to the way in which Art and—in some cases—Design are taught, these habits should not rest there and can be exercised from Reception onwards across all areas of the curriculum.

What are the elements of reflection? Students need to develop the habit of distilling what they have learned before proceeding to the next stage of their work. They need to develop the habit of generating flexible plans that provide them with a structure but which can evolve as they make progress. They need to be able to monitor their progress—when working individually or in groups—in order to make sure that they are on the right lines, proceeding in the right direction, and think about whether they need to change course. They need to be open-minded and willing to review what they have been doing before making any revisions and changes along the way.

Although many of us do reflect in these ways when we are faced with immediate and urgent challenges, young people have to be helped to learn how and why they are of value. We need to coax them into making these practices habitual.

An essential attribute of reflective learners is their ability to know themselves so well that they are able to make good choices and decisions about how and what to learn, based on that reliable self-knowledge. BLP teachers encourage their students to develop and act on that self-knowledge. (This is where BLP differs from some other approaches to 'learning styles': we encourage young people to develop and trial their own awareness of how they learn best, and don't stick crude labels like 'Kinaesthetic Learner' on them that limit rather than stimulate their ability to think about themselves, for themselves.)

In a Year 10 classroom at Park High School in Harrow, students were involved in a collaborative mathematical investigation. One girl, Sarah, was sitting at a table on her own while others were actively involved in groups. When asked why she was working independently, she said, 'When we have investigations to do in groups, I know that I don't think for myself about the problem but I tend to get sucked into what everyone else says. I've had a word with Miss and she lets me have some time on my own to think things through before I join my group'. Sarah was being encouraged to develop her own self-awareness, and to gain a more sophisticated ability to be reflective and responsible about her own learning.

An overview of the learning powered teacher

In the chart on page 116, we have pulled together some of the strands that we have reviewed, over the last two chapters, that seem to contribute to the development of powerful, transferable learning habits in young people. In the left hand column we have listed a number of characteristics of 'good teaching' as traditionally conceived. Lessons are well planned, interesting, and well-paced and they make regular use of group-work. Teachers have a secure grasp of their subject and explain concepts and activities clearly, answer students' questions, help them when they get stuck, and encourage them to explore the subject-matter more deeply. They are conscientious markers, their students make good progress in their grasp of the subject, and they are always keen to improve their teaching so that student engagement and achievement improve still further.

No one would want to argue with that. Yet looked at from a BLP perspective, it seems as if lessons are all about the content, and teachers are doing a good deal of the work. The 'epistemic dimension' is conspicuous by its absence. In the right-hand column we have summarised some of our suggestions about how each of those aspects of good teaching might be 'turbo-charged' so as to focus on the development of students' confidence, capacity, and appetite for learning itself. We are not throwing out the content; we are simply adjusting the pedagogy so that it achieves a broader range of goals. Young people are helped to achieve as well as they can, *and* they are being systematically prepared to deal with the rigours and challenges of a learning life—whatever particular paths their lives may take.

Learning power teachers know their stuff; but they also reveal themselves to be open and enthusiastic learners. They design good lessons that both develop clear understanding and stretch a broad range of learning muscles; **and** they are explicit with students about the 'split-screen' intentions behind their lesson planning. Their planning leaves open appropriate opportunities for students to pursue their own questions, and to take increasing control of the way they structure their own learning. They are given plenty of opportunities to explain both what they know and how they learn. The nature of 'group-work' is varied creatively so that students learn how to move around in the social space of learning to their best advantage, and also how to monitor and improve the group processes in which they are taking part. Teachers are helpful—but they do not rescue students from difficulty too quickly, encouraging them to build up their learning stamina, and to become ingenious about how they can rescue themselves (and each other). Displays are used to encourage students' pride in their achievement and also to demonstrate progress and ingenuity in improving their own learning. Marking encourages students to think for themselves about how they could improve what they have done.

Finally, student progress is tracked in terms of subject-based achievement, and also in terms of the strengthening of their learning habits. We have not yet said much about how this can be done. That is the subject of Chapter 7.

Traditional good teaching

Turbo-charged teaching

Reveal yourself as a Learner

115

A subtle shift

Statements in the left hand column are about conventional 'good teaching'. Those in the right hand column describe the subtle shift needed to build students' learning power.

From *Building 101 ways to Learning Power*[7]

Good teaching		Boosting learning power	
1A	My lessons have clear objectives based on a scheme of work	1B	My students know which learning disposition we are trying to build in each lesson
2A	I am secure and confident in my curriculum knowledge	2B	I show students that I too am learning in lessons
3A	Students answer my questions confidently	3B	I encourage students to ask curious questions of me and each other
4A	I ask questions that encourage exploration of the subject matter	4B	I ask questions which help students explore their learning process
5A	I show students how to remember things	5B	I guide students to build their capacities to learn
6A	I ensure students work together in groups	6B	I help students understand how to learn effectively in groups
7A	I'm always available to help students through a learning challenge	7B	I help students develop their own strategies for coping with being stuck
8A	I build variety and change of pace into lessons	8B	I vary methods of working in order to develop different learning capacities
9A	I mark work regularly with supportive comments and targets	9B	My marking poses questions about students' progress as learners
10A	I display students' best work on classroom walls	10B	I display work in progress on classroom walls
11A	My records show that students make progress with attainment	11B	I chart progress in the development of learning capacities with my students
12A	I work hard to get things right	12B	I learn from my mistakes with my students

Chapter 6

Designing the learning-powered curriculum

In this chapter we explore:

- how the curriculum can be adapted to better allow the development of learning habits
- creative adjustments to the timetable
- how learning can be taken outside the classroom
- how learning can be made more authentic
- how students can play a greater role in their own education

Back in 2005 Park View Community School in Chester-le-Street was doing well. Students were getting good grades and Ofsted saw features that were outstanding. Nevertheless, school leaders and teachers felt that something was missing. As deputy headteacher Kim Cowie said, 'We were doing too much for the students and making them dependent on us—that's no good for them in the long run.' The school began to research possibilities for a radically different curriculum for students at Key Stage 3. Kim explained, 'We had the freedom to do things differently. What we needed were bigger chunks of time to really deepen learning opportunities, a more integrated curriculum that would make sense to students, and a common approach to learning across the curriculum.'

Having looked at a range of current frameworks and visited some innovative schools, the senior leadership team at Park View decided to work with Building Learning Power, and to base their new curriculum on BLP's 'common language for learning.' After a year of research and development, the school launched a new Year 7 curriculum in September 2007. Subjects were combined around three unifying areas—**Explore** (Humanities), **Design,** (Art and Design) and **Perform** (Music and drama)—which were to be taught in cross-faculty teams. Teachers planned their programmes around the learning habits as described in BLP and began to teach students in an integrated, enquiry-based way, making this the foundation on which to build more sophisticated learning habits in the future.

The impact on students and teachers became readily apparent when a BLP consultant was invited in to help the school review these approaches towards the end of the first term. Students were taking much more responsibility for themselves, making decisions about what and how to learn, talking about themselves as learners, and building on their primary-school experiences. As Kim remarked, 'We'd never made the most of their learning potential in the past.' Teachers were operating differently too. With bigger units of time and the opportunity to work in teams, they were enjoying creating fresh and challenging experiences for their students. Moreover, as they taught less—and enabled students to learn more—they were able to see more clearly *how* students were learning, and thus to intervene and genuinely personalise the learning more appropriately.

Key Stage 3 as the foundation for learning

Following a rigorous review of progress and impact, it was decided to extend this approach to Year 8 in 2008. The school has now established this 'Foundation of Learning' course as the core of Key Stage 3. Assuring progression and continuity has been at the heart of this work. Students are encouraged to reflect on their own development as learners and to identify for themselves the 'learning muscles' that they want to focus on developing next. They have used a variety of online tools to enable learners to track their own development and are currently working with *Goal Assess*.

120

Although these curriculum changes have focused on Key Stage 3, there has been considerable impact in later years. Teachers who have modified their approaches to teaching the younger students have naturally carried over many of their new habits into their work at Key Stage 4 and post-16. By planning for the integration of the learning habits into KS4/5 teachers have been able to naturally develop this approach. Essentially, teachers have come to think of themselves as learning alongside students—rather than just explaining what they already know—and what they have come to call 'Park View Learning' has become the focus for all staff development in school. As a Leading Edge and SSAT Regional Hub school, Park View's approach to learning has also percolated out into the wider community of neighbouring schools and colleges through its outreach training programmes.

Plan for integration

The battleground of the curriculum

Over the past few years, in the UK as in many other countries, there have been several high profile attempts to reform the curriculum in ways that acknowledge the importance of learning habits of mind. Most recently, in April 2009, the Rose Review of Primary Education went some way towards freeing up the curriculum from the straightjacket of an overdependence on subjects. In Rose's words, 'Subjects are essential but not sufficient'. Instead, Rose proposed broad areas of learning within which knowledge could be explored. Rose also suggested that interdisciplinary studies were essential as a means of thinking creatively 'outside subject boxes'. Many primary schools welcomed the opportunity to reshape their curriculum in the light of The Rose Review—although some felt that this didn't go far enough towards focusing on young people's learning habits.[1]

The primary curriculum

At the same time as the Rose Review, the highly regarded independent review, led by Professor Robin Alexander and known as the Cambridge Primary Review, proposed even further-reaching reforms, demanding 'a curriculum of breadth, richness and contemporary relevance, which secures the basics and much more besides.'[2] However, the Rose and the Cambridge Reviews became casualties of a change of UK government in 2010. The new Secretary of State for Education, Michael Gove, reasserted the primacy of content.[3]

> *'One of the reasons why we have such concerns about the Rose review of primary education,' he said, 'is because it presages a further abandonment of subject disciplines and a retreat into the fuzzy and abstract learning we descended into in the past.'*

What is Education for?
Michael Gove, 2009

But the concerns about a content-driven approach to the curriculum refuse to go away. In the last decade there have been a significant number of useful initiatives from government and the voluntary sector which have greatly contributed to expanding our conception of effective learning. For a few years it seemed as if, at least at secondary level, the more dispositional approach to educational outcomes advocated by BLP was becoming more valued. The new Key Stage 3 curriculum in England, for example, placed the cultivation of Personal, Learning, and Thinking Skills (PLTS) at the centre of the curriculum, and the development of this curriculum explicitly drew on BLP, as well as on other frameworks. But, as with the primary reviews, a shift in the political climate has led to PLTS being largely ignored and marginalised, persisting only in those schools where the understanding of their importance remains strong.

Personal, learning and thinking skills

Internationally, recent attempts at curriculum reform have seen the same kind of vacillation. In 2008 New Zealand launched a new national curriculum designed explicitly around the development of 'key competencies'. In Australia, different states saw the introduction 'the new basics' (Queensland), 'essential learnings' (Victoria and Tasmania) and 'learning to learn' (South Australia). The Finnish curriculum speaks of 'learning to learn competencies' and the OECD has developed a list of its own key competencies. The International Baccalaureate has a 'Learner Profile' which seems very close in spirit to the approaches espoused by BLP. This profile includes for example, inquisitiveness, thinking, communication, open-mindedness, adventurousness, and reflection.

International curriculum reform

Within the UK, there are several initiatives that have a kinship with BLP: the Royal Society of Art's Opening Minds, Philosophy for Children, Assessment for Learning, the Campaign for Learning's Learning to Learn Project, ELLI, Whole Education, Creative Partnerships, Learning Futures and Open Futures. The flowering of so many helpful non-governmental initiatives suggests the degree to which schools are searching to define the real purposes of twenty-first century education. Yet many of these have struggled to survive, some have shrunk back into an instrumental concern with more efficient attainment, and others have fizzled out entirely.

Kinship with BLP

Principles of curriculum design to develop learning habits

One of the aims of this book is to explore the extent to which BLP can contribute to the development of greater robustness in these kinds of learning focused approaches to educational innovation. An important piece of this jigsaw puzzle is the ability of schools to adapt their curriculum as a whole, as well as encouraging habit change in individual teachers. Our review of the implementation journeys of some BLP schools has suggested five future-based principles that schools have tended to use to guide their curriculum reform as they develop curricula for the twenty-first century.

BLP principles of curriculum reform

> **Principle One: Preparation for a lifetime of learning.** What capabilities do we want our learners to acquire that will serve them well in uncertain futures throughout their lives?

> **Principle Two: Fusion of learning habits and curriculum knowledge.** How can we best integrate acquiring knowledge and learning skills across the curriculum?

> **Principle Three: Extension of learning beyond the constraints of school time and place.** How can we design experiences beyond the short classroom lesson to create extended learning and reach into the informal learning lives of young people outside school?

> **Principle Four: Making learning more authentic.** How can we make sure that the learning experience in school matches more closely with learning in the real world?

> **Principle Five: Learner participation in curriculum design and delivery.** How can we design our curriculum so that students become leaders of their own learning? Which elements of curriculum will students have a role in designing and delivering?

On the following pages we offer glimpses into how these principles have been enacted in schools.

Principle One: Preparation for a lifetime of learning

What capabilities do we want our learners to acquire that will serve them well in uncertain futures throughout their lives?

The changes in the curriculum that have taken place at Park View Community School—and many similar schools—have been driven by a simple question:

> *Given that we are preparing young people for a lifetime of learning, what kind of learners do we want our students to become by the time they leave our school?*

When we have asked this question of teachers in schools across the country, their response is always very similar to that of Goffs School in Cheshunt, which is summarised in the spider diagram opposite.

Whilst there is the obvious need to secure curricular knowledge, skills, and understanding, all teachers—and school leaders—know that there are habits that support learning which all young people need to acquire if they are to thrive in an uncertain world. Some of this learning leads to examinable attainment; but much is long-term, personal, and focused on real-world problem-solving of many kinds. The learning habits on which the curriculum focuses should extend beyond study and scholarship. And, as we saw in Chapter 4, they need to be couched in terms that suggest practical things that busy teachers can do.

Habits in the BLP framework contribute to higher-order 'competencies'

Schools are finding that some of the frameworks and lists of competencies already mentioned are too grand or vague for them to get a practical handle on, but the habits in the BLP framework can help to underpin and clarify them. Being Creative, Independent, Investigative, Open-minded and Reflective, for example, all require good 'questioning muscles'. Being Caring, Principled, Open-minded and Communicative all draw on the ability to adopt multiple perspectives and see the world through other people's eyes: they require good 'empathy muscles'. In this way the same learning habit can contribute to several higher-order 'competencies'.

By the same token, each 'competency' is itself a composite. Take the Personal, Learning, and Thinking Skill called being a Creative Thinker. Research suggests that becoming a creative thinker involves being able to notice details and patterns, taking risks, questioning and playing, learning through imitating others, revising your ideas, and imagining possibilities. Each of these is treated in BLP as a separable 'learning muscle', each of which is capable of being stretched and strengthened. Thus BLP learning habits make explicit and coachable the very foundations of those qualities of mind that schools want their students to acquire. They form the elusive but essential 'underfelt' on which the 'carpet' of the more familiar curriculum is laid. It is this practical image of the mind that so many schools find interesting and helpful.

The design of the curriculum involves taking decisions not just about the knowledge, skills **and** habits of mind you want young people to acquire, but critically how these will be embedded into all types of learning opportunities over terms and years.

Find new ways

Don't give in

learn from mistakes

Persevere

optimistic

Show focus & commitment

Flexible

Ask questions of themselves ~Curious

Creativity — Imaginative

Inventive

By the time our students leave...

~Use range of resources

Able to organise Themselves

Confident

Willing to take risks

Plan ahead of action

Prioritise

Work well with others

Listen

Collaborate

Know what they need to do

Exercise choice

Show discernment

Have clear goals

Question what they are finding out

Communicate clearly

Principle Two: Fusion of learning habits and curriculum knowledge

How can we best integrate knowledge and learning skills?

Alderbrook Leading Edge School and Arts College in Solihull started their BLP journey by thinking about how they might map the coverage of learning skills across the curriculum. They had little idea of which skills were already being well exercised and in which subjects. The guiding question that they chose to pursue was: 'What would happen if subjects only addressed the skills that fit easily with their content or delivery style?' The school asked each subject area to feed back on two key questions:

- Which 6–10 of the 17 BLP learning habits are most readily exercised through your subject?
- Which of the 17 would you find it really hard to exercise?

Which learning habits do different subjects cover?

The responses were illuminating: some subjects were able to agree a set of frequently and infrequently exercised learning habits for their subject as a whole. Some responded year by year; others considered the question module by module. The over-riding picture from the feedback was that different subjects exercise a different blend of skills, and that each of the 17 behaviours fell into the 'readily exercised' set for a number of subjects, with the interesting exceptions of the ones we have called *meta-learning*, *capitalising* and *interdependence* (see page 73 for a reminder of what these refer to). In other words, if subjects were to play only to their perceived strengths, the breadth of the curriculum would ensure that the majority of the behaviours would receive sufficient attention if made explicit.

Do learning habits grow naturally?

With this in mind Alderbrook began its BLP journey by encouraging subject teachers to play to their perceived strengths. At this stage teachers were often unaware of the extent to which they were already developing specific learning habits. Many believed that, through their subject disciplines, the learning habits would naturally grow, but were short of evidence to support their belief. And students were completely in the dark about what learning habits they were developing—if any at all. This side of the curriculum was largely implicit, and rather hit and miss. This raised three further questions:

- How might subject departments be encouraged to develop and support the habits that are normally less readily exercised?
- How might the school better support the transfer of learning habits from one area to others?
- What do we need to do about meta-Learning, capitalising, and interdependence? Why should these three behaviours be problematic?

On closer inspection the school found that these three habits relied on others being already well-established. *Capitalising* was seen as an indicator of independence, requiring a *discriminating* use of resources.

Interdependence needed students to be able to *balance* social and solitary learning, thus requiring a prior understanding of both. And *meta-learning*, they thought, would emerge when students better understood themselves as learners.

As time went on, and all staff were trained to use the language of learning and to be comfortable with split-screen teaching, ongoing learning power reviews began to show evidence that the range of learning habits being explicitly developed through individual subjects was growing as teachers' confidence increased. By 2010, the reviews illuminated some surprising and encouraging feedback: namely learning habits that were initially regarded as difficult or even impossible to develop in a given subject were now being developed and regarded as perceived strengths. A broader range of learning habits were evident in written schemes of learning, were being made explicit in the classroom, and were being systematically exercised and developed in most years by most subjects. Recently the school has been debating this question:

> *Are there any habits that need explicit, whole-school attention because they are critical to success in a large number of curriculum areas, and which are showing up as a general weakness amongst students?*

This concern was revealed through students' responses to the on-line Blaze BLP questionnaire which the school uses annually (see page 166). As a result, a half-termly rolling programme of coaching in specific learning habits, delivered through tutor time, has been introduced to maintain and deepen the BLP focus at a whole-school level. The 2010–2011 rolling programme is shown below.

Term 1	Noticing	Persevering
Term 2	Listening	Collaborating
Term 3	Capitalising	Distilling

Each teacher maintains their own appropriate coverage of learning muscles lesson by lesson, but the themed habit of mind is highlighted repeatedly in lessons for that half-term.

Cleverly, the school has linked the learning focus for the students to a teaching focus for the staff. For example, earlier this year, when teachers were working on raising the level of challenge in the classroom, students were focusing on developing their perseverance. Alderbrook maintains a fairly traditional curriculum timetable and syllabus but has adopted a forward-looking approach to learning. Their approach to mapping the habits across the curriculum ensured a smooth introduction to BLP by playing to people's strengths: a pragmatic approach that others may find useful.

Subject areas were developing a broader range of learning habits

A traditional curriculum with a learning twist

Principle Three: Extension of learning beyond the constraints of school time and place

How can we design experiences beyond the short classroom lesson to create extended experiences and reach into the informal learning lives of young people outside school?

Giving time for and coherence to challenging learning

The opportunity to deepen learning habits is limited when the curriculum is divided into hour-long lessons and when an individual subject is given one or two lessons a week. Although it is important to train students to work with urgency and commitment, short and infrequent lessons tend to invite a more teacher-led style of pedagogy, with teachers focusing on curriculum coverage rather than the development of deeper learning habits.

Constant student movement from subject to subject in the course of a school day limits coherent learning experience. Students may see as many as 14 different teachers in the course of the week, and while variety is clearly valued by students, this feature of the traditional timetable may hamper the development of learning habits.

More and more schools are now re-timetabling lessons to last for half a day or even a whole day. This gives students more opportunity to pose questions, explore issues and investigate for themselves (see the case study of George Pindar College, from page 143). Even where schools do not wish to be as radical as this, they are often asking themselves where and how they might create more extended learning opportunities within their curriculum. In Design Technology, students often work for a whole term on crafting a tangible product; why should they not have the same opportunities for extended, challenging, creative, and reflective learning in English, or Spanish, or Science? Can we judiciously sacrifice a little bit of breadth for the incalculable rewards of a good deal more depth, they begin to wonder. At Park View, for example, their thematic projects give students extended opportunities to work independently and collaboratively in ways that stretch their learning behaviours.

Extending the ideas of Design Technology

When Year 9 Standard Assessment Tests (SATs) ceased to be a statutory requirement, Macmillan Academy in Middlesbrough developed their Year 8 and 9 'baccalaureate' which builds on the learning foundation laid down in Year 7. During these two years, students experience a wide range of learning opportunities where the exercise of choice is central to the learning that they then pursue. The curriculum comprises five component parts: Academic, Enrichment, Enterprise, Project, and Service. The traditional academic curriculum—which still accounts for 50% of the Baccalaureate award—is substantially augmented by an enrichment programme, substantial enterprise learning opportunities, a voluntary contribution to the wider community, and extended projects—one each year—that form a major part of students' 'home learning'.

This extensive re-interpretation of the curriculum is designed to develop transferable learning habits that are personal to the needs and aspirations of each student. As they progress through these two years, students accumulate learning-powered credit points so that they graduate with Gold, Silver, or Bronze awards at the end of Year 9. The highest awards do not necessarily go to those who are conventionally high achievers but to a wider range of individuals who are building their flexible learning muscles. The Macmillan prospectus proudly explains:

> 'Students who excel in the five baccalaureate sections will have developed the skills and components to equip them not just for Key Stage 4, but for their lives beyond school.'

Transferable learning habits

Enquiry-based learning

Developing curiosity, independence, and transferable research skills is at the heart of 'enquiry-based learning' (EBL), so it is no surprise that EBL features heavily in curriculum design in BLP schools. St Paul's Catholic School in Milton Keynes (which we meet in the case study in Chapter 8) has been developing enquiry-based learning for the last four years. Their EBL Handbook explains:

> 'At St. Paul's we are committed to creating a challenging environment where innovation and flexibility are celebrated. An approach to learning that focuses on student enquiry provides both teachers and students with an opportunity to think outside the normal confines of the curriculum. Teachers are encouraged to work collaboratively to break free from content-driven curriculum planning, and to focus on the skills that they would like their learners to develop.'

Students in Years 7, 8 and 9 experience several weeks each term when different curriculum areas come together to provide investigative work designed to generate a spirit of enquiry and experimentation. The humanities come together for an eight-week block to explore issues of migration under the driving question: Why don't people stay at home? Science, PE and Mathematics have combined for a unit called A Question of Sport where students investigate the science and maths of certain sports. They experiment, for example, with the ways tennis would change if ball weight and racquet sizes changed. RE and Humanities come together to consider a wide range of disastrous events—a tsunami, the Holocaust, the crucifixion, and explore the question: Does every cloud have a silver lining? After two weeks of research, groups present their findings to their peers, parents and teachers.

Intriguing questions

Enquiry-Based Learning at St Paul's Catholic School

Project	Year Group	Departments	In Summary...	Tasks	Learning Habits
'Why don't people stay at home?'	7	RE & Humanities	Migration of people around the globe. The reasons for this and the problems that arise	Group-work Research Diary reports Flash presentations	Questioning Collaborating Capitalising Distilling
'A question of Sport'	7	Maths & Science	Investigate sporting equipment and the science behind it— suggest modifications, generate hypotheses & test results	Research Planning Investigation Analysis Presentation	Collaboration Absorption Perseverance Taking Risks
'A Midsummer Night's Dream'	7	Expressive Arts	Design and market a 'Theatre in Education' package to present to students in schools	Select & perform Create support material Communicate USP & advertise	Collaboration Time Management Distilling Listening Imagining
'Does every cloud have a silver lining?'	8	RE & Humanities	Explore the nature of ... in the context of geographical, historical and religious factors	Extended research Newspaper reflection of past events Extended written presentation	Collaboration Noticing Questioning Planning
'Biodiversity'	8	Maths & Science	Design an experiment to compare biodiversity in two or more sites	Data collection Multiple presentations Peer assessment	Noticing Link making Planning Questioning Hypothesising
'What does it really mean to be human?'	9	RE & Humanities	Nature of humanity & exploration of destructive attributes of human race	Choice of topic to cover 3 subject disciplines Presentation transcripts Peer assessed	Questioning Reasoning Distilling

Taking learning outside the classroom.

Honing learning habits in a variety of circumstances (not just in classrooms) for a variety of purposes (not just for exams) is essential if students are to develop learning power that is transferable to out-of-school settings. There are a variety of contexts that can be used profitably to surface and hence to broaden learning power. Some schools have encouraged students to recognise the learning habits they are using in preparing for a musical or dramatic performance. Others have used work experience in Years 10 and 11 and the sixth form to build a range of learning habits.

Macmillan Academy has an international reputation for its specialist focus on Outdoor Learning. David Exeter manages their substantial facilities and leads on designing students' access to learning beyond the walls of the classroom. The Handbook says:

> *'Outdoor Learning is about developing learning through an organised, powerful approach in which direct experience is of prime importance. This is not only about WHAT we learn but importantly HOW and WHERE we learn.'*

Each year, students experience learning challenges that literally—as well as metaphorically—stretch their learning muscles. They are put in outdoor circumstances when they have to make decisions for themselves and with other people: 'learning what to do when they don't know what to do'. These challenging experiences are carefully debriefed so that students are able to recognise the generic habits they have used, identify how they might strengthen them, and determine when and where they can be used elsewhere.

Using enrichment activities to build learning power

Many primary schools use curriculum enrichment opportunities to extend their learning-power approach. Learning weeks of all types — Forest Schools, school camps, and visits — all help to broaden the use and understanding of the different learning habits.

Nayland Primary School in Suffolk is fortunate to have several acres of woodland attached to the school grounds that teachers use in conjunction with a 'Forest Schools' project. Children are encouraged to use this facility as often as possible so that they have the experience of trying out their learning muscles in non-curricular activities. If the children are challenged to build a boat out of natural materials found in the wood, they have to stretch their abilities to *imagine, plan, reflect* and *persevere*. Whether climbing trees or toasting marshmallows on a camp fire, they are *analysing risk, thinking* about safety, and learning to *collaborate*. The woodland area is also used to build habits such as *attentive noticing* (of plants and animals,

Learning power in work experience

Outdoor learning

131

say), *making links* with other experiences, and *capitalising* on available resources from home and community to strengthen their learning.

Mosborough Primary School near Sheffield encourages pupils to use their learning muscles outside the classroom by organising a range of challenging activities during their 'outdoor learning week'. Activities include erecting tents, den building, and orienteering. Recently staff brought into school a collection of different tents and set the challenge to teams of pupils to erect tents with minimal adult instruction and guidance. This task especially challenged pupils to use their *planning, collaboration, reasoning,* and *perseverance* muscles. Staff reported that pupils who showed outstanding practical problem-solving and leadership qualities were not always the ones who were confident classroom curriculum learners.

Using these curriculum enrichment opportunities helps to broaden learning power habits and give it a real-life flavour. Of course, many schools, both primary and secondary, provide such enrichment activities for their pupils. Far fewer have a rich and clearly articulated rationale for them. BLP helps to shape answers to the question: 'And apart from being fun and engaging, what exactly are the educational residues you are building through such experiences, and how do they arise from your vision of what the educated twenty-first century citizen needs in order to flourish?'

Reaching the informal learning lives of students

Students themselves are taking their understanding of learning habits outside school and using them to boost their own informal learning activities. They are encouraged by their teachers to go looking for the real-world value of *persisting, distilling,* and *noticing* (for example), and they readily seem to find it.

Sarah is a member of a drama club out of school and was rehearsing a play in which she was a vampire. In one scene she had to 'bite' a boy on the neck, which involved a level of intimacy she was finding difficult to handle. She discussed this with a school friend and recalled their BLP learning experiences to see if it could help. Using their *imagining* capacity they visualised the scene and then rehearsed it together. Sarah then tried it with her male partner and she became more comfortable in the role.

Mariza had signed up to take part in a 5K 'Run for Life' to raise funds for a cancer charity (her grandparents had died of cancer). She wanted to run the whole distance, but initially she found this difficult and convinced herself it would be OK to walk the 5K. She was reminded in school of the *persevering* capacity and this caused her to pick up the running again; she still found it difficult but she thought of her grandparents as she ran (i.e. using her *empathising* capacity). She also decided to run with an older cousin as often as possible (i.e. applying her *imitating* and *collaborating* capacities).

By consciously recalling and using her learning habits she became more confident of running the 5K run—and run it she did, all the way.

Winston's hobby is playing in a steel band. When the band was asked to learn a new piece, there was often an initial reluctance to attempt it. From thinking about his BLP experience in school, Winston has developed the habit of modelling the 'learning a new piece' process by publicly having a go at it during the practice sessions. He says he often makes mistakes but he has adopted a 'this is normal' approach and shows humour rather than humiliation. Through his example, the band has gained greater confidence at tackling new pieces with less fear of mistakes. Winston is also developing a respected leadership role in the band.

George is a former student of Dr Challoner's Grammar School who is studying maths at St Edmund Hall, Oxford. On a return visit to the school, he commented that he was thankful he had been introduced to BLP, especially as he had learned that 'making mistakes' is not evidence of limited ability but provides an 'opportunity to learn'. He reported that many of his peers at Oxford were struggling to learn this lesson. Like Winston's band members, they were very reluctant to dive in and make mistakes, or even to admit it when they had. They still feared that floundering or not-knowing would be Interpreted as a sign that they were not as 'bright' as they were supposed to be. George said: 'I've never felt so comfortable being stuck. It's going to happen anyway, so you just have to deal with it and learn from it.'

Principle Four: Making learning more authentic

How can we make sure that the learning experience in school matches more closely with learning in the real world?

This principle reminds us of the other side of the 'transfer' issue. Not only do we want students to find and flex their learning muscles out of school, we also want to ensure that what happens in classrooms echoes, the kinds of learning that happen 'out in the big wide world', that learning is bigger than school, it and is ultimately about what we do in the real world out there. In his book *Making Learning Whole*, David Perkins argues compellingly that it is the job of the teacher to give learners as real or 'whole' an experience of learning as possible. He uses the analogy of Scrabble® to show how boring it would be if, before you were allowed to play, you had to learn lists of three, four and five letter words beginning with different letters. Far better to start right in playing 'Junior Scrabble', get the feel for the whole game, and then build up your sophistication as you play. Perkins summarises the approach like this:

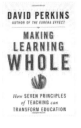

1. *Engage some version of the holistic activity, not just bits and pieces.*

2. *Make the activity worth pursuing.*

3. *Work on the hard parts.*

4. *Explore different versions of and settings for the activity.*[4]

BLP teachers find the idea behind this principle clear; the belief that they are preparing learners for the real-world learning they will face throughout their life is, in a sense, very much what motivates them to adopt BLP approaches. Nevertheless, even with the best will in the world, it is too easy to slip back into teaching *about* things rather than letting learners experience them at first hand if possible (what Perkins calls 'aboutitis') or, in the interest of being precise, breaking tasks down into such detail that the big picture is lost (Perkins calls this 'elementitis'!). An example of this latter type would be teaching football by only letting players dribble, shoot and tackle in a series of carefully orchestrated exercises but never letting them play a real game of football.

Authentic learning

Katie Hudson, a Year 6 teacher at Simpson School has been experimenting with trying to make learning more authentic using a week-long literacy module on newspaper report writing. She introduced the module by telling her pupils about the whole purpose of what they would be doing. They would become 'real journalists' on a newspaper, interviewing people about an event, writing a full report for the newspaper, and printing the paper for circulation. The classroom would become the newsroom of the paper with mobile phones for contacting people, computers to write up their reports, and printers to produce the paper for circulation to a deadline.

She made sure she had included a wide range of real challenges that journalists have to work with:

'Real' challenges

- Arranging and conducting interviews
- Converting interview material into copy
- Making the copy factual yet engaging
- Fitting the copy into the space allowed
- Word-processing the copy for the newspaper
- Working to a deadline

The pupils formed their own teams, by selecting the event they wished to cover. Before making a start in covering the event the teams had to decide which newspaper they worked for. This involved scrutinising newspapers, looking at reporting styles, images and captions, and deducing interviewing techniques. Earlier Katie had briefed members of staff, governors, and even one or two parents to act as interviewees. Some would be interviewed over the phone, some would be available in person.

The pupils also needed to work out and practise what Perkins refers to as 'the hard parts': practising interview techniques, listening carefully to what people say, skilful questioning to elicit information, empathising with the victims and eyewitnesses, drafting copy to get the right tone, and so on. The teams were expected to help each other with the tricky bits. Katie's role after planning the 'whole game' was to coach, prompt and nudge, encourage revising throughout, and finally help pupils to reflect on the whole experience.

The hard parts

As you might expect, the pupils loved the experience. Almost all writing levels increased, and Katie reported that the most encouraging result, from a narrow attainment point of view, was the fact that every child was able to include a quote in their writing, a concept they had previously struggled with.

Vocational learning

One would be tempted to think that vocational education ought to approximate to authentic real world learning. It is, after all, aiming to prepare young people with the skills to pursue a particular vocational path after school. Yet we have found that Design Technology can sometimes become as passive and formulaic as other subjects. But it needn't be: as Bill and Guy noted in a 2010 report for the Edge Foundation.[5]

'As well as teaching how to fillet a plaice or undo a corroded bolt, tutors in PVE should be teaching how to attend carefully; how to learn from mistakes and develop projects; how to mentally rehearse

tricky skills; and how to turn theoretical knowledge into practical on-the-job talking and thinking. But they can't do that unless they have a language in which to formulate those intentions.'

It may only take a small adjustment to teaching method, and BLP schools are beginning to implement the approach in vocational courses.

A teacher of Health and Social Care at Park View decided to stop telling students how to wash their hands. Instead of providing a set of instructions for her students to follow slavishly, she provided them with a range of opportunities to discover the best techniques for themselves, experiment with members of their group, identify the best ways of operating, and then prepare for an authentic real world assessment with an adult other than their class teacher. They had to;

- cope with increased, time-related pressures
- pose questions, link ideas and actions together, make use of all available resources
- explore possibilities constructively and assess their peers
- distill the key issues, adopt a plan, and revise it on the strength of experience.

The students were not just acquiring a practical skill; they were exercising habits of mind that would enable them to respond flexibly to much wider sets of circumstances in the real world.

Principle Five: Learner participation in curriculum design and delivery

How can we design our curriculum so that students become leaders of their own learning.

In *Visible Learning,* John Hattie's overall conclusion is that:

> *'It is what learners do that matters. The aim is to make students active in the learning process until they reach the stage where they become their own teachers, i.e. they can seek out optimal ways to learn new material and ideas, they can seek resources to help them in this learning, and they can set appropriate and more challenging goals [for themselves].'* [6]

Giving students increasing access to 'the controls' of their own learning gets better results, and prepares them better to be responsible and imaginative learners for the rest of their lives. Trying to do this bit by bit produces a range of interesting shifts in the way the curriculum is designed and delivered—and who it is designed and delivered by. In a rapidly increasing number of schools across the world, pupils are:

- learning to lead their own learning: exercising choice about what, when and how they will learn

- teaching others: taking a lead role in the classroom and beyond

- assessing themselves as learners; monitoring their own progression in learning power as well as in learning achievement

- acting as learning mentors and coaches: supporting the learning of other students and teachers

- reviewing learning in lessons: evaluating effectiveness and feeding back to teachers

- being part of curriculum review teams: having a genuine voice in decisions about the structure and delivery of the curriculum.

Student engagement

In schools like these, students aren't expected to passively receive a curriculum that has been designed solely to measure and test their examination skills; instead they are involved as active participants and, at best, the architects of their curriculum (even if they begin by playing a 'junior version' of the curriculum development 'game').

Active participants

Becoming active participants in their own learning and having a real 'learning voice' are central concerns of BLP approaches. Here we offer glimpses of how some of these curriculum changes are being put into place.

Students gaining a sense of themselves as learners.

Many secondary schools have amended their student induction programmes to spend time introducing the learning habits and explaining the school's approach to learning. Some have developed a Learning to Learn course for Year 7 as well as infusing learning power into lessons. These Learning to Learn programmes, often a lesson a fortnight, are seen as an efficient way of building understanding about learning. This saves time in lessons where there is limited opportunity for individual teachers to explain the learning muscles in any detail.

Walthamstow School for Girls offer a lesson every fortnight for Year 7 students to undertake 'fun activities'. Each student selects a learning behaviour to practice. The activity may be something light-hearted like 'with your friend, build a tower with cards' but the real purpose is to improve collaboration skills—and get the girls thinking and talking about what it takes to be a good collaborator.

Other schools have established occasional 'learning days' as a way of exploring groups of muscles through fun activities linked to what the students are experiencing in everyday lessons. Daily tutor time is another aspect of the curriculum which has been used to discuss learning habits. Through these kinds of introductory opportunities students gain a secure grounding in the use and value of learning habits.

Students gaining more responsibilty for learning

'Risky June' in Dubai

Wellington International School is a fee-paying, high-achieving, English-language secondary school in Dubai, where the staff were introduced to BLP in 2009. Parental pressure to get top results is considerable, so the risks of tampering with an effective, if traditional, model of education are keenly understood. Nevertheless in June 2010—after the most important exams had taken place—the principal, Mel Curtis, asked all the Key Stage 3 teachers to take some risks with their teaching along BLP lines, monitor the effects, and share them with each other. Essentially, teachers were asked to be more explicit with students about the learning habits they were using, give them more responsibility for organising their own learning, and encourage them to 'have a go' at learning something new, or learning in a different way from normal. An extra challenge for the teachers was to have students involved with them in planning the learning that was going to happen. These are some of the teachers' observations.

Taking risks

Drama: 'As two boys left my Drama lesson they were asked to describe what they had been doing and were so excited to share: "We had to keep going, and we were out of our comfort zone. It was hard, especially when we felt we were running out of time. We liked the freedom we had but instead of messing about it actually made us focus. It was really good because we could choose what exactly we wanted to work on to improve." '

Science: 'Two students helped us in the planning phase to decide the types of activities we could do and then these ideas were added to by the rest of the class...they loved it!'

They loved it!

Business Studies: 'Instead of teaching my Year 10 topic using PowerPoint [as usual], I set the students to research the topic for themselves in their own way, and then teach the rest of the class about what they had learned. I was quite hesitant about handing over so much to the students, especially in economics as there is so much content to cover. But I found that the students were very motivated as they were in charge... *they acquired all the knowledge necessary and it took less time than my traditional way of teaching.*' [emphasis added]

It took less time

Mathematics: 'We usually plan investigations that are very well structured for students to do on their own. This time we just gave them heaps of data and they had to work in groups to plan their own investigation. They had the list of 'learning capacities' and they had to identify the ones they were using. The planning has actually been easier... and I think this will lead us to think about how we can let students work things out more and learn from their own mistakes.'

Easier planning

Modern Foreign Languages (MFL): 'It's not easy to change what you are doing when it delivers excellent results. Why should we change anything if it works? For the good reason that we get this type of comment (from a Year 10 student) when we do things differently. "I feel that I have learned more and although it took more time than if the teacher had taught us, it was more efficient. If I sit and listen to her I take notes but I don't know what she is talking about. It goes in one ear and out the other..." From Risky June we have learned that students can be given a lot of responsibility without leaving it all to them... it takes longer initially as we need to develop a greater and deeper understanding of the learning process. But it's like anything: once we get into the habit, it becomes easier. As teachers we are here to prepare students for life—not just to get them into university.'

Preparing students for life

These experiments are significant. They show that, even under intense pressure to get high levels of conventional achievement, such small steps are making teachers more confident—and enthusiastic—about amending the delivery of the syllabus to make room for students to use a wider selection of their learning behaviours and hence gain take greater control of their own learning.

Students become their own teachers

When a school is committed to developing the leadership potential of *all* members of its community, its pays more than lip service to the notion of student leaders. Leaders of learning do not just participate on the School Council, they are given opportunities in many lessons to take responsibility for their own learning; to make decisions for themselves and others, rather than slavishly following their teachers' instructions.

Sophisticated skills

Some schools we have worked with have taken Hattie's observation seriously and enabled students to become their own—and others'— teachers. This requires the development of some fairly sophisticated skills: a clear sense of end goals; a flexible planning approach; heightened skill in distilling information, ideas, and opinions; clarity of expression; empathetic understanding of other people; an understanding of how to motivate, intrigue, and inspire. In other words, it is not enough merely to ask students to find out for themselves and pass on the information to others.

Students at Cirencester Tertiary College, for example, are encouraged to work under their own steam to prepare a presentation on a complex issue to their peers. (This is a formal English Speaking Board assessment, so the pressure is high.) Their presentation is aimed to provoke animated discussion and lead to a demanding question and answer session. The students rise astonishingly well to this challenge—but are only able to do so because they have been coached in the skills they will need, and have had ample opportunity to take this kind of responsibility for their own learning. To them, such tasks are clearly authentic, and consequently engage their full learning energies.

Students becoming learning coaches and reviewers of learning

In our experience, students are usually highly astute observers of learning— both their own and others'—and know quite clearly how and when they learn best, and what kinds of help they need from teachers. In traditional schools, this capacity to be their own and each other's teachers, and to contribute responsibly to the improvement of teaching and learning in the whole school, is often grievously underestimated. They may be given little or no opportunity to show how perceptive and mature they can be. But the wind of change in a good many schools, especially in BLP schools, means students develop an acute understanding of those subtle nuances in teaching that really make a difference when building learning capacity.

As we saw in Chapter 5, at North Oxfordshire Academy students are being trained to act as coaches to each other. They are learning how to respond to another person's needs, to evaluate their levels of skill and motivation, to listen and question to unearth understanding, and to enable others to realise their goals. As they develop their skills, they are being given opportunities to learn how to coach their teachers too. The power of students as observers of learning is already clear to one of the school's senior leaders:

'The students are great—I've had some really useful lesson feedback from them and one of our middle leaders told me yesterday that a student had picked up on exactly the same thing that a member of the senior leadership team had noticed in a previous lesson. The teacher then said that whereas she had half-ignored the SLT feedback, the student comment had really motivated her to change!'

Self-evidently, the creation of a culture in which students know how to give perceptive but respectful feedback to their teachers, and in which teachers are willing to listen to students and take seriously what they hear, does not happen overnight. It takes time, coaching, and support on both sides, and there are often hiccups along the way. But we have yet to visit a school that has dared to move in this direction and regretted it. On the contrary, they universally agree that the journey has been hugely worthwhile.

But they build the culture judiciously. In North Oxfordshire, as in many other schools, teachers reserved the right to select the first student learning evaluators. Faculty leaders were asked to nominate a couple of students from different Year groups with whom they would like to work. Though not all high-achievers by any means, these students have always felt privileged to be involved in these ways. One commented:

'The observation training was really good. I really enjoyed it and it was a good experience to know what teachers do when they observe other teachers. It was a long day that day but it was fantastic and we got to work with teachers and other students that we didn't know, finding out about how they think about teaching and learning.'

At Wren Academy, students from Year 7 onwards have played an important role in the school's regular learning power reviews, and in feeding back their findings to teachers. The enthusiasm of the initial group has led to many more students coming forward and asking to be involved. And the positive effect on the culture of the school as a whole is tangible. As a recent Ofsted report on Wren Academy observed:

'At Wren, everyone is a leader and everyone is a learner... In lessons, students demonstrate exceptional skills of leadership, teamwork, and reflection on their own and others' learning...'

There are other schools—like South Dartmoor Community College— where students are involved as regular reviewers of learning in faculties. At South Dartmoor, teams of students manage their own investigations into classroom practice and make recommendations to faculty and school leaders. Here too, Ofsted have recognised the value and impact of students being given this 'apprenticeship' in observation, participation, and responsibility. The effect on the development of their 'learning muscles' is palpable.

New roles for
students

As learning power schools mature, teachers become less threatened by these new roles for students and see the relationship with them as a partnership that benefits both school and students. Where students are encouraged and enabled to have a voice in shaping their curriculum, they have a genuine commitment to helping to develop the kind of education that they know they need. The case study of The George Pindar Community Sports College opposite makes this abundantly clear.

We have mentioned the importance of infusing BLP attitudes and practices throughout the curriculum if we are to build learning habits successfully. We know that skills-based courses expose students to tricks and tips that are seldom applied outside of the course. Commitment to an infused approach has caused some schools to consider how they might recognise the development of habits, help students acknowledge them in use, and target their further improvement. We begin to look at this in the next chapter.

In this chapter we have illustrated some of the ways in which the school curriculum as a whole can be adapted to help pupils build their learning power. Teachers can get so far by changing their individual habits of planning and delivering lessons, but there are other changes that need structural and policy changes at the whole-school level to enable and support them. If students are to be given greater responsibility for organising their own learning, some discussion and support at senior level is required. If they are to begin to help teachers improve their practice, and help monitor the nature of teaching and learning, there needs to be commitment from the staff as a whole, and worries and objections have to be addressed. If teaching is going to happen outside the classroom, and for different lengths of time, detailed planning and decision-making about the timetable will be essential.

Whether or not headteacher Hugh Bellamy at George Pindar Community Sports College is right in saying that 'anything is possible', it is clear from the examples in this chapter that a great deal is. Much less is set in stone, in the way learning is organised, than teachers have sometimes thought, and it is liberating and productive, if at times a little nerve-racking, to explore the benefits that such structural changes can bring. But all this requires leadership; and we turn to that topic in Chapter 8.

A study of curriculum redesign: George Pindar Community Sports College

In 2004, just 12% of the GCSE students at The George Pindar School achieved five good GCSEs. In the summer of 2009, 100% of students achieved 5 or more A* to C grades—57% including English and Mathematics. The intake of the school has remained the same: it continues to serve a deprived council estate at Eastfield on the outskirts of Scarborough. So what has made such a dramatic difference to the achievement and life opportunities to young people in this area?

A dramatic difference

A strategic approach

Headteacher Hugh Bellamy's strategy was to put learning at the heart of the curriculum. He was also committed to responding to the needs of the local community. The latter was quickly symbolised by changing the name from The George Pindar School—known locally simply as Pindar—to George Pindar Community Sports College to indicate a new seriousness focused on learning. But Hugh's approach was not a quick fix; the impact, he hoped, would be immediate but the real transformation of the school culture that was needed would take years.

Transforming the culture

Opening Minds plus BLP

As we have said before, the foundations of any cultural change have to be laid in classrooms. Work on the new curriculum at Pindar began in preparation for the school year 2005–6. Year 7 and 8 students would experience a competence-based curriculum that was initially based on the RSA's Opening Minds competency framework. However, the school quickly came to the view that this framework did not go far enough in identifying the precise habits that students would need to develop. It was at this point that the College adopted the language and concepts of Building Learning Power to complement its work on Opening Minds. Teachers were introduced to this language for understanding how students learn and were required to plan their lessons as split-screen experiences: paying attention to **how** students would be learning as well as **what** they were to learn. Although these habits were consciously developed within the competence-based Year 7 and 8 curriculum, the fall-out was soon felt in the way teachers taught in other years.

Starting with RSA's Opening Minds

Deepening the approach with BLP

In essence, teachers were trying to equip their students to take more responsibility for their own learning. Teachers were encouraged to use the BLP approach to spur innovation in a variety of ways that were consistent with the overarching aims of the College. The head knew that the only way to break with the past's record of under-achievement was to liberate both teachers and students to take calculated risks and try doing things

Liberating learners

█gpcsc

Keeping learning
under review

the scary guy.com

differently, in order to engage students in learning, and to get them interested in how they could build their learning power. At every stage, the College has kept learning under review; that is to say, it has always looked closely at how students are learning, and measured the impact of changes in pedagogy and curriculum on their learning habits and attitudes before moving on to the next stage.

These changes in the classroom went hand in glove with three other complementary features:

- The development of 'student leaders' who would have a voice in how the College was run and—ultimately—what kind of curriculum would suit their needs

- The involvement and engagement of the local community through activities that were targeted in response to local needs

- The support of an American motivational speaker called The Scary Guy, who helped the school to confront issues such as apathy and bullying in the wider community (see www.thescaryguy.com).

In all these ways, the College was aiming to raise the self-esteem of young people and their parents as never before. 'Anything is possible' was the key to Hugh Bellamy's vision for the Eastfield community. For example, the College has always made the most of its limited resources and constantly adapted its site to meet the learning needs of its students. Since 'anything is possible', in response to student and community requests space has been found for new facilities for Hairdressing and Construction, as well as the provision of enhanced sports facilities that are shared with local and regional educational, sporting, and business partners.

Creativity with time

Extended Key
Stage 4

At the ceremony at the end of Year 8, Pindar students 'graduate' as competent learners. Then they embark on an extended Key Stage 4 that is shaped to meet their individual needs according to a range of curriculum pathways. The College was keen for students to have a bigger voice in shaping the future direction of the curriculum. They needed to be asked what was going well and what could be improved to make things even better. They were quite clear: learning works better when you have got longer periods of time in which to explore your understanding. So the curriculum was redesigned to provide students with the time to hone their learning habits, explore their interests, and arrive at the qualifications that would be necessary for their emerging futures.

In September 2008, in its most radical move to date, the College implemented the whole-day lesson: students would regularly spend a whole day working in a single curriculum area. Student and teacher attitudes to learning had come a long way since 2005, and for some teachers this was just the opportunity they had been looking for to make their subjects more relevant and engaging. But for some curriculum areas and individual teachers this change proved demanding. Maintaining interest, variety, pace, and challenge for a whole day involved some serious thinking about the role of the teacher, and some struggled to adapt their habitual teaching style. Support was always available—both within and between departments—to ensure that no teacher was left to flounder on their own, and many were able to change their ways. Nevertheless, a minority of teachers found this shift too demanding and chose to move to different schools where a more conventional curriculum was still being pursued.

Even though the new approach became as natural to most teachers as their previous style, the process of continuous review and adaptation lead to some amendments for the school year 2009–10, with some curriculum areas reverting to half-day lessons.

gpcsc

A new way of
teaching

The Impact

Although incremental improvements in attitudes and results had been taking place between 2005 and 2008, the College was always aware that this radical change in learning would only begin to have a substantial effect on their GCSE results after four years (when the first group of BLP Year 8s would sit their exams). Since results at GCSE hadn't gone beyond the trigger 30% for five or more A* to C grades (including English and Maths), in 2008 the school was designated a National Challenge school. This provided both a threat and an opportunity. The threat was obvious and would have tempted less robust school leaders to abandon some of the radical approaches to learning that had been adopted. This they refused to do. The opportunity was to access resources that would enable them to provide even more personalised one-to-one support for individual students. This was already a feature of the College but now became something they could afford to pursue more wholeheartedly.

The impact of Hugh Bellamy's long-term strategic plan, coupled with a resilient and determined leadership team and additional financial resources, was an impressive set of results in the summer of 2009, towards which the College had been aiming for five years. An Ofsted inspection in May 2010 deemed them 'good with outstanding features'. Of particular note in their report was the transformation of teaching and learning, with teachers who had been considered satisfactory at a previous inspection now considered outstanding. The inspection took place as the College was embarking on an inter-disciplinary week when students were required to apply their learning

From satisfactory
to outstanding

gpcsc

Commitment to
a set of values

habits in challenging, real-world contexts alongside students with whom they were unfamiliar. Inspectors reported their admiration for the way the students rose to this challenge.

The Roots of Success

The Pindar story is a remarkable tale of commitment to a set of values that have been carried through with singular focus and purpose. The values that inform this coherent practice have as their cornerstones: community regeneration, relentless concern for continuous improvement, a drive to realise everyone's full potential, and a belief—by all partners—that anything is possible. Structural changes have been made, and additional resources received. But at the heart of Pindar's success lies their clarity of focus on the development of young people's capacity to learn, to regulate and organise their own learning, and to contribute to the school's continuous improvement. To summarise, some of features that have made this a standout success story are as follows:

A core focus on improving learning habits that is understood and enacted by all

- A foundation curriculum that introduces and assures those desirable learning habits
- Curriculum pathways that cater for the particular needs of individuals
- Flexible use of time to enhance learning opportunities and build learning confidence
- The use of student leaders to effect changes at curriculum and pedagogical levels
- One-to-one contact between teachers and students
- Confident, opportunistic, and inspirational leadership underpinned by clear and unambiguous values.

Chapter 7

Assessment and progression: How do we know it's working?

In this chapter we explore:

- the purposes of assessment
- some useful dimensions of progress
- different types of evidence
- examples of assessment in practice

Why track progression?

There are several reasons why schools are finding it useful to start documenting progression in students' learning power. They find that it:

- motivates and encourages students to put in the effort to continue improving their learning power

- gives students feedback on their learning power progress so that they can decide which 'learning muscles' they are going to target in the next period

- encourages teachers to realise that their efforts to improve learning power are being effective

- gives teachers information about individual students or classes that will enable them, the teachers, to discuss and guide learning power development more precisely and helpfully

- validates the progress made by students in terms of conventional attainment measures.

All of these purposes are legitimate and useful but they suggest different kinds of information gathered over different timescales. In devising a policy for tracking the development of learning power, schools are therefore beginning to create a multifaceted portfolio of indicators rather than a single metric. In this chapter we will discuss some of these different ways of tracking the development of learning power across different timescales.

What do we mean by progress?

From 'can do' to 'do do'

What do we mean when we say that a student's disposition to persist, or to question, has developed? Questioning, persisting, collaborating, making links and so on are things that people do. They are behaviours, either mental or physical or both. When we talk about dispositions or habits of mind, we are talking about the ways in which the deployment of these behaviours is becoming more frequent, more subtle, or more 'second nature'. As a teacher said of one of her pupils, 'Ruby has now got to the point where she can't not ask questions'!

If BLP is successful, students don't just show us that they 'can' make use of reflection or manage their distractions, and then we tick a box to confirm that they 'can' . We are looking to see whether, over time, they spontaneously make more and better use of these learning skills and tools. As we said earlier, unless we can see that students have made these tools their own, can intuitively see the point of them, and call them to mind for themselves when they are needed, we don't think the job of BLP has been completed.

Three dimensions of progress

From the experiences of schools which have introduced BLP we can see three distinct dimensions of progress.

The first dimension of growth is *strength*. To begin with, a learning muscle might only get used when it is specifically prompted or encouraged. Later, as in Ruby's case, the muscle gets used even when it is not being explicitly supported. Ruby's disposition to ask questions is now so much a part of the way she functions that she will insist on asking questions even when it might be a little inconvenient! She doesn't just ask questions; she has become a deeply inquisitive person. Or take Ciaran. He is capable of imagining how things might be different—but more than that, he now has a strong inclination to do so. He has grown, with help, into a keenly imaginative child.

Using the muscle more often

The second dimension is *breadth*. It is often the case that a child will possess one of the learning muscles already, but it only gets displayed in a narrow context. Watching Sam practising his penalty kicks, you can see that he is well able to persist in the face of difficulty. But he doesn't yet bring that same resilience to bear on his arithmetic or his writing. But fast-forward a year, and (with some BLP conversations and coaching) Sam has been helped to see how he can take the same resource which he has in his football, and apply it much more widely. He now perseveres with his sums and his painting just as much as his football.

Using the muscle in more contexts

Having the words with which to name these mental resources seems to be extremely useful in helping transfer to occur. That is why BLP places such emphasis on the vocabulary of the learning muscles. The particular words are not important; there is no right word for 'staying intelligently engaged with something despite the fact that it is harder or more frustrating than you thought it would be'. But having a word, one which the people around you use and understand as well, is very helpful.

And the third dimension of dispositional growth we call *depth*. This refers to a growth in the sophistication or skilfulness of each learning capacity. Ruby's inclination to ask questions has become not just broader and stronger, but her questions are more subtle, more appropriate, better designed to get her the information she needs. When Sam is on the verge of getting upset and giving up, he now has more strategies up his sleeve that can help him calm down, take stock and do something intelligent. He can close his eyes and take three deep breaths. He can count to ten. He can just stare out of the window for a minute to let his brain cool down. He can remember the voice of a 'learning coach' telling him 'You can do it!'. Like an Olympic athlete, he has a rich and varied repertoire of ways in which he can regulate his own emotions, so he can get back to being the best writer, artist, arithmetician, or footballer he can be.

Using the muscle more skilfully

151

And, of course, progress also means expanding the whole repertoire of learning habits of mind, so that students' learning prowess is becoming more multifaceted. They are learning to play with a fuller and more varied deck of learning cards.

So, overall, a teacher or a school can be looking for several types of progress. Each learning muscle is becoming stronger, and broader, and deeper. And the whole suite of learning muscles is expanding. As learning power coaches, teachers can constantly be thinking about how to help students develop along each of these dimensions. And as 'formative assessors', they can be thinking about how to help students take stock of their own development, and how to gather data across students so they can monitor and develop what they do to help students progress.

Using more muscles

Summarising progress

Some schools have used the 'Learning Power Wheel' shown opposite to summarise and record these types of progress periodically. The wheel is divided into sectors corresponding to the 17 learning muscles, grouped together under the emotional, cognitive, social and strategic dispositions. Teachers can fill in the wheel each term using the grading scale shown underneath.

However, the shading is not just an intuitive judgement by the teacher; it can be backed up by observations made by the teacher and learning assistants, by a student's own responses to an on-line learning power quiz, and by comments from parents. Sometimes the wheel can be coloured in jointly during a learning power conversation between a student and teacher. This dialogue gives students an opportunity to talk about their learning behaviours, identify strengths and gaps, and think about setting new 'growth' targets.

This diagram, simple though it is, has been found useful by both teachers and students and could form the foundations of a more sophisticated system.

Learning Power Profile

Name: **Lesley Wilson**

Date of birth: **20/05/2003**

Date of profile: **December 2010**

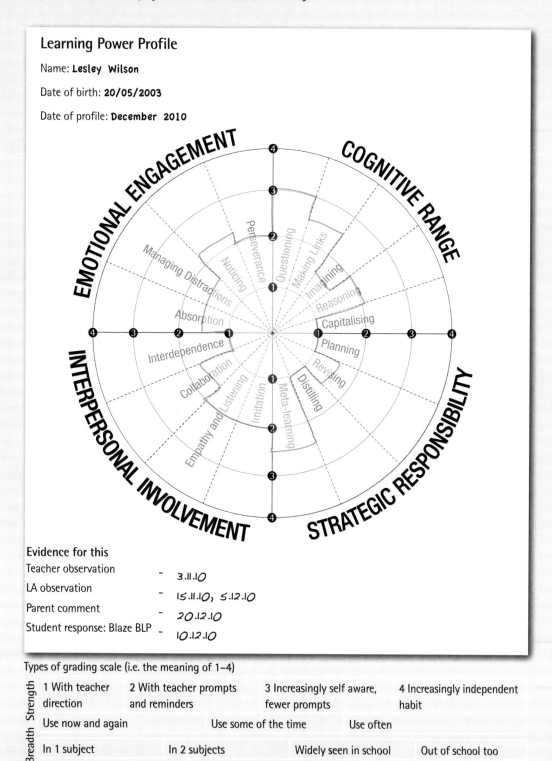

Evidence for this

Teacher observation	– 3.11.10
LA observation	– 15.11.10, 5.12.10
Parent comment	– 20.12.10
Student response: Blaze BLP	– 10.12.10

Types of grading scale (i.e. the meaning of 1–4)

	1 With teacher direction	2 With teacher prompts and reminders	3 Increasingly self aware, fewer prompts	4 Increasingly independent habit
Strength	Use now and again		Use some of the time	Use often
Breadth	In 1 subject	In 2 subjects	Widely seen in school	Out of school too

153

Types of evidence

What types of evidence can teachers collect in order to make the kinds of judgements that the wheel represents? We might think of these in three broad categories.

1. What students think about themselves as learners

Given the opportunity students are often happy to reflect on, talk about or write about themselves as learners. Learners' own self-reports offer a rich and legitimate source of evidence through, for example:

Self-awareness

- extracts from students' learning logs
- digital records of personal best moments taken by students themselves
- student responses to self-report questionnaires (such as *Blaze BLP*, which we describe later in this chapter).
- testimony recorded in their school planner
- student testimony when voluntarily submitting themselves for 'proficiency badges' in particular learning muscles
- students' UCAS personal statements
- testimony from alumni of the school—reports on how their learning power development helped their transition from primary to secondary or from secondary to the worlds of further study or work.

2. What teachers observe of students as learners

Taking on the role of a learning coach offers teachers more time to observe students developing their learning habits. As they mark students' work they will also be noticing and commentating on their use of various learning muscles. They may be awarding stickers for the determined use of learning muscles or undertaking dynamic observations of students as they grapple with a new challenge. Such evidence might include:

Teacher awareness

- students' products or performances
- photographic records of 'personal best' moments
- dynamic assessment—observations and records made of students in the process of learning

    When and how they ask for help

    The kinds of questions they ask

    Their 'think aloud protocols'
- a record of to whom, when and why recognition stickers were awarded.

3. What other people perceive of students as learners

Evidence of using their muscles more widely can be drawn not only from other teachers but from people who see the students outside school. It might include:

Others' awareness

- unsolicited comments from parents
- digital records from home or school clubs or out-of-school activities
- testimony from employers regarding a student's attitude to work during work experience
- testimony from piano teachers, sports coaches, youth club leaders, and the like.

You will have noticed that 'students' achievement levels' do not feature as a source of evidence for their developing learning power. This is not because we don't think it is important, but because it does not necessarily correlate with learning power. Students' achievement might have improved because the school has got better at spoon-feeding, for example. Nevertheless, we would hope that greater confidence and skill at learning would result in better performance. In Chapter 11 we will provide evidence that it usually does.

The when of assessing learning power

Schools have found it helpful to think about assessing learning power over different timescales.

Day-to-day assessment where the emphasis is on self- and peer-assessment and helping students to develop fine-grained understanding of their learning habits and how they grow.

Assessment timescales

Mid-range, periodic where a teacher might look at broader aspects of progression; for example, whether students are using particular learning habits more strongly, with greater depth, and with increasing independence than others, as discussed earlier.

Transitional assessment (e.g. annually or at the end of a Key Stage) where the outcome might influence students' future opportunities and choices and allow the school to adjust and develop its practice.

Challenges of observation

We have come to believe strongly that, if we want to support students' development as learners, the most appropriate forms of learning power monitoring are formative and ipsative assessment. We think that the idea of creating national grades or levels of learning power (or 'personal learning and thinking skills'), against which students' development is measured, is fraught with danger. However the process of tracking and recording learning power development is organised, this pitfall must be avoided at all costs.

The labelling of personal characteristics such as resilience or curiosity should only be carried out within a climate of immediate concern to support further development, and to encourage that development by showing students the progress they have made.

As with any form of appraisal, if those supportive and formative purposes are not clearly understood by the students there is a real danger of the process being perceived as punitive or as labelling them as more or less (in)adequate learners. Where the supportive and developmental nature of the assessments is clearly understood by all concerned, on the other hand, some provisional 'grading' may well be useful in focusing students' attention on the gains they have made and where further efforts might be rewarded.

We also think there is merit in each school involving students themselves in developing ideas about how progression can best be articulated and monitored. They often have clear intuitions about what the next level of 'noticing' or 'questioning' could look like, and these intuitions can be gathered over time into a model of progression that suits the school and is owned by the students.

On pages 158–159 we pull together the types of evidence and the different timescales into a sketch of one possible way in which a school might go about recording progression in learning power.

An impossible improvement?

At St Mary's Church of England Primary School in Thornbury, Gloucestershire, Jane Leo taught a Year 6 class. In 2007, a couple of weeks after her pupils had taken their KS2 SATs, she gave them a KS3 Levels 4–6 maths paper to do 'just as a bit of a challenge'. The children worked alone, with the exception of a few of the lowest-achieving children who were allowed to work in pairs. If any of the children asked her questions, she just said 'think carefully and just do what you think is right'. (She might be asked: 'Do they mean just add the two co-ordinates?' and she might reply: 'Re-read the question and if you think that is what it's asking then go ahead. Can you think of anything else they may mean? If not, go with what you think.' 'But that's too easy though' was one reply. Jane marked the papers (strictly), and compared the children's levels with those they had gained in their 'proper' KS2 SATs from two weeks before. Out of 22 children, all had gone up by at least two sub-levels. 13 children had gone up by at least a whole level (all but five of the children now performing at level 6!) Four of the class had gone up by four sub-levels.

This small–scale enquiry shows that Jane Leo knew her students well. She had observed them carefully throughout the year of 'doing BLP' and recognised their adventurous spirit and flexibility would allow them to succeed. She would never have set them up to fail, but she was surprised by just how well they succeeded in her experiment.

How does Jane account for this astonishing result? Obviously, the absence of emotional stress and the pressure of strict timing helped. But so did the way she had been teaching them for the previous year. They had learned how to make the best use of what they did know in order to 'give it their best shot' when they didn't immediately know the answer from memory. In her report, Jane wrote:

> 'I believe that their willingness to have a go stemmed from a year's worth of teaching them how to learn, and knowing themselves as learners. Through BLP techniques they know how to tackle a challenge; what questions to ask themselves; how to apply what they know to new situations; how to be flexible in their thinking, not always taking the expected route and being comfortable with that; knowing when to move on to something new and let their brains reflect on a problem whilst working on something else. They know themselves as learners and they see learning as a journey, not an end. If they couldn't do a question, they knew it wasn't because they would never be able to do it but that they hadn't seen the way there yet. '

Jane recorded the children's comments after they had completed the 'too hard' test. One said, 'Strangely, I really enjoyed that.' Another echoed, 'That was good—it makes you see the links between everything!' A third, 'I can't believe I could do so much of it...and it wasn't boring!' A fourth, 'I don't think I always did it the easiest way, but I still got there.' One child asked anxiously, 'So what do we learn next year then?'

An illustrative pattern of learning power assessment

	Timescales	Students tracking their own development
Day to day	Moment to moment	• Note when they are using a learning behaviour • Watch for learning behaviour being used by others. Capture on camera or note
	Lesson by lesson	• Work with learning-skill ladders or learning skills mats and note progress • Note when they have achieved a learning 'growth' target
	Day by day	• Reflect on learning for 2–3 minutes with a learning buddy (what was interesting, tricky, how they coped) at end of day
Periodic	Week by week	• Make entries in learning log/diaries. Note stand-out moments or personal best moments. Use photos, products, performances, vignettes. Self assess progress—breadth, strength, depth
	Term by term	• Take on-line quiz to estimate how much they think they use their learning muscles. Discuss with peers, teachers, parents. Set learning power growth targets • Submit evidence for 'learning proficiency' scheme • Note in learning logs—progress over the term
	Year by year	• Prepare 360° assessment of their use of learning power. Testimonial from peers, family teachers etc. Add to school/personal e-portfolio • 360° assessment PowerPoint presentation shared with next Year/phase teachers
Transitional		• Report on how learning power development will help or has helped them in transition from primary to secondary school or secondary school to further study or work • Write about themselves as a learner in UCAS forms or similar

158

Teacher tracking students' development	Illustration
• Note samples of conversations, code for frequency of learning language	*See Briar Hill Infant School example, page 160*
• Award learning behaviour recognition stickers. Keep a log of usage	
• Use learning-skill ladders or mats to promote deeper behaviours	*See Bushfield School example, page 164* *See St Mary's Swanley example, page 163* *See Simpson School example, page 173*
• Note what comes up in buddy reviews	
• Observe/record students grappling with difficult challenges. (Length of persistence, number of ways tried, when & how they ask for help, kinds of questions asked, etc.)	
• Mark work with comments related to use of learning behaviours	
• Sample entries in Learning Logs, note patterns	*See example, page 162*
• Note unsolicited comments from parents and others	
• Use feedback prompts from Blaze BLP to structure learning power conversations with students. Note attitudes, progress, gaps	*See example, page 168*
• Note evidence of students' projects or learning interests	
• Collect samples from learning portfolios (with permission)	
• Add to school's learning power portfolio to build a richer range of success indicators, e.g. independent, reflective, investigative, creative, team-spirited learners	No one kind of information will be suitable for all the purposes mentioned above, but these examples show a range of ways in which schools are beginning to address the issues.
• Teachers and school use information to assist in adjusting and developing its provision of learning power	

Tracking the development of learning power

Tracking progress day-to-day

Timescales for 'day-to-day' assessment include 'in the moment', 'daily', and 'weekly', and the approaches put the student at the centre of developing their learning behaviours. The ipsative and formative approaches:

- involve students reflecting on their learning habits as they happen
- offer them immediate feedback for relevant next steps
- motivate students to continue improving
- help teachers to see the effectiveness of, and adjust, their short term plans day by day.

Becoming aware

If students are to build their learning behaviours into habits they need to be aware of using them in the first place. So the growth of learning habits begins with students becoming aware of using them. This process is greatly helped by being able to name them. 'You really persisted well then, Maisie' gives the child a label that they can then use to recognise other instances of 'persisting'. Students become aware of their behaviours by linking the language of learning power to their actions, finding out what they feel like, talking to each other and their teacher about what they are doing.

At Briar Hill Infant School near Leamington Spa you can see this process in action. As soon as a learning behaviour has been introduced the children are encouraged to notice when they use it, and to briefly record what they have done—imagined something, used a good question, managed a distraction and so on—on a sticky note which they stick on a Learning Tree wall display. Teachers are on a constant look-out for the behaviours they have been explaining, encouraging and enabling, which they, too, capture through photographs or on sticky notes and add to the Learning Tree. This 'looking for learning' is further enhanced by 'learning detectives': two children who are assigned this role each day and who look for good learning behaviours in others and again add them to the Learning Tree. At the end of the day the Learning Tree offers a rich source of information to reflect on, explain, and reinforce through a whole-class learning power discussion.

At the end of the week the sticky notes are carefully saved in a large scrapbook. This gives the teachers a running record of what the children have been doing and noticing about themselves. Although this has only been in operation for a term or so the teachers are using their analysis of the weekly data to plan further development. They are refining their professional view of how their students' learning power behaviours can be converted into instinctive habits.

This 'consciousness-raising' process, in which children learn to recognise and name their own learning behaviours, is also at work in Annamaria Scaccia's class at Tremorfa Nursery School in Cardiff. She carried out a teacher enquiry on a group of four-year-old boys who showed low levels of perseverance and concentration. She simply took digital photos of them, and the rest of the group, on the occasions when they were visibly persisting and focusing on what they were doing, and displayed them on the Learning Wall. This simple manoeuvre turned out to have the desired effect: the boys wanted to have their photos on the board, so they tried harder to stay on task. Sometimes when they consider themselves to be working really hard at something they will ask to have their photo taken. One boy was heard to say, 'Quick Mrs Heathfield, ask Miss Scaccia to take a photo'. Unprompted, the boys use the Learning Wall as a constant source of reminders. Annamaria wrote, 'The wall wasn't initially intended to be used for reference; this is something the boys have decided for themselves. They look at the wall to remind them of the times when they were working hard... The photographs displayed give them ideas of things to do when they don't know what to do, which consequently is expanding their learning capacity.'

The effort to notice when different kinds of learning are happening helps the children to observe (and be proud of) their own progress. It also helps to train the attention of teachers. Teachers are often used to noticing if children are 'on task', 'working well', 'playing nicely' or 'looking happy'. It may be less familiar to them to be also noticing when they are imagining, making links, thinking carefully or using their empathy. This process of consciousness-raising helps everyone to refocus their attention on the nature of learning itself.

Over the following three pages we show examples of some day–by–day assessment approaches used in schools.

Assessing day-to-day: Examples from schools

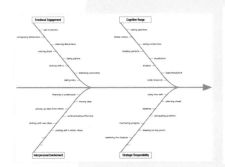

Observing learning

The 'fishbone diagram' can be turned into a useful learning observation tool. The 'big bones' show the main areas you are looking for, e.g. emotional, social, cognitive or strategic.

The little bones identify the actual behaviours you are hoping to witness. This type of format has been used and adapted by teachers and students. The layout makes for easy recording.

From TLO's Foundation Course material

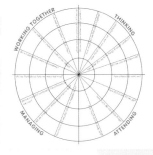

Learning wheels to stimulate self-reflection

This familiar learning stretch wheel, from TLO's Transition Activity Bank, has been used and adapted by hundreds of schools. It is often used after a group activity to help students reflect on how much they have used each learning muscle. Recording tools such as this can be used to gauge how students view their efforts or to plot a team's progress over time.' Perhaps more importantly they offer a way of structuring conversations about learning power.

Reflective Learning Log—to build self-awareness and capture behaviours

Many schools use Learning Logs in which students record their thoughts, feelings, and progress about learning. Some schools use the more formalised learning log pages from TLO's on-line Transition Activity Bank. Different pages prompt students to notice themselves using a learning behaviour over the course of a week—at school, at home, and elsewhere—and to note briefly what they did. For example, for Making Links they might note; 'When I built on the knowledge I already had', 'When I used an analogy to better understand something', 'When I met something new and asked myself how is this the same, and how is it different from things I already know?'

From TLO's Transition Activity Bank[1]

Empathy sticker

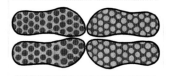

Interdependence sticker

Learning observers record learning.

Pairs of pupils go into different classrooms and record what they see, hear, feel. They may look for something specific like how children manage distractions. Observer forms with tick-boxes encourage systematic recording. This type of activity helps to build understanding of the learning muscles.

Learning stickers and awards to recognise learning

Many schools have set up pupil awards for learning well and/or for being good at spotting when they are using different learning muscles. They use stickers, certificates, a mention in assembly, or tea with the headteacher. Self-awareness and understanding of the detail of the learning process is further developed by asking pupils to articulate what they have done to earn the award.

Learning ladders in primary schools

St Mary's CE Primary in Swanley, Kent has been developing learning ladders to build a deeper or more finely grained understanding of each learning behaviour. Each learning muscle has been broken down into 6–8 progressive learning behaviours in the form of a ladder. At the end of each lesson pupils (in Year 4) are encouraged to assess and record the level at which they feel they have been using the muscle[s]. They do this by putting one of their small self-portrait photographs onto their learning ladder at the level that best describes their behaviour.

I can confidently use a variety of questions to enhance my learning.

I can use a range of strategies to create questions.

I am able to make sensible decisions about the relevance of my questions.

I constantly ask questions about why things are happening.

I use questions in different situations to show I am focused on my learning.

I can identify when a question will answer a problem and which questions will give the right answers.

I use a range of prompts to help me ask questions.

I ask questions when prompted.

Learning Mats to prompt learning and reflection

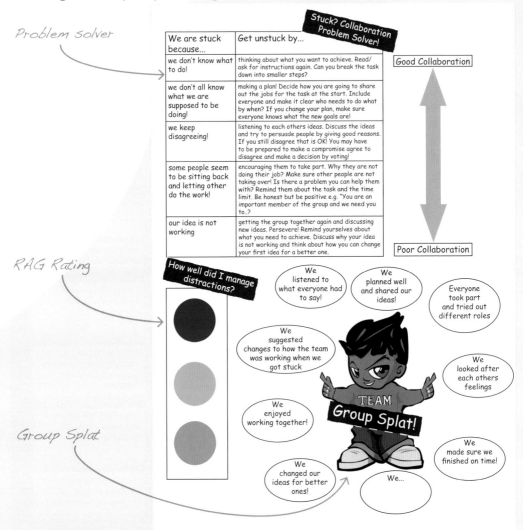

Problem Solver

RAG Rating

Group Splat

Learning mats, like this one from year 5 at Bushfield School, Milton Keynes, are A4 or A3 laminated sheets depicting various aspects of a learning muscle. They live on the tables where pupils are learning so that they can refer to them throughout the day. This mat shows different aspects of *collaboration* which serve to prompt pupils about how and when to use them during team working. The problem solver offers ideas for getting through tricky aspects of team working.

A Group Splat is used during or at the end of the activity to help pupils self-assess their learning and how they are progressing. The RAG rating panel encourages the pupils to assess their management of distractions. The collaboration arrow invites the group to gauge their progress on a simple line and explain the basis of this self-assessment. Similar tools have also been developed by teachers in secondary schools to help students reflect on their learning.

Tracking progress periodically

The point of periodic assessment is to allow pupils to stand back and take a longer-term view of their learning power development over time. These occasional reviews reveal strengths and areas for improvement, and also enable students to detect (and celebrate) progress that has been gradually built over a number of weeks. They also reveal patterns of development across contexts, and offer teachers information that will help them to adjust their medium-term plans and approaches.

Gary Scott is a Year 6 teacher at Princeville Primary School in Bradford who has been watching the growth of his pupils over the past two years. Last year he realised that although he could talk about the learning power progress of most of his students, he had nothing tangible with which to support or evidence his views. He began to observe his students more systematically using simple recording methods like fishbone diagrams (see page 162). Each half term he used these records to complete a partial Learning Power Profile for each student (similar to the one shown on page 153) They were partial because he only recorded progression for the muscles he had been concentrating on during the previous few weeks. However, over the course of the year every muscle group was covered. This six week periodic assessment gave him a good idea of the extent to which his attempts to build each of the muscles has been successful and with which of them students might need more assistance or practice.

Short-term periodic

Many of the day-to-day assessment approaches can also lend themselves to slightly longer-term periodic assessment. Schools have:

- asked students to look back over entries in their learning journal or equivalent, and write or draw a summary of their progress.
- asked teachers to undertake a dynamic assessment of students working with particular muscles which they have been practising in the last few weeks.
- totted up and discussed the numbers of learning power recognition stickers that have been awarded.
- got students to look through teachers' comments on their written work and estimate which learning muscles they seem to have been strengthening (and which not)
- got students to undertake peer analyses of each other using the learning wheel or similar tools to scaffold the conversations. This is often done in tutor-groups.

Turning day-to-day into periodic

Long-term periodic

Longer-term periodic assessment—termly or annually—benefits from using other more comprehensive data-collecting methods including:

- on-line assessment resources such as Blaze BLP.
- observing learning behaviours across Year groups and discussing results.
- inviting different subject teams to observe learning behaviours in a subject that's not their own.
- undertaking learning reviews across a subject, Year group, or set (see the discussion of learning reviews on page 209)
- undertaking more formal learning conversations with each student

Using BLP quizzes

As we have seen earlier, an important element in building progression in learning power is through conversations: between students, between students and teachers, and between students, teachers and parents. However, when not all parties are fluent in their use of the learning power vocabulary, it can be difficult to get these conversations going. That is where the on-line quizzes which we have developed can be of help: they are fun for students to do, they provide interesting feedback, and this feedback forms the natural basis for further conversations and reflections.

Blaze BLP is a suite of online quizzes which contribute both to the process of building learning power **and** tracking students' self-reported progress. There are five quizzes, one of which is an overall guide to the development of the learning muscles, and the other four zoom in in more detail on each of the four muscle groups: resilience, resourcefulness, reflection and reciprocity. After they have done each quiz, the software offers back to the pupil a pen-portrait of how their learning power is progressing, and some immediate suggestions as to how they might be able to 'exercise those learning muscles' even more. It is this feedback and advice that can form the basis of very productive conversations.

At Alderbrook Leading Edge School and Arts College students use the quizzes periodically to give a sense of the progress they are making in building their learning power. At the start of the year students complete the general Learning Power Quiz, the result of which gives a broad picture of how students view themselves as learners. Teachers scrutinise the results to find out if one group of muscles need stretching more than others. A week later students complete a second quiz which relates specifically to the weakest muscle group, and the results are used to pinpoint the particular behaviours that students are finding tricky. Teachers then use this information to design a series of challenges that are infused into lessons over the next few weeks. Towards the end of term the students re-do the quiz and teachers use the feedback information to confirm, sharpen or challenge their own observations. This on-line resource offers continuing information which helps to shape medium-term planning and support coaching conversations with students.

Learning power conversations

Termly or annual conversations are a cornerstone of developing and assessing learning power. After taking a Blaze quiz, students receive immediate and encouraging feedback at one of three levels related to their current use of each learning muscle. The computer might report that they are using that muscle

- Frequently and broadly
- Sometimes and variably
- Occasionally or only in a single domain

The purpose of learning conversations relating to these 'levels' is to encourage upward movement—to get students thinking about how they might make their use of that muscle stronger, broader and deeper. This intention shapes the conversations that ensue.

Conversations to strengthen learning power

Where the student is showing infrequent use of a learning muscle the teachers' coaching prompts (see overleaf) encourage a discussion on:

- exploring the meaning of the learning muscle
- thinking about why the muscle is/will be useful to them
- gauging what would help them to use it more often

Where students are showing variable use of the muscle(s) the coaching prompts focus the discussion on:

- deepening understanding of that learning muscle
- trying to remembering to use it in different domains
- exploring the benefits they might gain from using it
- seeking to find out what could trigger them to use it more broadly

A critical stage

This is a critical stage. Exploring what triggers the use of a muscle begins to nudge casual or reflex use of a muscle into deliberatly strengthening and broadening the habit of using it.

Teacher prompts to generate learning power conversations

Radar graph indicating self-reported strengths & areas to work on.

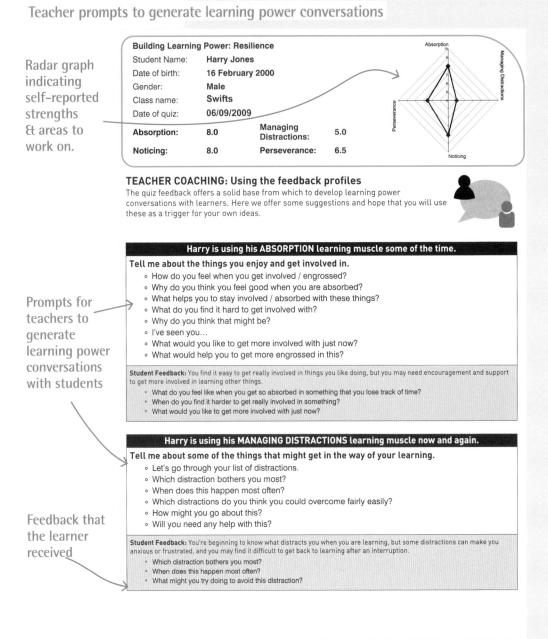

Building Learning Power: Resilience

Student Name: **Harry Jones**

Date of birth: **16 February 2000**

Gender: **Male**

Class name: **Swifts**

Date of quiz: **06/09/2009**

| Absorption: | 8.0 | Managing Distractions: | 5.0 |
| Noticing: | 8.0 | Perseverance: | 6.5 |

TEACHER COACHING: Using the feedback profiles

The quiz feedback offers a solid base from which to develop learning power conversations with learners. Here we offer some suggestions and hope that you will use these as a trigger for your own ideas.

Harry is using his ABSORPTION learning muscle some of the time.

Tell me about the things you enjoy and get involved in.

Prompts for teachers to generate learning power conversations with students

- How do you feel when you get involved / engrossed?
- Why do you think you feel good when you are absorbed?
- What helps you to stay involved / absorbed with these things?
- What do you find it hard to get involved with?
- Why do you think that might be?
- I've seen you...
- What would you like to get more involved with just now?
- What would help you to get more engrossed in this?

Student Feedback: You find it easy to get really involved in things you like doing, but you may need encouragement and support to get more involved in learning other things.

- What do you feel like when you get so absorbed in something that you lose track of time?
- When do you find it harder to get really involved in something?
- What would you like to get more involved with just now?

Harry is using his MANAGING DISTRACTIONS learning muscle now and again.

Tell me about some of the things that might get in the way of your learning.

- Let's go through your list of distractions.
- Which distraction bothers you most?
- When does this happen most often?
- Which distractions do you think you could overcome fairly easily?
- How might you go about this?
- Will you need any help with this?

Feedback that the learner received

Student Feedback: You're beginning to know what distracts you when you are learning, but some distractions can make you anxious or frustrated, and you may find it difficult to get back to learning after an interruption.

- Which distraction bothers you most?
- When does this happen most often?
- What might you try doing to avoid this distraction?

Where students are already showing frequent use of the muscle the conversation the coaching-prompts might encourage:

- seeking examples that validate the quiz's judgement of frequent use
- talking in more depth about the muscle in action
- exploring how they can become even more skilled in using it
- probing what triggers its use
- discovering where else it might be useful

We find that such conversations tend to deepen teacher-student relationships, help develop the common language for learning, and invigorate students' interest in their learning power.

Annual Periodic, or Transitional

We have met some schools where students are required to manage and record a 360° feedback on themselves as a learner at the end of each year. Students prepare a PowerPoint® presentation in words and pictures to show themselves as a powerful learner. The presentation often includes descriptions of their interests in school and out, and the learning habits they think they use successfully. They are expected to justify their views with evidence and testimony from teachers, family, friends and others. The presentation ends with a summary of the learning habits the student wants to improve in the future, and how they intend to go about it. This comprehensive exercise is often shared with parents and is posted as evidence in the student's e-portfolio for future use. In some cases the information is shared with Year group leaders, helping to smooth the transition from one year to another.

Building deeper skills

In the practical illustrations of how to track progression, and how to make good use of that information, we have focused on the first two of our three threads of progress: strengthening and broadening. We have reviewed a range of ways in which teachers can help young people to consolidate their learning behaviours into robust habits, and how to expand the range of contexts in which those dispositions spontaneously come to mind. Finally we offer a few thoughts about the trickier issue of how you might be able to demonstrate whether pupils are genuinely building up their level of expertise in imagining, noticing, or distilling the learning essence out of experience. What does 'getting better at persevering' involve? What does it look like?

The tricky issue of building expertise

Some schools have been rising to this challenge. They have been considering what the learning behaviours consist of at yet more finely grained levels. Take 'collaboration' as an example. It is made up of a skein of sophisticated social behaviours which can take years to perfect. Without a sense of what all these skilful threads actually are, there is less chance of improving them. Without an understanding of the finer skills of teamwork, it is hard to know how we can help other people develop them.

Following this train of thought, some BLP teachers have been asking themselves:

- What are the various aspects of collaboration?
- What does/should effective collaboration look like, sound like, feel like?
- What do we or should we expect of students and by when?
- How can we build deepening behaviours into the way we design lessons?
- How will we know progress when we see it?

Similar conversations may be had, of course, about reasoning, imagining, persevering, and so on. What do these learning capacities comprise? How would we organise or sequence the process of getting better? What does 'getting better' look like in different Year groups? These are complex issues which few teachers have considered previously. While this sort of teasing out of ever finer grains of a learning behaviour is in its infancy, there are some useful pointers which may help others travelling the same road.

The innards of learning

The examples opposite, taken from the BLP *At A Glance* cards,[2] show what well-formed habits such as planning and collaboration might be made up of. These descriptions, we have been told, have helped schools to begin thinking about what progression or 'getting better' might look like. Starting with this more detailed breakdown of what the full-blown habit consists of has helped them to imagine what 'earlier versions' or less well-formed versions might look like.

Some such conversations about the innards of learning have resulted in developing the ideas of Learning Mats and Learning Ladders as we saw on page 159. Sometimes these have been developed by groups of teachers 'in private', as it were, who felt the need to challenge themselves to unpick learning before sharing this with students. Others have been compiled by students and teachers together. Although such tools are in their infancy they have been seen to offer students a deeper sense of a learning capacity and a route map for the development journey.

A well formed Planning habit involves being ready, willing, and able to:

Have a sense of the longer term — considering options and possible consequences before taking action.

Know that it pays to start with the end in mind; identify end goals or objectives before considering possible action.

Make use of a wide variety of skills and tools to gather ideas and information, or sequence activity in order to decide what needs to be done.

Consider timescales and possible obstacles in drawing up a realistic plan.

Think laterally as well as logically so that the task in hand benefits equally from creative and rational thought.

Be open-minded and flexible about how things might happen so that opportunities can be seized and fresh directions taken.

Stop and take stock of progress in the light of experience, adapt the planned course of action, or even abandon it if it turns out to be inappropriate.

Evaluate the process and outcomes of an endeavour in order to learn from the experience and adapt behaviour in the future.

A well-formed Collaborating habit involves being ready, willing, and able to:

Work effectively with others towards common goals, acting flexibly in response to circumstances.

Seek to understand what others are saying; sharing, challenging, supporting and building on ideas.

Hold and express opinions coherently, compromising and adapting when appropriate.

Adopt different roles and responsibilities in pursuit of agreed goals and the well-being of the team.

Act proactively and responsibly; exercise initiative, see opportunities, and persevere in the face of difficulties.

From *At a Glance* cards,[2] Planning and Collaborating

Learning ladder for Imitation. Version 1

At Simpson School teachers have had several attempts at compiling learning ladders. Their first prototype description for collaboration is shown on page 108. At first they thought of progression ladders as being linear: you have to climb up rung by rung in the right order. The one below describes their take on the progression of imitation.

Better imitation

Better individuals' imitation →

- Naturally notices and adapts others ideas/ approaches without being solicited
- Sees imitation as an essential way to learn
- Can adopt a method/strategy to make their own, uses again (a resource from which to capitalise)
- Pre-empts the final 'thing' being imitated
- **Thinks ahead when imitating, predicting what might happen next**
- Looks back, adjusting and checking, reviewing
- **Concentrates for prolonged periods**
- Highly motivated to imitate to learn
- **Can motivate themselves to task when required**
- Sees imitation as adopting an idea, not copying
- **Concentrates/ attentive whilst imitating**
- Makes effort to use senses, e.g. making sure that they can see, listening attentively etc.
- **Is motivated to imitate to learn**
- Cannot maintain concentration
- **Gives up trying to imitate when encountering difficulties**
- Doesn't use all their senses effectively (listening etc.)
- **Gives up easily**
- Sees imitation as copying, not adopting
- **Does not readily learn from what they see**

From ladders to stages

But after a while they realised this didn't reflect the way their pupils were actually learning: they were seeing something more interwoven and less predictable. They now talk about learning stages rather than ladders. In putting these together they drew inspiration and information from a number of sources: TLO's KS1 Activity Bank where there are progression starter ideas for every behaviour,[3] extracts from 2008 DCSF Making Good Progress series, and from their own observations in classrooms. The stages broadly map the growth of learning power, but within each stage there is no specific order in which the elements have to be developed (see opposite). Teachers use these stages to remind themselves of what to look for and what to say in nudging students forwards to perhaps a more appropriate behaviour in the stage or indeed a behaviour in the next stage. Preparatory work has been completed on many of the behaviours and their model will soon be ready for testing.

Learning stages (Imitation)

Stage 4

- I try to adapt other people's ideas for myself.
- When I need to, I look at other people's learning to monitor my own progress.
- I choose to imitate as a way of learning.
- If I need to, I can focus all my senses and attention on what I am imitating.
- I actively look back, adjust, check and review when imitating.
- If I need to, I can motivate myself to learn by imitating others.

Here children are fully aware of the value of the behaviour and are able to use it to advantage when necessary

Stage 3

- I try to learn by watching others.
- I sometimes learn from other people's ideas or instructions.
- I try to ask questions so I fully understand what I'm imitating.
- I manage to use what I have learnt from other people.

At this stage children are aware of the value of the behaviour and are becoming less dependent on the teacher

Stage 2

- I know that imitation is using an idea, not copying the answer.
- I am aware that I can learn by watching others.
- I can ask others if I am on the right track.
- I need help to use all my senses when imitating.
- I can ask for instructions to be repeated if needed.
- I am aware that I need to concentrate on the person I am imitating.

At this stage children are aware of using the behaviours but need help, prompts, encouragement, scaffolding

Stage 1

- I might take notice of what other people are doing.
- I need to know that I can learn from what I see others do.
- I might ask for help.
- I might listen to other people's ideas.

What to avoid

- Thinking that imitation is copying.
- Letting others do the learning for me.
- Showing no interest in how other people do things.
- Giving up quickly when somebody is trying to show me 'how'.
- Getting annoyed when others show me how to do things.

At this stage children are usually unaware of using these behaviours

Better imitation

Developed by teachers at Simpson School, Milton Keynes

In the secondary sphere, teachers at Alderbrook School in Solihull have been experimenting with progression trajectories for each of the BLP learning muscles. They have tried to explain to themselves what progression in students' behaviour might look like and link this to their growing independence.

What teachers need to do to help students through the stages

The key difference in the learning ladder shown opposite is that the thinking was not just about what students will be doing at each 'level' but what teachers need to do to help move students from one level to another. The example is a summarised version of their progression statements for questioning habits.

This has not been an easy task and is far from being completed, but this type of exploration has proved to be valuable in having teachers look more deeply into their role. The school reports that the struggle involved in writing one of these ladders has been of much more value than simply buying someone else's version 'off the peg'. It has certainly generated many Aha! moments, as teachers discover new ways of organising their classrooms and designing activities with learning power in mind.

The example is very much a work-in-progress. However, they have developed some rules of thumb that have helped make the struggle run more smoothly.

1. Start 'at the top' with aspects of a well formed habit

Tips for building your own ladders

2. Move to the bottom—the 'entry level'—but don't write this simply as a negative, in terms of what such students can't or don't do. Describe how students actually do behave, if they are not using the behaviour.

3. The level of detail you choose is important. The more stages you try to differentiate, the harder it will be to articulate all the differences between them.

4. When writing the teacher side—how teachers can help students make progress—think in terms of 'telling' and 'directing' in the early stages; commentating, nudging and coaching in the middle phase, and inviting students to take on self-coaching as the habit becomes more and more expert.

These examples show the beginnings of deeper thinking about how learning behaviours might unfold and how teachers might assist the process. They have given teachers a better idea of what to do and look for in deepening learning habits.

Progression in questioning

	Levels of questioning behaviour	What teachers need to do to move students up the levels	
Fully independent habit	Understand value of good questioning. Willing to reveal uncertainties. Rarely accept things uncritically. Lead others in these skills.	Students progress to the highest levels through repeated practice and modelling in order to deepen the habit in themselves, and to help and support others to acquire and develop similar skills and habits	Encouraging self coaching
Increasingly independent habit	Curious about all manner of things. Unafraid of not knowing. Relish getting below surface of complex high order questions.		
Increasingly reflective, self aware, few prompts necessary	Display curiosity about a range of things. Speculate about possibilities. Get below the surface. Willing to play around with things to see what happens.	Provide opportunities to broaden own areas of interest, investigate problems at a deep level	Commentating
Developing skill that needs prompting and reminding	More willing to ask questions on unfamiliar areas/subjects. Beginning to seek/develop information. Seeking skills. Can use open and closed questions with prompting. Less inclined to accept things at face value.	Provide opportunities for open-ended tasks, practising their own questioning techniques, setting their own challenges, experiencing teamwork	Coaching
Only with teacher support	Beginning to ask higher order questions. May draw simple conclusions. Prefers to work at surface level.	Provide opportunities to practise uncovering facts and evidence, develop basic research skills, (index, library, internet). Use various questioning routines.	Supporting
Only with teacher direction	Rarely seem curious. Stick with the familiar. Low level closed questions. Accepts things uncritically.	Provide opportunities to use closed and open questions. Needs topics of personal interest. Support experience of certainty and doubts.	Directing

Developed by teachers at Alderbrook Leading Edge School and Arts College, Solihull

Part 3
Whole-School Activity

So far we have discussed seven layers of Building Learning Power's '10-ply' approach to culture change. The chapters in Part 1 focused on getting the beliefs and understandings right, so that everyone involved sees why learning power is so important, and is clear about what is realistically possible. Part 2 looked in some detail at what BLP actually asks of classroom teachers as they talk to pupils, plan lessons, design the curriculum and check to see if 'building learning power' is really happening. Classrooms are the engine rooms of a school's culture, so it was right to devote a good deal of attention to what goes on in them. But individual teachers' impact on pupils is limited if the whole-school culture does not support them. A learning-powered school is more than a series of learning-powered classrooms. It is these whole-school issues that we explore in Part 3.

In Chapter 8 we address the crucial issue of school leadership. Where some approaches to leadership treat it as a technical matter, and others as a matter of personality, BLP puts the vision first, and then asks: What kind of leadership is going to be effective to achieve the specific aim of helping young people achieve in a way that also builds their confidence, capacity and appetite for real-life learning? In a nutshell, if we want students to become powerful learners, school leaders have to work at creating a community that thrives on enquiry. Chapter 9 continues this theme by looking at the kinds of professional development that help to bring that community into being, and at how to support teachers who might initially be sceptical or reluctant to change their ways. Recent work by Dylan Wiliam and others on building professional learning communities is very helpful here.

'No school is an island', John Donne might have said, and culture change affects not just those who work in a school but all those who have a stake in it. Pre-eminent amongst those are parents, and in Chapter 10 we take a look at some of the ways in which BLP schools have worked to explain the approach to parents and to get them on board with the vision and values of BLP. From redesigning the school's website to running workshops for parents to help them build their learning power, many schools have found it very worthwhile to invest in helping parents understand what twenty-first century education could be.

Chapter 8

Leading the learning powered school

In this chapter we explore:

- the importance of leadership

- changing views of leadership

- leadership BLP-style

- a vision for learning

- approaches to innovation
  – creating a dialogue
  – supporting a culture of enquiry
  – keeping the learning on track

- looking at the school through the BLP framework

I t is the beginning of the school year. Principal Liz Coffey at Landau Forte College in Derby stands on the hall stage to welcome the new Year 7 students.

> *'Welcome to Landau Forte. Over the next five or more years we are going to get you used to being stuck and enjoy finding ways of getting yourselves unstuck! The first challenge this morning is to build the highest tower possible out of the resources that we have prepared for you. You can work in groups of three but you cannot talk to each other. Off you go!'*

This is the first in a series of challenges that the principal will offer her students. Each conveys a strong message that learning at the Collage is about coping with things that are difficult—and enjoying being at the edge of your comfort zone. Coffey wants her students to think of themselves as members of a learning powered school. Whereas in the past, she would have said: *'Welcome to Landau Forte, we are a successful school and if you work hard, we will help you make the most of yourself'*, these days her approach has changed.

The importance of school leadership

Leading a school is one of the most challenging and exciting roles that anyone can undertake. It is also one of the most important. Parents know this and pay particular attention to it when choosing schools. Students know this and can often tell you just what their headteachers are good and less good at. Studies of school effectiveness constantly remind us of the importance of leaders in education. The National College for Leadership of Schools and Children's Services owes its existence to the high value that the UK government places on school leadership. And Ofsted regularly comments on the different ways in which school leadership directly impacts on a school's ability to deliver high-class learning for its students.

Yet for all the books and reports about leadership, it remains, for a number of fairly obvious reasons, an uncertain art. The **first** reason why leadership can never be 'by the book' is because what leaders do has to depend on the unique collection of circumstances in which they find themselves. As Canadian headteacher-turned-inspector Dean Fink summed up:

> *'Successful leaders use a variety of strategies and styles depending on what it takes to create an environment for learning, and they actively search out the many good practices that are out there, but they also adapt them to their particular contexts.'*[1]

Multiple leaders

Secondly, leadership is hard to pin down because, in any organisation, there is never a single leader. Leadership has to be distributed and delegated across many layers of a school, including heads of department, bursars, administrative supervisors, chairs of governors and parent-teacher associations, not forgetting students themselves, whether as 'prefects', class captains, or captains of clubs and sports teams. In addition, there are all those who may have no formal title, but are leaders none the less by virtue of their knowledge, skill or character. A headteacher has no choice but to be a leader of leaders.

Moral purpose

'Leadership is about creating a sense of purpose and direction.'

Sir Michael Bichard

The **third** reason why there can be no universal blueprint for successful leadership is that it depends on where you are trying to go. Many leadership manuals talk as if leadership were merely a technical skill, as if one could specify the 'how' of leadership independently from a consideration of 'whither'. But other authors, like Michael Fullan, see that the heart of leadership is what he calls 'moral purpose'.[2]

The first job of leaders, says Fullan, is to gain real clarity and focus about where they want their schools to go: what kinds of young people they are ultimately trying to develop. Their second job is to turn that vision into a narrative that will engage and inspire the people whose job it will be to make the vision a reality. Leadership is about getting 'buy-in'. Thirdly, leaders need to be good at creating structures and activities that will enable, encourage, support (and if necessary impel) those people to move in the right direction. They need to know what it will take to make it happen. Finally, they need to be able to find ways to monitor, recognise, and celebrate progress, and to adapt their strategy in the light of this information and experience.

Turning vision into reality

A good many of these ideas are enshrined in the distillation of the 'qualities for effective school leadership' that was produced in 2010 by the Northern Ireland Assembly, reproduced on the panel overleaf.[3]

Leadership BLP-style

The emphasis on the importance of clarity about 'moral purpose' is critical when we come to think about the special demands there might be in leading the learning-powered school. For BLP is not designed merely to create more efficient learning and improved examination results. Its goal is to broaden the scope of education; not just to improve the means to the traditional goal of achievement and attainment. The idea that 'our school' is dedicated to producing confident and creative learners, as well as delivering high standards, does not live in the land of Mission Statements, website Home Pages and Good Intentions; it has to be an ever-present ambition and a demanding day-to-day challenge.

Beyond mission statements

BLP leaders cannot get away with vague, aspirational talk about 'good to great', 'world-class education', 'transformational' or 'inspirational' schools,

Key points from Northern Ireland Assembly Paper 2010

- The leadership of schools is second only to classroom teaching in terms of its influence on student learning, with the greatest impact found in schools where the learning needs are most significant.

Broad range of skills

- The role of school leaders is becoming increasingly complex and demanding, and principals require a broad range of skills and attributes in order to carry out their duties effectively.

Adapt practice to context

- It is important to note that there is no 'one size fits all' approach to school leadership; leaders need to adapt their practice to the context of the school in which they work.

Personal qualities link to leadership success

- There is a strong link between leaders' personal qualities and leadership success.

Shared characteristics

- The evidence indicates that the most effective school leaders share a number of key characteristics, including that they are open-minded, ready to learn from others, have strong values, and are emotionally resilient.

People-centred values emphasising equality and respect

- Leaders of schools in disadvantaged contexts share many of the same traits as principals of other schools; being driven by core values that are people-centred, with a moral focus and an emphasis on equality and respect.

- Research suggests that effective principals of schools, in challenging circumstances in particular, share the following attributes:

  » Passion and risk-taking – Personal humility – Emotional intelligence – Tenacity and resilience in advocacy – Respect for others – Personal conviction.

Distributive leadership works

- Effective distribution of leadership throughout the school is another key characteristic of effective school leaders and is linked to the improvement of educational outcomes for pupils.

'best practice' or 'next practice', because, unless you specify very clearly what the goal actually is, it is all too easy to think that you are merely talking about schools that get better results (as conventionally defined). BLP is not primarily about improving a school's position in the league tables, whether they be local authority tables, or the OECD tables of international comparison. For those fancy phrases to mean anything, you have to spell out 'world-class *at what?*', 'transformational *to what?*', and 'next practice *for what?*' That's why the first chapter of this book stressed the clarity and the validity of the BLP vision.

The lenses of the BLP leader

School leaders who have embarked on the BLP journey see the world through a specific set of lenses.

- Their vision of building powerful real-world learners needs to be compelling enough to attract a wide following, even when it is different from what the school down the road, the local authority, or the current government are saying. You need to make strenuous and persistent efforts to win the hearts and minds of colleagues, governors, parents, and local advisers. This takes courage and conviction.

  A compelling vision

- Their approach to innovation will tend to echo the values and approaches to learning advocated in BLP. Creating a learning-powered school is a learning journey. You cannot just buy the BLP manual and implement it. To create the kind of culture change that is necessary, you have to read, and think, and argue, and experiment, and adjust, and try again. A BLP school needs to be growing in its collective resilience, resourcefulness, reflection, and relationships, at the same time as it is trying to cultivate those qualities in its pupils. In short, they create a dialogue about learning, they actively encourage experimentation, and they involve everyone in monitoring improvements that are not always measurable in the traditional ways of measuring attainment.

  Involving everyone in discussing, trying things out and seeing what works

- Their leadership style involves modelling these learning virtues to the best of their ability. Leaders in BLP schools tend to be passionate learners themselves, interested in learning processes, keeping up with research, and able and willing to talk about their own learning lives to staff and pupils alike. Learning-powered leaders tend to see themselves as leaders of learning, encouraging everyone in the community to be less afraid of risk or uncertainty by their own example.

  A passionate learner

- Their model of leadership tends to be a distributed one. They usually encourage others to manifest and model learning qualities in their own professional lives. This will include students, especially in their dealings with those younger or 'newer' than themselves.

  Enabling others to lead

- Their approach to professional development for staff centres on growing their confidence and expertise in BLP. This usually means

Dynamic professional
learning

creating dynamic professional learning communities, ongoing teacher enquiry projects, targeted use of coaching.

- A commitment to undertaking regular learning reviews to see the degree to which BLP approaches are really embedded in the school.

Dual-focus leading

It seems to be very useful for learning powered leaders to keep in mind the 'frequently asked questions' that we discussed in Chapter 3. Pre-eminently, we have found that it can be surprisingly hard for some colleagues to get out of the 'either / or' mindset: *either* we are going to focus on raising standards, in which case the fine aspirations of BLP will have to take a back seat; *or* we are going to try to develop confident real-world learners, in which case we are likely to jeopardise the precious results. The leader's

Pursuing two goals

job is to keep challenging this assumption with data (like that which we present in Chapter 11) and research (like that of John Hattie) which shows otherwise. For BLP heads, the heart of their leadership is the capacity to ensure that both goals are pursued simultaneously.

This dual-focus leadership is analogous to what in Chapter 5 we called 'split-screen' teaching. In similar vein BLP leaders have to do split-screen leading, ensuring that the learning power agenda is at least as prominent as the more usually dominant curriculum and assessment ones. In short they have to create a culture in which:

- students systematically develop the confidence and capacity to learn: more 'mind gym' than classroom
- teachers learn how to act as more and more effective learning power coaches in their dealings with young people

A changing culture

- good results are achieved by cultivating BLP habits of mind, not by spoon-feeding, 'boosting', 'narrowing the gap' or 'teaching to the test'.

'For us the results have been fantastic. We have changed the ethos from a school that had attainment and behaviour as its prime foci, to a school that focuses on learning. In 3 Years our 5 A*–C's have gone from 17% to 51% (more than twice the level of attainment of comparable schools). All this is largely attributable to BLP.'

Armando di Finizio, The City Academy Bristol

Getting leadership right from the start

In the systematic evaluations of our sample of BLP schools, we asked the senior leaders in the school to fill out a detailed questionnaire which then, wherever possible, formed the basis of a follow-up interview with the headteacher. Several of the questions were designed to probe the school's experience of implementing the BLP approach, and particularly their reflections on the kinds of leadership which they had found to be successful in getting the approach infused into the life-blood of the school. Much of the rest of this chapter draws on this interview and questionnaire data.

Reflections on leadership

Dissatisfaction and readiness

'We were looking for a framework for building children's independence as learners. We frequently despaired that children were not transferring what they had learned; that they seemed so dependent on adults; that they asked so few questions to do with learning; that teachers were doing most of the talking. We had a strong feeling that we were missing out on some of the more important things.'

Primary headteacher

Several schools said that part of BLP's success was that it came along 'at just the right moment'. This could mean a number of things. Some schools had already been engaged in a consultation process with staff, governors, parents and, in some cases, the students themselves, about the vision for their school and even the root purpose of twenty-first century education. Often, they had worked their way towards a concern with the cultivation of 'life skills' as well as literacy, numeracy, and exam results. Many were worried by pupils' dependency. The head teacher of Nayland Primary School, for example, said, *'Our school was ready for BLP as our children were like little birds waiting to be fed—and we wanted them to learn to feed themselves!'* Many of the secondary schools said they had come to the realisation that they may actually have been cultivating this attitude of dependency through too much 'spoon-feeding', and were keen to find another way. Dr Challoner's Grammar School said they knew they were producing *'successful students, but not necessarily good learners'*. In most cases, this readiness was not just fortuitous. The headteachers of these schools had deliberately stimulated the kinds of debates within the school community that produced the readiness.

The right moment

Stimulating readiness

In addition, several schools said that BLP offered them just the kind of language they had been looking for: it articulated clearly exactly the kinds of common values they had been developing. In particular, they seized on BLP because it gave them a vocabulary for thinking and talking about children as learners (rather than just as high, average, or low 'achievers').

Along with this 'fertile ground', several schools also expressed a growing dissatisfaction with other initiatives which they had tried, but which had begun to feel too superficial—not really getting to the heart of the matter. Or they felt rather piecemeal, and BLP seemed to offer a coherent overarching picture which 'made sense' of these other approaches. Landau Forte College, for example, said they were fed up with 'gimmicks' and 'one hit wonders'. Or they wanted to create a whole-school approach to 'learning to learn', and not leave it to a few enthusiasts.

A few of the schools saw BLP in the first instance as their preferred strategy for raising attainment. They either wanted or needed to improve their examination performance, but they had decided to take what, for some, felt like the risk of aiming to do so by building up students' responsibility for their own learning—rather than retrenching into an ever more teacher-driven, teacher-directed model.

Creating a vision

BLP's big ambition, core values and frameworks helped school leaders create their own personal vision of how these could play out in the school. They felt that BLP chimed with their values and personal convictions about education. Important was their realisation that BLP went way beyond a few tweaks in the classroom: it would involve whole-school culture change and would take several years to implement and guarantee sustainability. Indeed this understanding has been shown to be a key difference between schools that have been successful with BLP and those where it has fizzled out. BLP needs passionate leadership commitment to long-term culture change. Leaders who shared their commitment to long-term culture change with staff have been the most successful in developing BLP.

Commitment to long-term change

Time and again, teachers told us that the commitment of the headteacher (and the senior leadership team more widely) was crucial to the success of BLP. The support of the head, expressed frequently, visibly, and genuinely, seemed to be a make-or-break requirement for staff to take the approach seriously, and to put in the thinking and experimentation required. For the approach to spread beyond the natural enthusiasts and the 'early adopters', there had to be a clear message that 'this is not just another initiative that is going to blow over', but is here to stay. As one head put it: 'Our approach was (1) we all do this, (2) this is for the long term, and (3) we all start together and learn together'. Another saw it as important that she continually kept BLP high profile within the school and 'stayed close to its development'. She regularly visited classrooms and talked with individual teachers about how they were weaving BLP ideas into their lessons, and developed with them ideas about how they could take it further.

Being visible

First steps to implement the vision

Visions of the future can be necessarily hazy at first. Successful leaders realised the ideas would have to be crafted, explored, and expanded by everyone in the school. They knew that simply telling people about their vision wouldn't work; eventually everyone would need to see it as their vision and understand their part in making it a reality. What was needed was to start a dialogue—firstly with a few colleagues and then more widely—about the what, why, and how of the changes.

Where headteachers delegated responsibility for BLP to a colleague, and did not seem to be personally involved, we found that the chances of successful implementation were slim. So were they when protestations of support for BLP were mingled with strong traditional messages about the importance of results at all costs. In one of our secondary schools, where BLP had been slower to take root than in comparable schools, one of the assistant principals said in her interview with the researcher:

Harmful mixed messages

> 'I think we have been giving a bit of a mixed message to the staff, if I'm honest. We are a high-achieving school, and teachers are under a lot of pressure to get the best possible results. But this isn't really compatible with taking risks and trying new things out in your teaching. So I think our progress has been slower than it might have been, because of that.'

Getting the dialogue going

Headteachers have used many concrete ways of getting things going, including sharing ideas in SLT, giving teachers BLP books, and engaging a trainer to deliver an introductory professional development day. However, the most successful way of getting started seems to have been to create a sustained dialogue about learning throughout the school. No big fanfares, no invited speakers, just talk amongst ourselves about learning. This in itself can represent a subtle shift in the school's approach to staff learning which echoes BLP's messages: it is a learning journey which no-one can do for us. Such dialogues were created through informal staffroom chat, or having colleagues take a learning walk around the school to look at learning (not at teaching, or at pupils' 'work', of course).

A dialogue about learning

The most successful approach to fostering the dialogue was often to commission a 'learning review' where a trained consultant worked with a group of staff to look deeply at the sort of learning that is going on in classrooms. These learning reviews (which we describe in more detail in Chapter 9) often had the effect of helping staff to focus on the kinds of learning processes that they were routinely asking students to use—and to identify where this 'mental exercise regime' might be partial or narrow, as well as where in the school it might also already be more broad and comprehensive. Learning reviews enabled staff to look at their teaching

Reviewing learning

from a different perspective, and this often served to stimulate greater interest and ownership of the changes that were being mooted.

At Walthamstow School for Girls, for example, before they had even introduced the language of BLP, the leadership team asked each faculty to undertake an audit of the learning skills which they were routinely requiring the girls to make use of, and the results were shared and discussed at several staff meetings. The fact that this was conducted in a spirit of genuine enquiry (rather than 'appraisal') enabled the entire staff to buy into the discussion, and it resulted in a real curiosity to explore ways in which they could broaden or deepen the learning habits which they were asking the girls to use.

A key feature of BLP school leadership is the extent to which leaders have continued to create a dialogue about learning and innovation. Effectively, BLP schools are practising the kind of 'could-be' language advocated by Ellen Langer (see page 69). They are putting into practice their belief that there may well be more than one way of doing things. The school is engaged in dialogues between students, parents, teachers, and other adults who are part of the school community.

Creating a culture of enquiry

The emphasis on dialogue is very often deepened and sustained through encouraging small action-research enquiries and the development within the school of teacher learning communities. Teachers in BLP schools are frequently keen to become involved in action research, specifically focusing their enquiries on the kinds of questions promoted by BLP (as Rhian Thomas did in the example on the panel opposite). Teachers are encouraged to ask 'what if' and to share the results of their enquiries with other staff.

There are many examples of such small-scale enquiries throughout this book. Here are some examples of the kinds of questions they might be prompted to ask:

Enquiry questions

- If I give my Year 2 children freedom to read in a variety of settings will they enjoy reading more?
- If my Year 6 students create their own 'stuck posters', will they become more resilient?
- If Year 9 students teach Year 7 students, will the Year 9 students become more confident about their own learning?
- If I help my students to design and deliver lessons, will they become more engaged in learning?

Replicating Carol Dweck's research

Rhian Thomas at Cantonian High School in Cardiff divided her A-level Psychology students into two groups matched on their baseline performance to date. Then, for three weeks, she tested Carol Dweck's advice by praising Group A for their effort, while praising Group B for their 'natural ability'. She then gave both groups of students more difficult questions to grapple with, and logged their questions and reactions. Finally, she gave them some of the easier questions on which they had started the trial. Her replication of Dweck's findings is remarkable.

'I found that the students in Group B who were praised for their ability became worried and concerned about grades and marks. They no longer enjoyed the task and didn't want to work on it for homework. They were also obsessed with comparing their grades with others...Many were starting to choose the easier tasks when they were given a choice. When asked why, they said they wanted to make sure they achieved a good grade. 85% of the students in this group said they felt stupid when they couldn't complete the difficult tasks... I also noticed in this group that attendance was becoming more erratic, especially when there was a deadline.

Students in Group A, however, who had been praised for their effort, seemed to feel more confident of their skills. Instead of focusing on their results, they seemed to be more interested in learning something new, and focused on different approaches and strategies for solving a problem. They showed greater flexibility when faced with difficulties... Attendance of this group had improved when compared to each student's individual attendance prior to the enquiry.

But the most alarming finding, according to Rhian, was the performance of the two groups when they were finally allowed to work on some of the easier problems. A third of group B students actually did worse on these questions than they had done originally. Their apparent ability had decreased. Group A, on the other hand, not only held their own on these problems; half of them did better than they had done originally. After a bare three weeks of being treated in a slightly different way, the two groups' chances of getting good A-levels were now markedly different. Rhian concludes succinctly, 'We should help students to value effort. Too many students think effort is only for the inept. Yet sustained effort over time is the key to outstanding achievement.'

Over three weeks;

Group A praised for effort

Group B praised for their 'natural ability'

Group B

- worried about grades
- no longer enjoyed tasks
- obsessed with comparing marks
- chose easier tasks
- felt stupid when tasks were difficult
- 30% did worse on questions done originally

Group A

- more confident of their skills
- interested in learning something new
- focused on different problem solving strategies
- showed greater flexibility
- 50% did better than they had done originally

Research based dialogue

Examples of approaches to creating deeper research-based dialogue include:

- creating a staff 'learning research club' where all teachers read the same piece of research and meet to share their reactions

- enabling and encouraging staff to enrol for higher degrees

- producing a digest of teacher reports into their enquiries (Bay House School, Gosport).

Other schools have established long-term Teacher Learning Communities where teachers systematically plan, try out and share their ever-deepening BLP practice. Such communities support and scaffold teachers' habit change (see Chapter 9).

Whatever the dominant approach, leaders in BLP schools have recognised the value of staff actively experimenting with the kinds of approaches advocated in this book. Teachers are empowered to experiment and create their own solutions. A spirit of openness and enquiry increasingly pervades the school. The growing culture in these schools is supporting the freedom to experiment, take risks, and learn from mistakes. Teachers are never taken to task for getting it 'wrong'. The schools are learning their way forward and staff view themselves as leaders of their own learning.

Keeping track of learning power

In BLP schools learning becomes a collaborative process to which everyone is invited to commit.

Teachers and teaching assistants. Working in a culture of trust and openness, teachers and teaching assistants become increasingly confident to experiment and take risks. But this is no free-for-all: the quality of learning in classrooms and around the school is kept under regular review. Teachers get used to being observed regularly, but come to trust that the spirit of this is as a learning support for them, and not a process of judgement or appraisal. Staff don't see this as being checked up on but as part of a dynamic, reflective process across all levels of the school.

Teachers self-monitoring their changing practice

As this culture consolidates, people get used to watching out for and recording changes in their practice, and changes in students' learning behaviour, motivation, or achievement. They might note, for example, the extent to which students are:

- showing greater interest in learning

- taking more responsibility for learning

- becoming less dependent

- asking deeper, more insightful, or more frequent questions

- showing more confidence in tackling difficulty.

Teachers may also undertake an annual self-review of their practice against indicators such as those shown on page 116.

Team leaders are encouraged to monitor lesson designs, the use of open-ended tasks, the use of 'could-be' language or split-screen teaching, and to look for how the habits of teachers are shifting. They too are seeking to understand learning more deeply, to search for connections between outcomes and practice, and identify development opportunities.

Monitoring at team level

At a whole-school level strategic leaders continue to monitor student achievement, behaviour, well-being, and a host of other familiar indicators of performance. But learning-powered leaders will also monitor:

Monitoring at whole-school level

- improvement in self-reported learning behaviours (possibly using Blaze BLP)

- increased involvement in enrichment or out-of-school activities

- types, preferences, and outcomes of student-initiated projects

- patterns in class and year awards for learning behaviours

- parents' responses to BLP-style reports

- increased student involvement in the design and delivery of lessons

- parents' take-up of web-site suggestions about how to help their child become a better learner (see Chapter 10)

- staff's voluntary take-up of involvement in a Teacher Learning Community or similar

- feedback from employers on students' attitudes on work placements

- effects of training students as researchers or learning coaches

- outcomes of learning sub-committee as part of Student Council

Such monitoring gives strategic leaders a valuable handle on how the overall development of students' learning power is progressing.

Growing a learning school

Some schools are going further by looking at the school itself as a learning organisation. These schools have begun to audit their cultural values, asking themselves difficult questions to ensure they practise what they preach. The panels overleaf give a flavour of the questions being asked.

A learning school?

Whatever approaches are adopted, the goal of successful leaders is to create a school in which individuals and teams of staff are highly reflective and self evaluative in a spirit of non-defensive curiosity and openness. We pick up this theme again in Chapter 9.

Applying learning power to the school

The emotionally resilient school

- Believes that it has control of its own destiny
- Fosters a positive attitude towards learning and improvement
- Is confident that it can rise to the challenge of its long-term goals
- Retains its focus and commitment in adversity
- Recognises and channels its emotional energy constructively
- Addresses issues openly and communicates frankly
- Is open to new ideas and criticism
- Is prepared to take responsible risks
- Bounces back from disappointments and retains an optimistic attitude
- Avoids complacency when things appear to be going well
- Is well-equipped to attend to details and notice what is happening in the parts as well as the whole
- Resists being deflected by external pressures for short-term results
- Regards mistakes as valuable ways of continuing to learn and improve
- Is prepared to take appropriate action when faced with challenges and difficulties

The cognitively resourceful school

- Constantly poses questions to secure deeper understanding
- Approaches everything with an appetite of enquiry and curiosity
- Is able to generate good ideas in response to different and changing situations and circumstances
- Looks for ways in which things might link together
- Adopts a logical and systematic approach when necessary in order to secure efficient outcomes
- Values intuition as much as reason and is prepared to back hunches and play with ideas
- Is inclined to say 'What might happen if... What could we do... What's possible...?'
- Is inventive and flexible in its use of people and resources
- Explores opportunities and options so as to capitalise on those external resources that may benefit the school
- Capitalises on the capabilities of all partners within and beyond the school
- Provides experiences from which all its people can learn

Adapted from TLO's *Learning-Powered School Audit.*

The socially reciprocal school

- Articulates its values and principles in ways that are understandable to all partners
- Explores things from a variety of viewpoints before making decisions
- Is led by a team that listens, openly consults, and conveys clear and coherent messages to staff
- Values all individuals and their contributions to an interdependent whole-staff team
- Enables people to understand how best to function within a variety of teams
- Moves people so that they learn from and with a wide range of people
- Is prepared to challenge individuals to go beyond their comfort zone
- Acknowledges and responds to people's feelings and emotions
- Ensures that everyone's contribution is acknowledged and rewarded
- Commits to the personal and professional development of all its people
- Uses coaching to support individuals' learning
- Knows where outstanding practice is in the school and ensures that it is used to help others learn and improve
- Seeks ideas from best practice elsewhere and applies them to the school's own context
- Benchmarks its own performance against outstanding practice in comparable schools

The strategically reflective school

- Has an inspiring vision and clear plan of how it can be achieved
- Is driven by a School Improvement Plan that is flexible and subject to regular, focused reviews
- Sets challenging goals and targets that provide learning stretch
- Is realistic about what can be achieved within the constraints of time and resources
- Monitors performance so that it is able to modify practice proactively not reactively
- Gathers data in order to identify strengths and challenges
- Makes use of frequent internal evaluations that inform further areas for improvement
- Ensures that teams within the school are being led and managed effectively and efficiently
- Uses a performance management system that is developmental rather than judgmental
- Is led by those who model that they are engaged in learning projects and personal development which are in line with the school's strategic goals
- Understands itself and is good at playing to its strengths and minimising weaknesses
- Above all else, keeps the quality of learning under continuous review

The BLP Sat-Nav: a route map for learning-powered leaders

Over these first ten years of BLP development, schools have taken up the challenge largely because the vision and values of BLP chimed with those of school leaders. They were prepared to take a leap into the unknown, and what we have described here are the things successful leaders have done to enable everyone in the school to thrive and develop as a learner. But our evaluation revealed that, for some, the culture change journey has felt harder and more hazardous because there have been no route-maps to guide them, and no milestones against which to check their progress.

A tracking device

In response to this need, we have recently been developing a way of tracking a school's development towards the creation of a learning-powered culture. We call it the **Learning Quality Framework (LQF).** The framework owes its existence to the pioneering endeavours of all the schools mentioned in this book and many others. It offers a set of staged descriptions of the development of a school whose prime educational goal is to develop better learners. It tries to capture the essence of what a learning school does to ensure all its people become better learners.

The LQF is organised under twelve principles which are concerned with different aspects of a school's culture, such as the school's vision for learning, how leaders lead learning, how classroom practice, assessment and the curriculum need to be designed in order to build learning habits, and how the school acts on its own learning. It is no coincidence that these principles themselves map closely onto the chapters in this book: it was largely the research for this book that uncovered the need for the map, and gathered together the data on which it is based. The principles are further described through indicators which show how the principles are realised in practice across four phases of development.

Based on research

The Learning Quality Framework aims to serve several useful functions

As a **diagnostic instrument**, the LQF enables a school to assess where it is now on its learning journey. By considering the principles and the four levels of indicators the school can gauge which aspects of its learning culture are now secure, which need development, and which need starting from scratch.

As a **formative instrument**, the different types and levels of indicators provide the school with a clear set of guidelines for planning their way forward. From the analysis of 'what is', which the framework provides, the school can develop a strategic overview of next steps.

As a **summative instrument**, giving schools a valued external view of their progress through the use of a LQF Quality Mark. Developing a culture in which real world learning thrives is a not insignificant job, so stages along the way are worth recognising and celebrating. Schools' progress can be validated and publicly recognised. The Quality Mark will be accredited by the Centre for Real-World Learning at the University of Winchester.

As an **evaluative instrument**, the LQF Quality Mark assessment report provides a deep observation of how the school is putting the principles of a learning-powered school into action. As you would expect this is not a simplistic box ticking exercise, and the purpose of the report is to help the school move forward and guide further action. As such the report can be used as proof of self-evaluation.

The panel overleaf gives a partial view of the first three principles of the framework. Of course there is much more to the Learning Quality Framework than we can show here but many schools have welcomed it as a route-map, a challenge or a worthwhile agenda. While we could describe its value in fancy phrases, we leave it to schools to voice its practical uses:

How schools view the Learning Quality Framework

'It made sense of my random thoughts. We have been struggling to think about what we needed to do next. We had lots of ideas but they were random and disorganised. The framework has drawn these all together. It's the school's plan for the future'

DH, Secondary School, Solihull

'This is my development plan for the next five years'

Primary HT, Winchester

'Aha! Now I see where I am going; it all makes sense. This gives me the big picture. We have been working in a small area of this and when you are working down in the detail you lose sight of the whole. This gives me a route map for so many aspects of school life'.

DH, Secondary School, Birmingham

'We will use this framework to guide our journey and we will want our progress validating. Going for assessment at various milestones will be our way of celebrating that progress.'

HT, Secondary School, Plymouth

It is perhaps worth mentioning that the LQF does not require a school to be using the BLP framework per se. The framework is based broadly on the learning sciences and the principles of learning organisations, not the particulars of the BLP frameworks. The framework is therefore of value to any school that wants to put learning at its heart. You can find out more from www.learningqualityframework.co.uk

Based on the learning sciences

A partial view of the Learning Quality Framework

Principles	Explanation	Bronze indicators
Commitment. The school is committed to using the learning sciences to develop its people's learning dispositions, and equip itself as a learning organisation		

CPa Vision for Learning

CPa A shared vision for 21st century education based on social, economic, moral, and personal learning imperatives guides the school and its community.	**A new vision for education.** How the school grows and uses a vision for the empowerment of learning.	**CBa1** *The school...*
	Spreading understanding of the vision in the school and community.	**CBa2** The emerging understanding of the need to review the school's vision for learning is spreading throughout the school.

CPb A Framework for Learning

CPb A coherent approach to building traits that affect how people go about learning, drives learning in the school and its community.	**The school's view of learning.** The nature of the school's learning framework.	**CBb1** *The school's...*
	Strategic influence of the framework. How the learning framework gradually influences many aspects of how the school works.	**CBb2** *Some staff...*

CPc A Language for Learning

CPc A rich language of learning recognising its emotional, cognitive, social, and strategic dimensions, permeates learning across the school and its community.	**A language for learning.** The extent to which the school's language for learning is used throughout the school.	**CBc1** Some teachers use an emergent language of learning between themselves and with students.
	Impact of the language for learning. The extent to which students use and profit from the language for learning.	**CBc2** *Target students...*

Silver indicators	Gold indicators	Platinum indicators
CSa1 The school's (new) vision for strengthening learning character is based on core values of learner empowerment and the expandability of intelligence.	**CGa1** The school's vision for learning is embedded in its culture and guides the school's improvement plan.	**CPa1** *Internal and...*
CSa2 *Understanding of...*	**CGa2** *School governors...*	**CPa2** The school works with others beyond the school in developing innovative learning practice.
CSb1 The school has adopted and/ or developed a coherent learning framework predicated on 'Learning is learnable' and informed by the psychology of learning.	**CGb1** *Within the...*	**CPb1** The learning framework is re-tailored to meet the school's needs in the light of up-to-date research into the learning sciences and in-house action research into learning.
CSb2 *The school's...*	**CGb2** The school's understanding of learning, as described in its learning framework, has influenced a range of policies and practice across the organisation.	**CPb2** *The school's...*
CSc1 *A shared...*	**CGc1** *A shared...*	**CPc1** The shared and dynamic language of learning is evolving in response to research and practice.
CSc2 Students are becoming familiar with the language of learning and some use it effectively to improve their learning.	**CGc2** *Students are...*	**CPc2** *The shared...*

Leading a Learning Powered School

Case study: St Paul's Catholic School, Milton Keynes

St Paul's is a comprehensive school that serves the Catholic community of Milton Keynes. Although many schools struggle in the city, St Paul's does well, gaining consistently good examination results and outstanding inspection grades by Ofsted. Despite this, headteacher Michael Manley felt that students were depending too much on the hard work of their teachers and that they were leaving the school ill-equipped to operate as independent lifelong learners. He decided that he wanted to shift the school culture from one where things were done to and for students, to one where things were done by and with students. As a result, in November 2005 the Senior Leadership Team decided to design a whole-school strategic plan that focused on building students' learning power. This has been a unifying focus for the school's development over the last five years—the results have been so successful that its impact has gone beyond the school to influence learning and achievement in many other local primary and secondary schools. (St Paul's is one of several BLP 'hub schools' around the country that help others in the locality along their BLP journeys.)

The main features of their Plan for Learning

Notwithstanding the considerable and conflicting pressures of being the headteacher of a large comprehensive school, Michael Manley recognised that it is what goes on in classrooms that really matters, and that this should be given prime focus. Over the last five years, he has personally been intimately involved with the powerful changes and subtle shifts in teaching and learning that have been taking place at St Paul's. All teachers and teaching assistants at the school understand from him that these approaches are central to the school's vision and will not disappear (as external initiatives often do).

The first step was to get all members of the extended leadership team on board. This team read and discussed several of the BLP publications in an attempt to raised their own ability to talk and think about students' development as learners. They were also the first to explore how to take these ideas into their own classrooms. The team then conducted a school-wide review of learning habits to gauge how students were behaving as learners. They observed lessons and gathered data from across the curriculum and representative Year groups on the learning muscles that students were being allowed, required, or encouraged to use and develop in lessons. The subsequent report highlighted areas for improvement and this was used as the basis for the first stage Strategic Learning Plan.

The school identified that it needed to adopt a common language for identifying students' learning habits. They also decided that this language

Dissatisfaction and readiness

A unifying vision

Clear message of long-term change

Beginning the dialogue

Looking for learning

would be used to interpret and bind in any other external initiatives that came their way, such as Social and Emotional Aspects of Learning (SEAL), the Specialist Schools and Academies Trust work on 'Deep Learning', the Key Stage 3 Curriculum's Personal Learning and Thinking Skills (PLTS), and the Department for Education's Assessing Pupils' Progress (APP). The school found that the BLP framework and vocabulary was not only highly compatible with these other frameworks, but actually gave them greater coherence and impact.

A language for learning

Always keen to assess students' levels of achievement, record progress and communicate clearly to parents, the school established a working party to identify the progression ladders for each of the habits that they were going to develop in their students across the curriculum. This tool has been used, reviewed, and enhanced regularly over the last five years and—along with regular whole-school reviews of learning—plays a major part in gauging the impact of these approaches on classroom practice.

Preparing to gauge impact

Intensive training of all senior and middle leaders took place over two days in May 2006. At the end of this, these school leaders were able to adapt and enrich their schemes of work and develop new learning resources in readiness for the coming school year. They had also been introduced to coaching techniques since this was to be the basis for staff development within and between teams in the school. The belief was that teachers would learn to be 'learning coaches' to their students in classrooms if they were participating in peer coaching groups themselves. This proved to be a successful strategy.

Initial training

Coaching development

Thus, with considerable strategic thinking and preparation behind them, the staff began the 2006–07 school year with a launch of the new emphasis on learning to learn. In order to ensure an infused approach—rather than a bolt-on course on the edge of the curriculum—the extended leadership team maintained a rolling programme of Learning Power Reviews that built on the baseline survey that had taken place six months previously. With learning coaching beginning to become embedded in teaching, the school had ensured that there would be many ways for all teachers to be talking about the ups and downs of learning—with their students and with each other.

Continual review

Keeping the dialogue going

Maintaining momentum

After the first full year, there was a recognition—amongst both staff and students—that the school ethos was changing significantly. Naturally, some areas were slower to move than others, but supportive and challenging line managers ensured that additional training was made available to encourage all curriculum teams and individual teachers to embrace the new approach constructively.

Managing performance differently

Adapting the curriculum

Integrating enquiry-based learning

Motivational factors

Coaching did indeed prove to be a successful way of supporting and developing teachers. Always prepared to take risks and do things differently, the leadership team decided to make two-way coaching the way forward for performance management. All teachers were entitled to use developmental classroom observation as a tool for professional dialogue and the basis for agreeing targets for improvement. The learning coaching skills of teachers in classrooms were enhanced enormously as a result. Teachers were clearly changing the ways in which they talked with students.

To begin with, the school was loath to change its curriculum and timetabling model. However, they began to recognise that, whilst the timetable continued to be based on the 50-minute lesson, there was little opportunity for students to get involved in the kind of extended project work that might stretch their learning muscles more effectively. So they decided to experiment with enquiry-based, cross-curricular learning projects that would enable teachers to work in teams with groups of students. Planning for this began in the summer of 2007 to prepare for an eight-week project for Year 8 students across all areas of Humanities. The focus topic was to be Migration, stimulated by the 'driving question': Why don't people stay at home?

This pilot was judged to be a major success: students were engaged, stretched, and achieving at higher levels. Since then, these enquiry-based, integrated projects have now become a regular feature across all years, involving increasingly interesting cross-faculty collaborations. Science and PE now work together on a project called 'A Question of Sport' which gets students to explore the science behind various sports. For example, they experiment with modifications in equipment, and explore questions such as: How would the game of tennis have to change if the balls were heavier? (See Chapter 6)

The roots of success

The school believes that the success of this long-term, sustained commitment to stretching students' learning muscles and building their learning power at St Paul's is the result of several motivational factors:

- The hands-on involvement of the headteacher
- The enthusiasm of teachers who can see the impact of this way of working in their classrooms
- The awareness by students that this makes learning enjoyable and relevant
- A willingness to keep looking afresh at the issues in order to keep the work live and dynamic

Regular internal publications have been produced which disseminate ideas for teachers and are also used to keep parents abreast of developments.

Most recently, the leadership team has identified the need to push teachers' understanding of the BLP pedagogy to an even higher level. The team has maintained its commitment to reading research about learning, and they have embarked on a new programme of professional development. The process will continue to evolve and deepen in ways that cannot yet be predicted.

NB. You can see Michael Manley talking about BLP and his school by going to www.buildinglearningpower.co.uk

Keeping staff and parents aware of developments

Summary

In this chapter we have tried to follow our own guidance about leadership, and concentrate on the kinds of leadership questions, dilemmas, priorities, and difficulties that seem to flow directly from the vision itself, rather than from an abstract specification of what the disembodied ideal leader might do, or the traits they might possess. Of course there is much more to be said, and even more to be learned, about the subtle craft of school leadership. But we hope that the examples we have provided here may provide both stimulation and some reassurance that leading the journey of learning-powered culture change is possible.

Chapter 9

Professional development in a community of enquiry

In this chapter we explore:

- the stages of professional learning
- the nature of habit change
- learning reviews
- teacher learning communities
- peer coaching
- learning enquiries
- the value of appreciative enquiry
- doing classroom observations
- overseeing professional development

A group of eight teachers and two learning assistants are exploring what they have been doing in their classrooms over the last month to build students' learning power. Each one relates a story of changing practice and its impact on students. Kristina is excited by the wall display she has made with students about the learning muscles they are concentrating on in their split-screen lessons. Arnie speaks movingly about how he is adapting the way he praises students and how this is having a positive effect on how his students see themselves as learners. Henry speaks of his first attempts at using a split-screen approach in a couple of lessons and how he decided which learning muscle to couple with the content. He had felt a bit daunted by the prospect of teaching in a new way, but was relieved to find that students cottoned on quickly and seemed to benefit from concentrating on the individual learning habits. Sheena, a learning assistant, talks hesitantly about how she is trying hard not to tell students what to do, but to ask questions like 'How else could you do that? What else might you try? What would help you to get this better?' She says it felt as though she wasn't doing her job to start with but over a couple of weeks she has seen the children taking more control of their learning and becoming more interested.

And so it goes on, everyone taking the opportunity to share what's been happening—triumphs and difficulties alike. Kirsten, who is facilitating the session, helps her colleagues to tease out some of the knotty issues and explore more deeply—not just what happened, but to mull over why and how and why not. The session moves from a familiar 'show and tell' format to a deeper analysis of what makes practice work and what might be needed next. It is a spirited engagement of professional colleagues who are deeply interested in what helps them to adopt new habits of teaching. They move on to planning what they will do over the coming month, and commit to meeting again to share and explore their endeavours.

These teachers are working in what has been described as a 'teacher learning community'. They are aware of the multifaceted nature of building students' learning power and appreciate that it will take sustained effort over time to adapt their long-standing practice. They are taking it step by step, learning from colleagues' actions as well as their own.

Learning together

'Teacher Learning Community'

Professional learning as habit change

Schools that have taken building learning power seriously have quickly realised the centrality of professional development (PD) in making it work. But they also realise that effective PD has to be more than a one-day course and 'away you go'. Thinking of the primacy of learning rather than teaching has implications not just for students' learning but for staff learning. Teachers' habits as learners have to become part of the picture; how they go about changing is as relevant to their discussions as what changes they are aiming to bring about. In other words, the staff learning has to undergo the same sort of shifts as students' learning. So the school has to think of PD in a split-screen way: **'what'** has to be learned and **'how'** it might be learned.

The primacy of learning

Changing the habits of a professional lifetime is not simple. It involves un-learning and re-learning: unpicking, readjusting, trying things out and seeing what works. It's about staff using their own learning power to effect changes in themselves. And the desired change is not just in what they think and believe; it is in how they spontaneously talk and act and plan. Even small shifts in the type of language a teacher uses take time to implement fluently. They have to stop using previous language, start using new language, hesitantly at first, then in different contexts, more frequently and with greater fluency.

Changing teaching habits

Becoming proficient, and then developing further so that the 'new' approach becomes second nature, takes time and effort. The scale overleaf, adapted from a model proposed by American philosopher Hubert Dreyfus, makes it clear how many stages a person has to go through before they achieve flexible and effortless expertise in a new skill. Developing expertise involves progressing from stilted, hesitant, and rigid behaviour (conscious incompetence, the 'clunky' stage) through the developing ability to read situational cues and routinise behaviour (conscious competence), and onwards to developing smooth, flexible intuitions that naturally make the most of situations (unconscious competence). It is perhaps worth noting that this progress is not inevitable; if it were, everyone would become expert eventually. Learning, as BLP suggests, involves the active habits of noticing, questioning, experimenting, reflecting, and discussing. In the process of becoming learning-power coaches, teachers very often find that they are developing their own learning power.

Realistic expectations about effort and progress

It can be useful to discuss models like this with staff, so that they pursue their BLP journeys with realistic expectations about the amount of time and effort that is going to be needed. Unconsciously assuming that change is easier than it is can quickly lead to demoralisation ('I'll never do it'), self-recrimination ('I'm just not clever enough to get it'), or resentment ('This is just stupid; why are they making us do this?').

Stages of progression

Intuitive understanding	Expert	• I do not need to apply any rules now • I have an intuitive and holistic understanding of the situations • I have a range of strategies which I use to change situations • I just know how to make the most of situations
A few rules of thumb	Proficient	• I can appreciate the whole situation now — not just its aspects • I know what is important and I can spot any deviations from the norm • I can use positive past experiences to help me • I use a few rules of thumb
Developing own routines	Competent	• I am better now at reading cues and acting on them • I have developed some routines and have standardised the way I operate • I appreciate the range and scope of the task and can concentrate on what is important
Finding what's important	Advanced Beginner	• I have experienced more situations now and am beginning to understand what I am doing • I do not need the facts and rules so much but I am not sure what is important and what is not
Rule-bound	Novice	• I do things according to the rules: I need the facts • I operate fairly rigidly • I am very aware of what I am trying to do but I can't read the situational signs • I can't use my own discretion • I am not confident

Increasing intuition (vertical axis, pointing upward)

(Based on Dreyfus's five stages of progression: see Eraut 1994)[1]

Professional development in the spirit of BLP

The spirit of BLP means that teachers do not just 'learn how to do BLP' without thinking. BLP has to be understood, critiqued, customised, and developed by teachers and learning assistants alike—and that, for many schools, has led to a radical rethink in PD practice. As we saw in the example at the beginning of the chapter, this means regular opportunities to share experiments, successes, failures, doubts and ideas, and then go back to the classroom and have another go.

For example, one school reported how whole-staff meetings were held each half-term to give input about a [new] BLP capacity, to explore together how BLP could be woven into existing planning, and to brainstorm ideas about how to tweak lessons: *'Turn them on their heads so that they empowered children to learn'*, as the head put it. *'We looked at what I called "simple in's to BLP"—simple strategies in lessons to embed BLP principles'* she said. *'We also shared success stories together. We did not have a set plan as such, and one of our strengths I think is that we have been good at encouraging "trying things out" both as individuals and Year groups, and then capturing what is working well and building it into the whole-school practice.'*

In another primary school there were regular 'walkabouts' after school, where the whole teaching staff visited each other's classrooms to see how they were embedding BLP principles and language in their lesson plans and displays. Teachers 'piggy-backed' on each other's creativity, and good ideas spread more readily and more rapidly as a result. Teachers of older Year groups were often surprised, for example, at the level of sophistication of the learning environment in younger classrooms, and so were challenged to 'up their game' with their own children.

Other schools have taken a more concentrated approach, enabling staff to meet regularly as the kinds of 'teacher learning communities' described above, encouraging teachers to delve more deeply into their practice and become skilled as facilitators of learning.

Schools have adopted a range of PD approaches to ensure the necessary culture shift and we explore some of these in detail later in the chapter. The shift to BLP practice in professional development has been guided by the following ideas:

Guiding ideas

- recognition that BLP takes time to implement and that the shift can be made in small cumulative steps
- the need to keep a dialogue going to ensure the change remains high-profile and continually progressing
- the need for teachers to feel able to experiment, reflect on, and distil their learning

- the need for the whole school to be involved in the same 'game' of learning.
- the need for staff to see themselves as learners and leaders of their own learning.
- the requirement to build professional trust and mutual respect.
- the need, eventually, to devise and agree standards of BLP practice.

Bringing people on board

In any school there will be enthusiasts, early adopters, cautious observers (waiting to be reassured or convinced), and maybe a few who actively resist changing their ways. This latter group, if it exists, may comprise people with well-articulated, principled objections, others who are just 'stuck in their ways', and some who may be vocally (or silently) cynical about any attempt at innovation. Headteachers told us that they have to work with different groups in different ways. Some colleagues may be helped to 'come on board' with some reassurance, perhaps being buddied-up with a more confident colleague. Some may need a stronger push from senior leaders in the school. And some may come to realise that they would be happier in a different school. One head told us that his guiding principle was 'Gentle pressure, relentlessly applied'! Several said that it was very important not to get impatient, and to see BLP as a process of gradual, cumulative culture change across the whole school that might take several years to embed.

Treading carefully

It can unnerve teachers who have been getting good results to discover (or be told) that there are hidden costs to their 'good teaching', in terms of doing too much for the children and thereby encouraging them to become passive and receptive, rather than proactive and questioning. Several headteachers told us that this needed careful handling, and they had to tread carefully in the way they introduced BLP. They had to make sure that teachers did not feel judged or blamed, and had plenty of time to understand for themselves why BLP might be a good idea, and why they might benefit from 'going deeper' in their understanding of learning.

The following types of professional development opportunities have been built into the PD programmes of many schools. Not all schools use all of these opportunities but it is often the case that the more successful the BLP implementation, the more of these professional development opportunities are used strategically to effect change.

Types of CPD

- Learning reviews
- Teacher learning communities
- Coaching partnerships
- Small-scale learning enquiries
- Appreciative enquiry
- Classroom observation and personal review

- Visits to other schools

We will take a brief look at each of these in turn.

Learning reviews

Working with schools to help them review the quality of young people's learning has proved to be the most powerful instrument for enhancing teaching and improving the learning habits of students. Although all schools are used to evaluating standards of achievement against Ofsted criteria, very few are in the habit of examining how students are actually behaving *as learners* and observing carefully what teachers do to deepen independent—and collaborative—learning habits. As Ian Veitch, Headteacher of Park View Community School, told us, '*The learning review was the most significant and serious piece of research and evaluation that has ever been conducted in our school'.*

Looking at learning behaviours

A learning review is conducted in the spirit of Building Learning Power. In other words, it is not something that is done to a school, rather is it done with and by a school. It is not a monitoring activity that is designed to check up on teachers; it is a piece of considered evaluation—conducted by teachers—of how students are as learners and what changes could be made in classrooms and throughout the school in order to expand students' learning capacity. In our experience, teachers welcome the opportunity to look at their students through fresh eyes. At Dr Challoner's Grammar School in Amersham, reviewing learning has become a continuous process and an essential part of continuing professional development. Teachers—and students—volunteer to be involved in the review process and are heard to say, '*When's the next review? How can I get involved?'* An external evaluator, who is experienced in observing learning habits in schools or colleges, usually leads an initial review. However, as at Dr Challoner's, once the expertise is there, subsequent reviews are organised in-house and become part of the school's cycle of self-evaluation.

Done with and by the school

An initial review of learning is a really useful starting point for introducing BLP into a school, since it:

Building internal capacity

- provides a baseline survey of the nature of learning and the development of dispositions and habits of learners
- indicates that this is not 'yet another initiative' but an enhancement of current practice
- involves key members of staff with different backgrounds and experience
- introduces a different way of looking at and thinking about learning
- encourages professional dialogue about learning habits
- stimulates growth and development in those who are involved in the process

- results in a report of findings that generates an action plan.

The review team

The review team that conducts the review is assembled and briefed, with the help of the review leader, in response to the school's perceived needs. In a secondary school the team usually consists of about five or six people, in addition to the review leader, and may comprise a cross-section of staff, a group of newly qualified teachers, a team that will become the school's learning power coaches, members of the senior leadership team, students, or a mixture of all of these. In our experience, the use of students as partners in the review process has always enhanced the quality of perceptions and debate—though, as we saw in Chapter 6, not all schools are ready to take this step at the start of the reviewing process.

A range of evidence

For the most part, the learning review focuses on the behaviour of students in lessons, but it also draws on the perceptions of students, teachers and support staff with whom structured interviews are conducted. The results of perception questionnaires are scrutinised along with the school's documentation relating to how students learn at the school—policies, schemes of work, resources, and staff development opportunities.

Preparing for the enquiry

The review team spends a good deal of time in preparation for their enquiry. They define the purpose and nature of the review and communicate this to all staff. They take care to establish protocols so that all teachers will see the process as thorough, professional, and unthreatening. They are trained to know what to look for in lessons: where and how to find evidence of learning habits in students and how to gauge teachers' intentions and students' awareness. The sample of lessons is always substantial and representative of the full range of ability and curriculum. They look for missed opportunities, and are prepared to feed back in constructive, non-judgmental ways in order to stimulate a genuine learning culture in the school. Before the review takes place, they conduct joint observations and observe and discuss learning in each others' lessons.

Triangulating information

Once the process data has been collected, a triangulation meeting takes place to distil the evidence and outline the report that is subsequently written by the external evaluator and returned to the school for discussion and action planning. This objective view of the school provides a wealth of information and ideas for the next stage of development.

Schools that have used this as their starting point have continued to keep learning power under review and made it a central plank of staff development, both for those who do the reviewing and those whose lessons are reviewed. At Wren Academy, for example, an annual review of learning power, by an external evaluator working with a team of teachers and students, has contributed considerably to the school's outstanding Ofsted inspection.

Teacher learning communities

Many schools have seen the benefit of supporting teacher learning communities in one form or another. The nature of such communities has been extensively researched by Dylan Wiliam: see for example the paper 'Tight but Loose'.[2] The essence is a small group of teachers who meet together regularly to deepen their understanding of an approach, trying out new things and reflecting on and sharing their experiments with each other. Wiliam finds that such communities work best when they are voluntary, grouping 8–10 teachers with similar subjects or age groups, who meet monthly for about 75 minutes over a couple of years. Here is an example of one of many ways in which a meeting could be structured:

A well-worked model

Introduction

Firstly the group members agree aims for the meeting, and quickly off-load irritations or frustrations about work that otherwise could hinder the progress and feel of the meeting.

Sharing how things are going

Each member gives a summary of what he or she has tried to achieve since the last meeting. Everyone is expected to report back to every meeting. The group question and probe their colleagues' summaries to encourage analysis and deeper reflection. They use BLP-type questions such as 'What do you think is getting in the way? What would make this better? How could this technique be modified to make it work for you? What do you think made that work so well?'

Learning from each other

New learning

The middle section of the meeting is where new ideas are introduced. There are many aspects to the BLP agenda—language, classroom organisation, split-screen teaching, tracking progression—and the groups work on these according to need. So this part of the meeting might include some input about how to design split-screen lessons, how to introduce visible thinking routines, or how to design activities to stretch a particular learning muscle.

Extending the approach

This changing middle section keeps the meetings fresh, but importantly aims to progress the breadth and depth of the approach.

Personal action planning

Each member then plans what they intend to try over the next month. This gives staff time to think and plan.

Planning action

Review of the meeting

Finally the group reflect on the original objectives of the meeting to see if they have been achieved.

This tight format makes clear the purpose of the exercise and everyone knows what is expected of them. Meetings such as these have been a prominent feature in many BLP schools and have helped teachers and support staff to take risks, examine their practice, and share both successes and tricky problems in an atmosphere of trust and commitment. These discussions substantially support the systematic development of learning powered teaching habits.

Westcliff High School for Girls have developed an interesting extension to their Teacher Learning Communities know as Silver Service. The ten senior teachers who each convene a small TLC meet periodically for lunch. This is a full 'silver service' lunch with tablecloth and good food during which they review the progress made by each learning community and plan new initiatives. They have spotted the need to inject more purpose and innovation into their groups to avoid them becoming traditional 'talking shops'. Their future plans include inviting student feedback on lessons as staff now have the confidence to benefit from this. This way of working has stimulated cross-curricular discussion and observation, something previously unknown.

Coaching partnerships

Just as classroom teachers build learning power by acting as coaches of their students, so their own professional development benefits from coaching partnerships with colleagues.

Learning Champions

Many schools have developed teams of 'learning power champions' whose enthusiasm for Building Learning Power has been used to inspire and guide other colleagues. These champions are often those who have conducted learning reviews and have learnt to look at classroom practice differently. Further training, development and experimentation is useful to deepen their perceptions about how students learn. Working together in pairs or triads they then extend each other's learning. They explore the challenges that they meet, share the trials and changes that they have made and observe each other's lessons in order to learn from and with each other.

For many coaching partnerships, the well-known GROW model is a useful structure for organising learning conversations.[3]

GROW

G ... an exploration of learning *Goals*

R ... a scrutiny of current *Reality*

O ... an examination of *Options* and *Opportunities* that have been or could be taken

W ... a commitment to future action: *What* will we do next?

Working in triads seems to be a good way to hone these champions' coaching skills. When one member of the group coaches another, the third observes the dialogue and provides feedback. Through rotating these roles over time, they become more skilful at coaching each other in preparation for adopting a wider role in coaching other colleagues. The impact is even greater when students learn to develop coaching skills alongside their teachers.

Coaching triads

It can prove hard for some teachers to see that BLP doesn't demand a wholesale replacement of familiar ways of teaching with new ways: it is much more about a subtle shift in the way you do what you have always done. So most schools find that continual coaching, modelling and reminding of staff about what is and isn't involved is important. Jane Snowsill, Assistant Principal at Wren Academy, puts it well:

> 'I have to help people see that BLP isn't a complete reorganisation of what you do. There are lots of opportunities to shift what you do or how you phrase something a little bit. Instead of saying, 'You need to do it like that', you could ask, 'Is there a better way of doing it?' Or, 'What do you notice when you are doing it that way?' Same number of words; no extra effort. But you are encouraging students to be more thoughtful about their learning, and to take greater ownership.'

Jane's colleague, Advanced Skills Teacher John Keohane, who is in charge of BLP staff development at Wren, agrees that this subtle coaching and reassuring is a major part of his role.

> 'At first, some colleagues experienced BLP as a Big Thing: they felt intimidated and didn't feel they were up to it. I find that part of my job is reassuring them that they are already good teachers, and pretty good at developing students' learning capacities. It's just becoming more aware of that side of things; tweaking your approach, developing it gradually, so it gets more focused on the kinds of learning that are happening. But once they feel more confident, the risk then is that they will think, 'Well, if I'm doing it anyway, what's the big deal?' Some staff swing between the two extremes of 'This is totally overwhelming and strange', and 'This is just what we do anyway'.'

Two extremes

Small-scale learning enquiries

Whereas teacher learning communities are formal structures to scaffold teacher's changing habits and gradually add new skills, small-scale 'action research' enquiries offer an opportunity for individual teachers to pursue a particular interest, to take an idea a bit deeper, or to link an enquiry to a particular group of students rather than say a whole class. We have reported many learning enquiries in this book, and it is through such enquiries that much learning about how BLP works has come to light. Here, is just one, illustrating how one BLP school has got the 'teacher enquiry' bug, and is taking it to a really exciting level.

Bay House School is a very large 11–18 comprehensive school in Gosport, Hampshire, with over 2,000 students on roll. Their Year 7 intake is broadly average, but by the time they sit their GCSEs their levels of achievement are well above national expectations. In 2011 Ofsted observed *outstanding lessons that stimulate students' thinking about the way they learn. Students are gently and effectively helped to become inquisitive, resourceful and collaborative.*

But it is not just the students who are developing these learning habits. Since 2010 the whole staff have formed into over 30 small 'professional learning communities' (PLCs) which are busy supporting and generating a whole range of different enquiry projects into how students can be helped to become better learners. Thanks to the energies of lead teachers Annie Bainbridge and Nigel Matthias, the school proudly publishes both a *Professional Learning Communities Newsletter*, which reports on the PLCs' activities, and their own *Bay House Journal of Educational Research*, which contains short reports of the teacher enquiries that members of the PLCs have undertaken. One PLC is working with students across the whole school on the question 'How can we help learners take more responsibility for their learning?' Another PLC is researching whether 'enquiry-based lessons' have a positive impact on students' engagement, attainment and attitudes towards learning. A third asks, 'How can the library support the development of lifelong learning attitudes, especially in boys?'

Introducing PGCE trainees to BLP

PLC 17 has been exploring the question 'How can we enable PGCE trainees to experiment with BLP approaches to teaching?' Trainees were interviewed about their impressions of the way BLP language, imagery, and teaching methods were being used in the school—a process that was useful both in focusing their reflections on what they had seen, and enabling the staff to get some feedback on the use of BLP through fresh pairs of eyes. The trainees were generally impressed that the rhetoric of BLP was being carried through into the day-to-day life of the classrooms, though they noted that *some members of staff were more successful / confident with the use of BLP than others.* The group is now devising a more detailed questionnaire for the next cohort of PGCE students, and also producing a podcast / vodcast to explain the Bay House approach to BLP for future cohorts.

The first issue of the *Bay House Journal of Educational Research* has reports of several enquiries, of which the following two are typical:

> Ryan Peet's enquiry is entitled 'Moving from clarification to enquiry: encouraging learners to question in mathematics at Key Stage 3.'

Encouraging learners to ask their own questions, Ryan found, 'creates shared ownership and increases learner motivation and engagement'. He also found that apparently 'silly questions' were often a stepping stone to more fruitful questions, and therefore were to be welcomed, not discouraged. He also showed—in line with the BLP philosophy—that the idea of 'stretching their questioning muscles' needs to be made explicit to the students, and is also greatly helped by some modelling by the teacher.

Aislynn Matthias shared with us the regret that 'assessment for learning' (AfL) had become *just another way of raising attainment in examinations*, so she experimented with getting students to use their initial self-assessments as a basis on which to plan their own future learning (rather than this being done by the teacher). Subsequently they were asked to reflect on the process of taking responsibility in this way, and the effectiveness of their own learning plans. She found generally 'a very positive reaction to being more involved in making decisions and planning', but that some of the weaker students felt initial anxiety at 'not being told what to do by the teacher'.

The effect of these initiatives on the staffroom culture at Bay House is palpable. There is a buzz of inquisitiveness, experimentation, and reflection that inevitably rubs off on the pupils—as Ofsted observed.

Appreciative Inquiry

Some schools we have worked with are using Appreciative Inquiry, an approach to exploration created by David Cooperrider and colleagues at Case Western Reserve University in the USA. Appreciative Inquiry (AI) is a relatively new way of managing change in organisations.[4] Its four stages are Discover, Dream, Design, and Destiny (Doit). Traditionally, the process of change starts from identifying a 'problem to be fixed', which runs the risk of making staff both defensive and fearful. By contrast the AI model assumes that organisations have many strengths which can be harnessed to meet new challenges. The trick, therefore, is to catch the organisation when it is working at its best. Rather than problematising issues, AI begins by trying to identify what happens when the organisation and individuals within it are working really well. This process normally involves a series of interviews, the outputs of which are stories, pictures, and key-words describing things that are already going well in the desired direction of travel.

Assumes many strengths

So teachers in schools embarking on BLP-type approaches might gather stories about what is already going well, prompted by questions like: 'What are you most proud of?' 'What do you do best in terms of how you develop learners?' 'What is it that you do that most helps to develop powerful learners?' 'What is the most empowering lesson you have taught recently?'

The only rule for such enquiry is that it has to begin by being wholly positive. For some people this is surprisingly difficult; it often tends to be easier to talk about problems than strengths. It's not that people are forbidden to talk about what is not going well; rather, discussions are framed so that when they do move into more critical mode they do so in a spirit of pride and optimism, having confirmed all the many good things they are already doing. And this can make a huge difference.

After 'Discover' you Dream: creating a wish-list of what you would like to do (with current constraints removed). This frees people's minds to think more creatively. After these first two stages, you have an agenda for action and change that isn't encumbered by the usual excuses for inaction. From here you move into familiar territory—Design, a key element of any school development work, and Doing that is reflective and optimistic.

A learning review is often framed in an appreciative way. Schools are keen to unearth and articulate the ways in which they are already helping students to develop confidence and independence as learners—but without the BLP language for learning, they might not have 'joined up the dots' and realised how much is already going on. From this encouraging realisation, it becomes easier and more motivating to think of ways in which they can build on existing good practice, rather than feeling that they are embarking on a whole new enterprise.

Classroom observation and personal review

As schools push deeper into developing teachers' learning habits, they come to question the status quo on what constitutes good or outstanding teaching. Many schools then begin to alter how and why they undertake classroom observation

Developmental Classroom Observation

In many schools, teachers have come to view observation of their classroom practice as an appraisal that leads to a graded assessment of performance. In addition, this appraisal is often linked to a performance management system that sets targets for teachers. Such a view limits the learning that can take place—none of us is at our most open-minded when we feel we are being judged—and inhibits teachers from engaging in professional dialogue about how students learn. Schools with whom we work on BLP have often evolved a more enlightened view. In such schools, classroom observation becomes a developmental entitlement, to be welcomed as the source of self-organised improvement.

Many schools in the UK have created classroom observation sheets to capture data in line with the official Ofsted criteria. The focus of observation is to help the observed teacher to meet these criteria better. In learning powered schools, however, the observer is often as much of a learner as the observed colleague is, and the observation 'schedule' is designed in a more open-ended way, to encourage reflection and imagination by both parties. Before an observation takes place teachers identify what learning habits they will be focusing on, and generate for themselves the most appropriate tools for capturing data to stimulate the ensuing discussion. A learning-powered observation is a two-way process for the observer and the observed from which they both can learn. It is observation *as* development, as shown in the diagram below. In many BLP schools, as we have seen, students are also involved in this process and engage in professional dialogue with their teachers as their learning coaches.

Teachers at King Edward VI Handsworth School in Birmingham have started using the rating wheel shown on page 153, with student observers to gauge the coverage of learning habits in lessons. A small group of student observers shade the chart and compare their perceptions with those of their teachers in order to identify areas for further development.

Observations such as this have caused teachers and support staff to ask themselves different sorts of questions about their practice and their development needs.

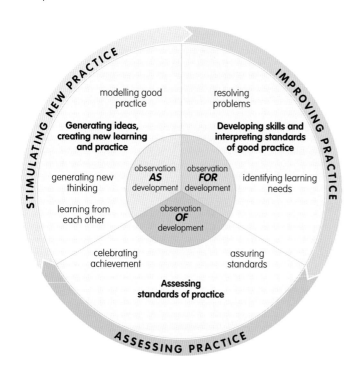

Plan what you want to find out

Questions to ask BEFORE the visit:

- Who will be the best people to visit the school?
- What are we trying to find out?
- Can we ask to go into lessons where BLP is happening?
- Will we be meeting the person who leads this work?
- Will it be possible to talk with other teachers and students?
- How will we be able to gauge the impact and outcomes?
- Can we look at their approaches to developing staff?
- Can we arrange a timetable for our visit?
- Can we arrange some reflection time for ourselves during the visit?

Questions to ask DURING the visit:

- Why and when did the school adopt these approaches?
- What has been the impact on teachers and students?
- What are the signs that this is affecting the environment and culture of the school?
- How is Building Learning Power evident in lessons—is it an awkward add-on or a seamless part of the way teachers teach and learners learn?
- How important is this to the school—is it central to their strategic plan?
- What are the key elements of continuing professional development in BLP?
- How is the school monitoring the effectiveness of BLP?
- In what ways are parents involved in this work?

Questions to ask AFTER the visit:

- What are the strengths, weaknesses, opportunities, and threats in adopting BLP-type approaches at our school?
- What impressed us most?
- What questions are we still asking ourselves?
- How will we report and feed back to others at our school?
- How can we bring the SLT on board—do we need an external input?
- How would we start if we were to adopt Building Learning Power?
- Who are the people who could champion this work for us?
- Should we start with a review of current learning habits?
- Can we sketch out a rudimentary action plan?

Visits to other schools

There are many schools around the UK that have been developing learning-powered cultures and practices for a number of years. Some of these have become recommended sites of good practice, referred to as BLP Learning Hub Schools. Details of these hub schools are available via the BLP website. When schools are looking to adopt BLP, they will often say: 'What does it look like in practice? Where can we go to see it in action?' Spending a day in a school that is, at least in some respects, further down the track than your own can be a rewarding experience. We have found, though, that it is essential to plan carefully and communicate clearly to the host school what you are interested in, in advance of a visit, and to maintain a clear focus during the visit in order to maximise gains from such an investment of time. It is easy to be distracted by aspects of a new school that are more eye-catching and to realise, on the way home, that you may have missed some of the BLP subtleties.

Learning hub schools

The page opposite shows an example of a list of questions that one school developed to help focus their attention and get the most out of their visits.

We are aware of other educational networked communities organised so as to enable schools—among other things—to share ideas and visit each other. Three UK-based networks that operate with 'learning-power-friendly' aims and spirit are:

- the Cambridge Primary Review network, www.primaryreview.org.uk
- Whole Education, www.wholeeducation.org
- the Expansive Education Network, www.expansiveeducation.net

These tend to cross-link to each other and to other similar communities, formally and informally—particularly via schools and organisations who participate in more than one. They are likely therefore to be useful starting points for finding other relevant networks not noted here (no doubt including some that do not yet exist at the time of writing!)

The What of Learning

So far in this chapter we have looked at ways in which schools have enabled staff to learn about BLP and blend this into their practice. It may be worth summarising some of the things (which we have described in more detail over the previous chapters) that teachers will be learning about.

The 'curriculum content' for BLP includes:

- introducing and using a language of learning
- using the physical environment to reinforce the messages about learning

BLP curriculum content

- designing learning opportunities to stretch learning behaviours ('split-screen' teaching)
- using learning language to nudge, encourage, and comment on students' learning
- developing growth mindsets (a la Carol Dweck)
- giving students more control over their own learning
- tracking progression in learning habits and using this information formatively
- using 'could-be' language to promote curiosity and enquiry
- bringing parents on board and harnessing their support in growing learning habits
- adapting the curriculum to support progress in learning habits.

Each one of these bullet points represents a significant shift in emphasis from much current teaching practice. For some teachers, these shifts will be highly congenial. For others, they will be more challenging. In the concluding pages of this chapter, we look closely at how one school put a PD programme together.

In this chapter we have described a number of ways in which BLP schools have tried to organise professional learning for their staff, so that they can gain confidence and flexibility with the BLP approach. We hope these illustrations will spark some further ideas in the reader's mind about how they can manage the process of professional development in their schools. As we have said, BLP asks teachers to become aware of habits that might be quite deep-seated and automatic—habits of observing, describing, interacting, organising, and evaluating—and to engage in some conscious experiments with their 'natural' style of teaching. Any such process of habit change feels awkward for a while, and all habit change takes time and practice to consolidate. But the vast majority of our teachers have found that the satisfaction of seeing students—high- and low-achievers alike—taking greater control of their learning, and discovering the pleasure of being able to figure out difficult things for themselves, makes their efforts enormously worthwhile. We have yet to meet a teacher who, having mastered the BLP way of teaching, decides to go back to 'chalk and talk ', wresting back the control of the classroom which they had begun to share with their pupils.

A radical overhaul of professional development

Case study: Simpson School, Milton Keynes

Simpson School has been involved with BLP since 2007 and there are numerous examples of their practice scattered through this book. For this reason we take time here to describe their difficult journey and their staff development programme.

In the summer of 2007 the school had to come to terms with some uncomfortable truths. Their maths results were their lowest ever at 25% L4+, and a staggering 65% missed their individual progress targets. Over a third of children attained below their targets in English, and the behaviour of many children was poor with 136 days of fixed term and 2 permanent exclusions.

The children were not coping with the experiences of school. Simpson draws the majority of its pupils from some of Milton Keynes's most disadvantaged areas. The number of children qualifying for free school meals is almost double the national average, and a third of pupils speak English as an additional language. The catchment area consists largely of housing association homes and temporary accommodation for families new to the UK. Indeed the estates are considered to be in the 20% most disadvantaged areas in the country. The school also suffers from a very high churn, with the proportion of children moving schools in a year reaching up to a third. Added to this, the number of children with special educational needs is above average, and many of them experience emotional or behavioural difficulties.

Children not coping with school

Many disadvantages

The school saw its results as a wake-up call but were at a loss as to what to do. They had previously toed the line and accepted the need to invest heavily in the knowledge and skills curriculum and in a team of Learning Mentors to offer pastoral support. They had diligently undertaken numerous intervention programmes including Better Reading Partnership, Early Literacy Strategy, Further Literacy Strategy, Raising our Level Fours and much more.

What to do?

What they realised was that through desperate attempts to raise standards, they had come to see the curriculum as content only. Positive learning attitudes, emotional resilience, social skills and positive self-image were not on their radar. Instead they did things for children, hid them from the struggle of learning, and fed them facts. Something had to change.

The problem

During the soul searching they came across BLP, a model that opened their eyes to the expandable and learnable human disposition to learn.

Better times

Their story is one of triumphs and hard work. Triumphs because attainment has improved dramatically (between 2006 and 2010 English L4+ results jumped from 40% to 68.8%, and Maths L4+ from 48% to 62.5%) and children's capacity to face challenges has done much to eradicate behaviour problems (in 2010 there were only 19 days of fixed term exclusions, and no permanent exclusions). Hard work because it has taken commitment and dedication to avoid being deflected back to their old ways of working despite pressure to do so from the local authority.

Development for everyone

Simpson School took their learning journey seriously, recognising this had to be a whole-school approach. They concentrated their efforts on developing all staff. Every year, at least one INSET day is devoted to some aspect of BLP practice, backed up by half-termly staff meetings; coaching partnerships have been built; staff meetings have been used as teacher learning communities; some staff have undertaken research enquiries; classroom observation schedules and practice have been altered to capture student learning; learning reviews, both external and in-house, have been undertaken at regular intervals; learning how to learn is a major strategy in the school's development plan. Simpson School has used just about every type of staff development approach described earlier in this chapter.

What has emerged from this work is not only a highly proficient BLP school, visited by people from all over the world, but an enviable staff development programme which they have developed from their four years' experience. Every new member of staff goes through the programme to ensure they are on board, and ultimately skilled, as a BLP practitioner. Records are kept of every member of staff at every stage of their journey and the learning journeys are personalised for everyone, including support staff.

Professional development pathways

The development pathways describe what staff need to understand and what they need to be able to do. They also specify the resources available to help staff on their journey and the professional learning opportunities they can be assured of at each stage. No one finds this threatening since everyone is on the same learning journey.

What is expected first

The **first stage** involves knowing the BLP framework, being aware of the need to cultivate a culture shift in the classroom, and being committed to the moral dimension of BLP. Staff are expected to develop stuck prompts with their class and act on 'stuck is a good place to be'. Staff are given various BLP books to read and discuss with their coach, and prompt cards for each learning habit to remind them of the language of learning they are beginning to use in the classroom. Dweck's work on growth mindsets has also been integrated into this first stage.

The **second stage** involves staff observing their students, noticing the learning behaviours being used, and giving praise for their use. They are expected to introduce four capacities in the class and plan a couple of lessons that make use of these capacities. To help this stage there are staff meetings to explain and practise re-designing tasks from traditional worksheets. Coaches help the process along by team teaching the new lessons and discussing the process. This is a lengthy stage, with each of the four capacities taking half a term to introduce and integrate.

Deepening teachers' skills

Stage three moves on to ensuring there is holistic coverage of the capacities in the classroom. Staff are introduced to the '9 Thinks' model for lesson design and are expected to use three aspects of this: driving questions, starter challenge, and stuck challenge.[5] They are expected to aim to deliver four lessons a week to this design and monitor how they are covering the capacities. Coaching pairs plan a lesson using this design and observe each other delivering the lesson. After about two terms, staff use a self-review tool to assess their progress and discuss this with their coach.

Broadening teachers' habits

By **stage four**, year 2 of the professional development pathway, the teacher is expected to contribute to creating a learning culture more widely in the school e.g. taking a learning power assembly and taking part in learning walks. They now plan lessons using the whole 9 Thinks model and apply this to lessons, sequences of lessons, full-day projects and all subjects. They are trained in how to observe other teachers and conduct focused learning walks around the school, and are observed giving formative feedback to those they have observed.

Coaching support

Trained in observing techniques

Finally staff learn how to plan for progression in learning habits and record children's progress. The school has developed an impressive range of learning ladders that are shared and re-created as staff come to understand better how different learning habits progress. At this point staff are considered ready to show visitors around the school and deliver showcase lessons.

Guiding visitors round the school

This comprehensive, cumulative programme with support at all levels ensures staff feel confident and motivated to contribute to a unique and growing body of knowledge about how to build students' learning power.

Chapter 10

Sending BLP home: Involving parents in their children's learning

In this chapter we explore:

- a new kind of parental engagement based on BLP
- some examples of practical initiatives to engage parents

'My kids seem to have become more grown-up. They get on better now. I've heard them talking about collaborating to get their bedrooms tidy.'

'Jamie comes home with lots of new words. He talks about persevering and managing his distractions. I thought this was funny at first, but I am realising this is seriously helping him to learn.'

'I really like the new reports we have been getting about my daughter. They tell me useful things about how she is learning. I think I've learned how I could help her to get better.'

'Please can 'Patsy' come home with Jenny again.' [Patsy is a doll that has taken on the attributes of a good learner. She is allowed to visit children's homes for a night.] 'When she came home last week, the children played more constructively. They didn't fight about which games to play and they went to bed without a struggle.'

Once schools have begun to develop their approach to implementing BLP, is doesn't take very long before they realise that there could be major implications for the way they interact with parents and carers. An overarching issue reported by all schools adopting BLP-type approaches is the need to develop effective ways of communicating and engaging with parents to ensure that:

- parents understand what the school is trying to do and
- what goes on at home and in the wider community complements the approaches being adopted at school.

The comments quoted above are just a few of those made by parents as they have become aware that something interesting is happening in their child's school.

A different kind of parental engagement

For more than a generation now, schools have been committed to actively involve parents. This involvement is often associated with school-generated requirements like school trips or parents' evenings or school photographs or social events. But BLP schools are looking beyond 'involvement' to 'engagement', which implies a more active and personal level of participation in their child's learning. Schools are interested in engagement because in recent years research 'has made it clear that parental engagement with their child's learning makes a significant contribution to the child's achievement',[1] and that parental engagement is a much bigger factor than school in shaping achievement.[2] Obviously, parents also have a powerful influence in shaping their children's character, and three aspects of character are especially useful for successful learning.[3] These are:

- self-regulation—the ability to regulate emotions; not to be subject to temper tantrums and to be able to survive reasonable setbacks.

- empathy—being able to imagine things from another person's perspective; to understand where they are coming from.

- persistence—being able to stick at things even when they are difficult.

BLP approaches have much to offer on each of these three vital aspects of what it is to be a powerful learner. Carol Dweck beautifully sums up the contribution of a parent intent on growing children who are powerful learners:

> 'If parents want to give their children a gift, the best thing they can do is to teach their children to love challenges, be intrigued by mistakes, enjoy effort and keep on learning. That way they will have a lifelong way to build and repair their own confidence.'

A gift

What parents do at home

What parents do at home has a powerful influence on students' emerging self-concept as a learner. Constructive activities at home that appear to help create successful learners include:

- using interesting and complex vocabulary

- encouragement to read for a range of purposes

- cultural activities such as visiting libraries, museums, performances or historic sites

- encouragement to develop hobbies

- providing opportunities to question and try out new things

- having conversations about things outside the home

- opening discussions about progress at school

All parents are different but there is growing research to suggest a kind of 'tough love'[4] is more likely to produce children who are self-regulating, co-operative, and socially responsible. This involves setting and sticking to clear boundaries, inside which children are encouraged to play and explore, along with a warm and affectionate approach to children's experiments and mistakes.

Tough love?

As schools know only too well, whether or not parents choose to get involved depends on things like their own experience of school, the shape of their working lives, and whether, in genuinely making an effort to engage them, the language used by the school is clear, welcoming and accessible. **Parents are more likely to become engaged if they see their children's success as learners, both in school and out, as part of their job as parents.** It is those children who are doing less well at school who may need their parents' active engagement most, and those in the middle—neither 'gifted and talented' nor having 'special educational needs' or 'learning difficulties'—who may not be realising their potential.

Slow to change

Many schools, and BLP ones are no exception, have been slow to change the way they deal with parents. The organisation of parents' evenings, the use of homework, and the way school reports are written, for example, can be deeply resistant to change. And while most schools have websites and use e-mail communication, when you scratch the technological surface, you often find that schools have not re-thought the kinds of things which it is worth communicating with parents about.

Types of parental engagement

There are, of course, many ways in which parents can engage with their children's schools. Joyce Epstein, Research Professor of Sociology at John Hopkins University in the USA, has developed a useful and widely cited framework for thinking about how schools can engage parents most effectively. In the table opposite we have re-ordered Epstein's six categories of involvement, and added a BLP twist to each. Over the following pages we offer glimpses of what schools are beginning to do in each category.

1   Communicating

The most basic thing for schools to do is communicate with parents about what they are up to—not just practical arrangements, but their vision: what it is they are trying to help their pupils become, and how they are going about it. In the case of BLP, this means explaining to them what 'learning power' is, what it consists of, and why it is so important. Some schools have included parents right from the beginning, involving them in the debate about whether to adopt an approach like BLP. The majority of schools, though, seem to have involved parents after trialling the approach for a term or so, when they feel more confident about its merits and potential impact.

Information sessions

Beyond the 4 R's

The most popular way of introducing BLP to parents has been through information sessions backed up by leaflets, newsletters, and the school website. The need to make the purpose and language of BLP accessible has proved challenging for some schools. Simply explaining what the 4 R's and the 17 learning habits are doesn't seem to engage parents' interest reliably. Schools have found it important to highlight that:

- the approach is about helping children to become better learners, in school as well as out; enabling them to understand, use, and become more skilled in using a wide range of learning behaviours; making the children more responsible and independent as learners.

- the approach will take some time to really embed into the culture of the school, and that it means teachers teaching a bit differently using the language of learning.

Epstein's six types (re-ordered)		... and with a BLP twist
Type 1: Communicating	Designing effective home-to-school and school-to-home communication methods which engage all parents regularly	Designing effective engagement processes to enable parents to understand the core concepts of BLP. Integrating BLP into all the school's reporting structures
Type 2: Learning at home	Providing good information to enable all parents to help with homework and offer other family learning activities	Rethinking homework to reflect the school's learning principles: a range of home learning activities designed to exercise students' learning muscles, choice, and responsibility
Type 3: Parenting	Helping all families to have the basic home conditions in place including active parenting strategies and regular communication with school	Helping parents to become learning coaches and specifically to understand core principles of reward and praise strategies
Type 4: Volunteering	Recruiting volunteer parents to help in school, in classes, and in extra-curricular activities	Recruiting and training volunteer parents to act as Parent Learning Champions in school and within the parent body
Type 5: Decision-making	Including parents in decision-making activities to build a sense of ownership, including being involved in governance	Encouraging parents to be involved in shaping the full BLP range of experiences, as part of inclusion in wider decision-making activities
Type 6: Collaborating with community	Finding and using resources from the wider parent community to enrich school life	Creating a talent bank of parents with passions and enthusiasms who can be local learning heroes and coaches

- the approach will have (or is already having) positive effects on children's behaviour, motivation, and stickability, *and* on their levels of achievement.
- parents too can help their children to become better learners and that the school would value their important assistance.

Questions parents need answers to

The most successful sessions have sought to answer the following questions for parents:

- What is Building Learning Power all about?
- What difference might I expect to see in my child's learning habits and language?
- What will the school be doing differently?
- What will the children be doing differently?
- What can I do as a parent?
- What habits am I nurturing by the way I behave with my children?
- Which of these habits might help and which might hinder the growth of learning power muscles?
- Why is this something I should value?
- What place does BLP have in my child's future?
- So what impact is it having or expected to have?

We have heard of many ingenious ways which schools have used to tempt parents to such sessions:

- organising the sessions at different times of day to ensure as many parents as possible can make it
- planning the sessions to include children giving some kind of performance about learning (always a successful draw for parents), and/or having the children explain the nature and benefits of BLP to their parents.

Gaining their interest

- buying small rubber brains and sending these home with the pupils with an invitation attached saying something like 'Come and find out how my learning brain works' or 'Find out how I can get better at learning'.

Where information sessions have been arranged after two or three terms of BLP, attendance has been helped by the fact that children have already started taking the language of BLP home and using it naturally, and parents have become intrigued to find out what it's all about.

In these information sessions parents have asked very practical questions, exploring, as one parent put it, 'how we are delaying the rescue'; what coaching style approaches are appropriate, how to recognise fixed mindsets and how to help their children re-frame their beliefs, what constitutes good home learning, how to model being a powerful learner, how to rise to the challenge of celebrating stuckness, how to rid themselves of anxiety about their child's ability and position in the class, and so on.

Schools have been slightly anxious about how parents might react to such sessions, but have been relieved and sometimes a little surprised at how fascinated and enthusiastic parents have been to become co-travellers on this learning journey.

No need to be anxious

Learning activity days

Primary schools in particular have held learning activity days to introduce the approach. Schools have recorded attendance of seventy or eighty parents at these events, where for past curriculum events they would have considered twenty a good turnout. These drop-in events are often organised around activities that aim to engage parents in the use of particular learning muscles through engaging and amusing activities.

High turnouts

Websites and newsletters

Having highlighted interest and enthusiasm through this type of introduction to BLP, schools follow it up with regular communication through newsletters and their website, updating things like the target learning muscles for, say, a week, and encouraging parents to point them out to their children when they are using them at home.

Reception areas

The large plasma screens now so familiar in school reception areas are being used to convey BLP messages. Snippets of video showing children using their learning muscles in a lesson or outside school have become a talking point for parents and an effective way of keeping the messages alive.

A talking point

Curriculum information sheets

Many schools produce half-termly information sheets that explain what pupils will be learning about. Some BLP schools have extended this valuable resource to include the focus learning muscles linked to the content areas, the language of learning associated with the muscles, and things to look out for and extend at home.

A different kind of report

A typical end of term report of the past would usually have concentrated on a pupil's progress in each subject area, and their likelihood of success in forthcoming examinations. Reports often revolved around four overworked concepts that we have come to call The Dull Quartet: Effort, Ability, Achievement and Conduct (or Behaviour). The child's learning was often boiled down to their level of attainment, and accompanied by cryptic comments such as 'Tom needs to improve on his connectives.' What, we wonder, is a parent to make of such statements? What could they do to

Nayland Primary School: an experiment in report writing.

Teacher comments that pick up previous areas to develop

Comments about progress that link learning capacities to content areas

Teacher comment flags up an area for improvement

The pupil's own ideas about which capacities to develop

Pupil: Albie Jones   Class: 3B

Progress in learning power

Albie has developed great **listening** skills which he uses carefully with both adults and children. He has also great **empathy** with others and this helps him to **collaborate** well when learning in both small and large groups. He knows how to take turns and share his ideas thoughtfully. Albie is developing the ability to become **absorbed** in learning by avoiding small **distractions** around him.

Maths

Although challenging, Albie has learned to **persevere** to develop his understanding of how to make addition and subtraction jump along an empty number line…

Science

Albie is getting better at coming up with lots of ideas when investigating. He can now make **reasoned predictions** and confidently communicate his ideas to others…

History

Albie has become particularly good at **making links** between different areas, e.g. how electricity has changed our lives and the changes and benefits of medicines…

Art

To take his learning to the next stage, Albie needs to begin to **reflect** on his own and others' art and to suggest ways to improve and develop his artwork.

Teacher comments

As Albie consolidates his learning habits he will become more confident in his own abilities and will be even braver to 'have a go' at new learning without feeling concerned or intimidated by the opinion of his peers…

Albie's future learning power focus

I am learning to use my **questioning** muscle to ask more complicated questions to find out about a topic

I am learning to develop my writing by **planning** it in advance I am learning to choose the appropriate operation to solve real-life maths problems and begin to explain my **reasoning**

NB: BLP vocabulary words highlighted in bold

help with Tom's connectives? Sometimes it seemed as if there was little parents could do other than endorse the report and praise their children for having done well, or exhort them to do better.

But BLP reports for parents are beginning to take a difference approach. The one shown opposite is a prototype that Nayland Primary School have been working on. It offers parents an insight into their child's use of and progression in learning habits. This is information that parents can more readily understand and, more importantly, do something with. It offers a talking point about what the child does at school and furthermore suggests how the parent might pick up on the points and coach their child to develop further.

A revolution in report writing

Christ Church C of E Primary School in West Bromwich attached each child's feedback from a Blaze BLP quiz to their usual end of year report, and used this as an introduction and invitation to an open evening to find out more about learning behaviours and what the school was doing to encourage their use. 90% of the parents attended and all were enthusiastic about the new approaches.

Although such reports are in their infancy they offer an important bridge between learning at school and at home, and many BLP schools are turning their attention to developing them.

2   Learning at home

Many parents have become deeply involved in 'doing homework' for and with their children. Perhaps because they have picked up how important it is to 'get things right' and do tasks properly, they help with homework to ensure answers are right, things look neat, and that there's enough volume. So homework is often seen as a chore for both pupils and parents alike. The pupils have little responsibility or choice other than to do it and get it right.

Debby Hughes, a Year 2 teacher at St Augustine's Catholic Primary School in Kenilworth, wanted to explore the possibilities of co-planning with her pupils in order to nurture their curiosity and encourage them to take greater responsibility for their learning. She decided to begin this shift with their home learning. In order to keep the task as open and potentially rich as possible she began by sharing only the title of the learning topic and then asked pupils to generate questions around what interested them about the topic. With the ideas scribed they went on to discuss how they could go about finding the answers. Lastly the group generated ideas about how they could demonstrate their learning to their teacher. The pupils were given the week to complete this self-generated home learning. They had free choice about which aspect of the topic they would research, how they would research, and how they might present their learning. And, as this exercise was all about making choices, they were also told that they might choose not to do this home learning.

Giving choice

At the end of the week, Debby collected in the outcomes. Only two children had decided to exercise their right not to do it and she found it difficult not to chastise them in any way. She had given them the right to choose not to do the homework and they had made that choice. However, it soon became evident that the children were disappointed not to be part of the exciting exchanges between their fellow pupils as they shared their findings and the many imaginative ways they had found to present their learning. Debby was delighted that the quality of the outcomes exceeded her expectations and realised that she had sometimes unwittingly put a ceiling on what they might be expected to achieve. The outstanding quality of the learning outcomes convinced her that involving pupils in co-planning their learning, and offering them opportunities to take on rich learning challenges, was welcomed by the children. They had genuinely engaged in the process, taken pride and delight in the outcomes, and had clearly worked independently rather than involving their parents. They were also keen to share their outcomes with others, using each other as a learning resource.

Outstanding outcomes

This gave Debby the confidence to extend the practice to strengthen the learning community of the classroom. Interestingly, she has continued to offer the children the option not to do their home learning but since then 100% of pupils have chosen to complete it. She firmly believes that the experience of being allowed to exercise choice appropriately has been a really valuable lesson for all the pupils. They are strengthening their intrinsic motivation which she believes to be so much more powerful than learning in response to extrinsic demands.

3   Parenting

The next focus

The common theme for any school using BLP approaches is that it is likely to want to focus on exactly what it is that parents can do to help their children become more powerful learners. Given that we know that it is what parents do at home that has most impact on their children's learning, it is not surprising that schools tend to focus next on offering ideas for what parents can actually do in the home to build their children's learning power.

Just as BLP changes the way teachers teach, so it can influence the way parents parent. For example, if parents want to help their children see the value of effort and to develop self-belief in their talents, then, as we have seen elsewhere, they may choose to praise their child specifically for those efforts which show them 'going the extra mile' rather than simply for 'getting a good mark'. Or if they want them to become more resourceful, they will create situations in which children have to work things out by themselves and hold back from helping them too soon.

Some schools are beginning to offer snappy hour-long sessions on specific aspects of the BLP approach such as

> 'How to praise your child',
> 'How to help your child when they are stuck',
> 'Helping your child to set goals',
> 'Recognising signs of distress'.

It has to be said that such approaches are in their infancy, but as BLP gains momentum we are hopeful of a widespread flowering of these important 'Parenting for Learning Power' workshops.

Influencing the way parents parent

Perhaps the most ambitious parental engagement work that we know of was done at Simpson School in Milton Keynes. As the case-study on pages 221–223 showed, Simpson School draws its pupils from some of the most deprived areas in the country and the approach that was trialled had to go right 'back to basics', in learning power terms: coaching parents in interacting more purposefully with their children, encouraging them to appreciate that helping their children to learn better was indeed part of the role of parents. They started by helping parents appreciate that 'play' was not a break or a distraction from 'learning': it was one of the most important forms of learning that children did.

Over the course of six weeks a group of parents and teachers played and learned together. They made dens and 'art work' with cardboard boxes which the parents had to obtain from supermarkets. During some of these highly engaging sessions, parents explored what it meant to collaborate and persevere. In other sessions, parents were each given £10 to buy suitable items for a dressing-up box from charity shops, and they explored imagination and empathy and their importance in learning. Parents were given prompt cards (see page 236) that would remind them of the main points from the sessions and offer ways in which they could use the ideas at home. The parents involved in the first course were subsequently involved as helpers in the second course.

Six half-days of play

Simpson has effectively taken on the core BLP ideas and asked itself the question: how might parenting change? What can parents do at home to strengthen their children's learning muscles? Their emerging solutions are creative and easily replicable by others. The trick seems to be to create an environment in which parents feel they can come and learn together, sharing the challenges of parenting and talking about their children. Then, while they are doing this, they can pick up really important BLP approaches which they can experiment with and adapt as they think fit.

Learning-power prompt cards for parents

Why is collaboration important in the real world?

- People come together all the time to get things done.
- We all have roles to follow in the family, at work and in the community; when we do our bit we get on.
- Learning alongside others gives you new ideas, this gives you a bigger bank of experiences to choose from when you face a problem.

More activities to build collaboration

- Prepare a family meal together.
- Build a town or zoo out of lego or wooden blocks.
- Build a train together using cardboard boxes.
- Create a large collage together.
- Try doing anything 'big' that you can't really do on your own.

And during the activities remember to:

- Get most things ready in advance, keeping a few things back to add a challenge.
- Think out loud: explain what you are doing and why.
- Praise each other's good ideas and efforts.
- Pick up and use good ideas from others.
- Listen and watch and learn from each other.
- Stand back and let them learn.

The sessions were a revelation to those involved. Parents realised that learning was not something that just happened at school:

> 'Learning can be done in different ways, it's not just what teachers give you to do,' said one mother.

> 'I've realised that learning is in lots of everyday life experiences such as work relationships,' said a Dad.

Other important shifts occurred; one parent began the course saying

> 'My children don't like working with other people because that's how I am',
>> and ended it saying

> 'I can help my children to become better at collaborating than I am',
>> and

> 'When you are not using your learning power, you're not really learning'.

This type of intensive course requires a great deal of planning and commitment, but Simpson School is convinced it was worth the effort. Not only did the parents come to see their parenting role differently, but the children of these parents showed marked improvements in their use of various learning behaviours in school. There was an immediate knock-on effect on the children which continued as the parents became helpers in the second course.

Websites and newsletters

Some primary schools and a few secondary schools, Bay House School Gosport being one, have started to offer tentative advice about parenting for learning power.

The content and tone of such areas can be tricky. The best have steered clear of 'preaching', and, just as we saw with teachers in Chapter 9, have had to make sure that parents do not feel judged or blamed. Many and varied examples of everyday activities with a BLP twist seems to be a valuable way to go.

What parents learned about learning

Parents now know they matter

4   Volunteering

All schools welcome parents who offer their time to help in the school or with extra-curricular activities. BLP schools find that they need to take more time with inducting these parents into the school, explaining how BLP works and what this means when talking to pupils. In the early days of helping out, parents find it hard to hang back and allow pupils to struggle. Since their original motivation was to be able to give children help, they, like teachers and learning assistants before them, have had to learn how to give pupils greater freedom, independence, and choice. They had to learn the sort of 'Learnish' language prompts that we discussed in Chapter 4.

So as schools offer more and more opportunities for parents to contribute their time and talents, they have to be aware of the need to take more time to ensure parents can engage with the practicalities of the school's new ethos and language.

Getting the most out of volunteering

5   Decision making

Parent and community representation on school governing bodies and in thriving Friends associations are an important feature of every school's life. Beyond this parents are now being consulted on a wide range of issues, made easier through school web sites. Although most 'Friends' of the school continue to play a mainly fund-raising role, some BLP schools are encouraging these organisations to focus their efforts on gaining greater parental engagement in learning. This seeding of an idea has great potential for the future.

'Friends' groups encourage parental engagement in learning

6   Collaborating with the community

All schools are finding interesting ways of making links with their communities. Some BLP schools are enthusiastically building what they call a 'talent bank' of parents and others in the community who are willing and able to visit the school and talk about what they do and, importantly, how they learn at work. Nayland Primary School enlisted the help of mums, dads, and other relatives who all work in scientific jobs, to tell their learning stories as part of a science week. This helped pupils to link school science to real life and recognise that people keep on learning throughout their lives. Again, we think there is great potential for this idea to flourish in the future.

Talent banks

Pulling the strands together

As we have said repeatedly in this chapter, it is still early days for BLP-style parental engagement. But from the evidence of what we have seen, schools that are being most effective:

- have a clear understanding of what being a 'powerful learner' is, what they mean by 'learning success', and share it with all parents

- subtly shift the focus of their conversation with parents onto how parents can best help their children become better learners

- create a 'split-screen' style of parental communications, altering reports, parent evenings, etc. accordingly

- communicate key BLP messages in a range of media, eliminating educational jargon

- sensitively offer practical ideas for parents to use at home

- develop, in partnership with parents, a clear strategy for engaging parents as learning coaches

- offer parent workshops on a range of BLP topics throughout the year.

What's most effective

We have scanned numerous school websites to gain a flavour of how schools are explaining BLP to parents. Many continue to use the original language of the framework and don't venture very far into explaining the purpose behind it.

Interestingly however, staff who have either attended or been involved in designing sessions for parents have reported how 'it was good to hear [or think about] the messages and dialogue again from a different angle'. Staff themselves have become more receptive to BLP when the 'training' was not aimed directly at them.

Engaging parents remains a tricky area for many BLP schools but our findings suggest that when it is done in a 'could be' way, when parents don't feel threatened, when the school explains the science and rationale behind the approach, parents are more than willing and enthusiastic to become involved.

A tricky area

Part 4
Reflections

In the final part of the book we take a step back from the practicalities of BLP, and adopt a more reflective stance.

In Chapter 11, we tackle the vital job of assessing the evidence for the impact of the approach. We report on the reactions and impressions of the schools themselves, and discuss various kinds of data which they have been collecting in order to inform and guide their own journeys. But we also look at the effect BLP has had on students' performance in public examinations, specifically Key Stage 2 SATs and GCSEs—remembering that the improvement of such 'results' is not the main purpose of BLP, but also that it would be problematic if those results were found to suffer. We also look at what school inspectors such as Ofsted have had to say in their reports on BLP schools. Overall, this 'mid-term' survey of the impact of BLP is more than reassuring; it is highly encouraging.

In Chapter 12 we carry out a short reflective round-up of the main arguments and issues raised in the book, and try to see what the future holds for approaches like BLP. While some national governments and political parties are either uncomprehending of, or actively hostile to, such approaches, we are cautiously optimistic that they will continue to prosper. BLP chimes well, we have found, with the educational values of many teachers and school leaders, and they are eager for the mixture of precise language, clear illustrations and practical suggestions that nevertheless is not prescriptive, and continually invites schools to craft and customise their own version.

Chapter 11

The impact of BLP: Does it work?

In this chapter we explore:

- the effect of BLP on students' academic performance
- Ofsted inspectors' observations
- independent evaluations of BLP schools
- some action research by BLP teachers
- students' self-perceptions
- teachers' and others' perceptions of students

Types of evidence

I t is well-nigh impossible to draw hard-and-fast conclusions that prove that BLP has had specific effects on students. Nevertheless, there are a variety of kinds of evidence that, taken together, give us increasing confidence that the approach is having beneficial results. They include the following:

1. **Students' performance on tests and examinations.** Whilst the practices of BLP are not aimed directly at raising standards as traditionally defined, but at building wider transferable dispositions towards learning, it is vital that we can show that these practices do not damage or jeopardise results—or may even improve them.

2. **Inspection reports**. It is not explicitly in the brief of Ofsted inspectors to look for the development of learning-oriented habits of mind—their main concerns are with achievement and safety—but it would be encouraging to find that they notice and approve of the effects of BLP strongly enough to make comments in their reports.

3. **External evaluations.** A similarly objective source of evidence can be provided by external evaluations of BLP. We report the results of several of these.

4. **Action research projects.** Small-scale research projects, in which teachers rigorously evaluate for themselves the effects of BLP-related changes and interventions in their classrooms, provide very useful fine-grain evidence both of impact and implementation. A good many of these have been dotted about in previous chapters to illustrate the finer points of BLP.

5. **Students' perceptions of themselves as learners.** Whilst are there are all kinds of well-reported problems with focus group interviews, self-report questionnaires and the like—are respondents taking them seriously, for example, or are they merely telling you what they think you want to hear?—it is clearly useful to know if youngsters *feel* as if they are being helped to become more resilient, resourceful, imaginative and so on.

6. **People's perceptions of the process.** Although testimony from leaders, teachers, TAs and parents does not, by itself, constitute incontrovertible evidence for BLP, nevertheless it would be helpful to know if they are seeing positive effects on their students. We have also noted comments schools have made on students' behaviour more generally.

We provide some evidence on each of these in turn.

1 Students' performance

'Students' test performance—best results ever! BLP really does work!'
Rachel Macfarlane, Headteacher, Walthamstow School for Girls

Before we present the data on student achievement, one crucial point may need reiterating. The point of BLP is not to raise conventional results; it is to expand the range of valued outcomes to include the development of the confidence and capacity to learn all kinds of things, out of school as well as in. Expanding young people's capacity to learn, and their appetite for learning, is seen as a valuable end of education in its own right; not just as a way of improving scores on existing indicators.

So the question of critical importance is: does attention to these BLP objectives interfere with performance on more conventional indicators? Do the results hold up, when we try to teach in a way that produces more confident, sophisticated and independent learners, or do they suffer? If we can show that examination performance is preserved, that will give heart to teachers and school leaders who sympathise with the BLP spirit, but are anxious not to jeopardise their 'standards'. So if the results stay the same, while learning power improves, that is a success. If they do not go up, that is not a failure. We have found that the pressure on schools to raise standards is so intense, it can be hard for teachers to hold onto this perspective.

Does BLP interfere with performance?

Having said that, it would be nice—and not terribly surprising—if the results did actually improve. It would not be much of a shock to discover that young people who are better able to manage, review and plan their own learning, and who are more resilient and resourceful in the face of difficulty, do better on the tests. Indeed, the research that we mentioned in Chapter 2 from John Hattie and others suggests that this is indeed what happens. We will see whether our own data corroborates this.

Do results actually improve?

We present the data that we have gathered graphically.[1] These graphs show the SATs scores for a range of primary schools, and the GCSE scores for a range of secondaries. The data is presented in the form of multiple base-line graphs from the period one year before the introduction of BLP to the most recent available data for each school (2009 or 2010 for primary schools and 2010 for secondary schools). The use of multiple base-line graphs 'across settings' (i.e. in different schools) is applicable as schools introduced BLP at different times.[2] This kind of graph enables easy comparison of SATs and GCSE attainments between schools over time.

Multiple base-line graphs

Primary schools

Graph 1 shows the total SATs points for the seven participating primary schools, together with the average points for English primary schools for the same period. It is clear that two of these schools, Bransgore and Bushfield, were too new to BLP to show any post-BLP trends. The others show a mixed picture. Mosborough, Princeville and Simpson, with very different starting points, show marked improvements in their SATs scores. Both Princeville and Simpson, with very low levels of achievement compared to national norms, deliberately undertook BLP with the aim of improving standards, as well as expanding children's capacity to learn.

Remarkable results

The Princeville story is particularly noteworthy. Between 2003 and 2006 their SATs results had deteriorated dramatically and the school was at risk of being placed in special measures. A new headteacher discovered that the psychological foundations of BLP resonated well with her own educational values, and introduced BLP to her staff and school community in 2007 as the way to improve the school's SATs results. The impact has been, in her own words, transformational. Pupils who were well behaved but passive learners have become enthusiastic, confident and resourceful learners, and in 2008 and 2009 attained above national average SATs results. The schools' 2009 Ofsted inspection graded the school 'good' with 'outstanding' elements and in the same year Princeville was reported to be the third most improved primary school in the country.

Why should this be?

St Mary's CE Primary School in Swanley seems to show a dip in their SATs performance following the introduction of BLP, though their latest result provides clear evidence of overall improvement. The headteacher's account of the results is as follows:

- St Mary's is a one-form entry school and consequently is susceptible to variability in the learning capacities of Year 6 pupils who sit SATs. 11+ passes in different years can range between 2 and 6 pupils out of a class of 30. This has a significant effect on SATs results.

- Coupled with this is the fact that St Mary's is located in Swanley, one of the most disadvantaged communities in Kent. It has a mobile population, including 50% Roma traveller families, and high incidences of parent illiteracy.

- Unlike many neighbouring schools in more affluent communities, the school does not run extended school activities for SATs coaching.

- The school's contextual value added (CVA) results are in the top 10% of similar neighbourhood schools; the school received acknowledgement for its commitment to BLP from Ofsted.

In this form the evidence clearly indicates that, over time, all schools' SATs results improved after starting BLP. The rate of improvement of all schools was better than the corresponding national average rate for the same period.

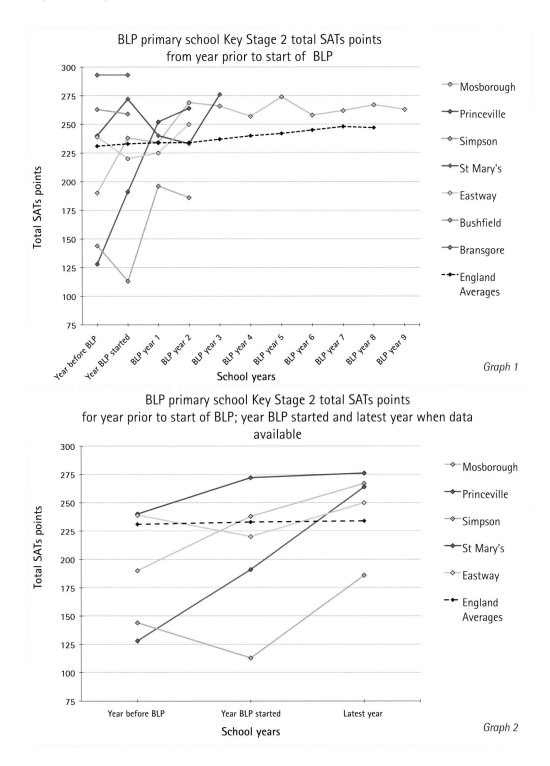

Graph 1

Graph 2

Secondary schools

Graph 3 below shows the percentages of pupils who obtained 5 or more GCSE Grades A*–C from the 9 BLP participating secondary schools from the year prior to the start of BLP to 2010. The graph also shows average percentages for English secondary schools for the same period. Clearly, GCSE performance at Dr Challoner's Grammar School and Westcliff High School for Girls has not changed since the introduction of BLP as their annual performance is consistently 99% or 100%. Interviews with school leaders revealed that, for these high-achieving schools, their primary motivation for introducing BLP was paradoxically to overcome pupil dependence on an 'exam results' focused curriculum and on 'outstanding' classroom teaching. Both schools were increasingly concerned that their 'intelligent' and 'exam successful' pupils tended to be passive learners and often struggled to apply their knowledge and capabilities in situations other than those familiar to them in school. In contrast, the newly appointed senior management team at George Pindar Community Sports College introduced BLP specifically to raise pupil attainments and avoid special measures. Graph 3 shows that since the introduction of BLP the school has consistently achieved national standards.

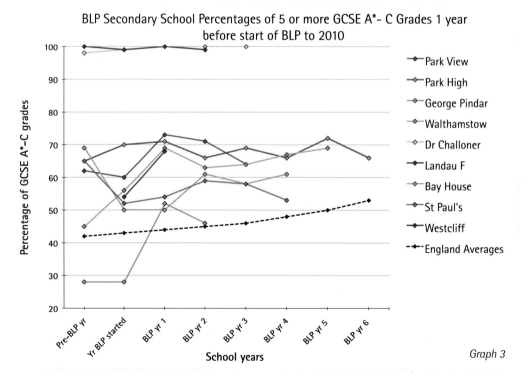

BLP Secondary School Percentages of 5 or more GCSE A*- C Grades 1 year before start of BLP to 2010

Graph 3

The A*–C percentage is a relatively crude measure of a school's performance. A more sensitive and revealing indicator is the school's total GCSE points score, and these results are shown in Graph 4. This more valid account of the impact of BLP on GCSE exam performance shows that exam performance in all schools improved following the introduction of BLP, albeit at different rates. (The complete England Average total GCSE point scores are not available but the scores for 2004, 2005 and 2007 are 336, 347 and 374 respectively, suggesting a slower rate of improvement than for BLP schools.) Even the high-achieving Dr Challoner's and Westcliff showed improvements on this measure. The table of secondary school Ofsted ratings (page 253) shows that the two schools with the most improved total GCSE points scores, George Pindar and Westcliff, also showed significant improvements in Ofsted gradings.

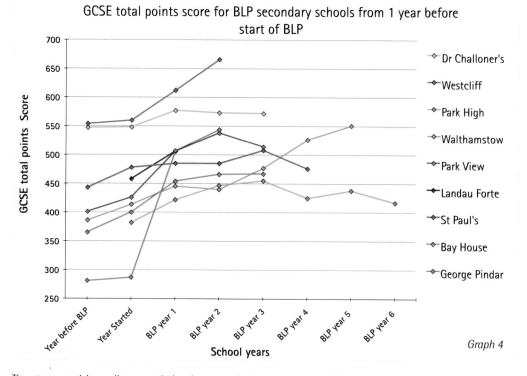

GCSE total points score for BLP secondary schools from 1 year before start of BLP

Graph 4

The strong and immediate correlation between the introduction of BLP and an increase in GCSE points scores in secondary schools—stronger even than in the primaries—seems somewhat surprising. There are more teachers to convince that BLP adds value to pupil learning, and we have found that some subject departments take more convincing than others. There may also be greater perceived risks in a secondary school, especially in ones that are 'performing well', as the fear of a sudden deterioration in performance is real. Set against this, however, our interviews reveal very high levels of commitment of secondary senior leadership teams, often led by a headteacher acting as a BLP champion, to implement change. All the BLP secondary schools in our sample have given priority to staff training in BLP and have established highly motivated steering groups to promote systemic and cultural change throughout the school. Additionally, giving priority to data feedback, staff mentoring, regular cycles of review and building relationships with other BLP schools may all have contributed to these unexpected findings.

A remarkable effect

One example of the effect of BLP on pupils' exam performance was reported by Park View Community School in Chester-le-Street, County Durham. On 25th January 2010, England's biology A-level students sat the first of their two exam papers. The following day thousands of these students launched an on-line protest saying that the exam was unfair, and over 3,000 students sent furious messages to a Facebook group about the exam set by AQA. Pupils described the exam as a disgrace, saying it bore no resemblance to specimen papers and feared it could jeopardise their chances of a university place. One student said:

> ' I'm actually more upset than angry, I've worked so hard and need an A to get into the university I've applied for, no chance of that now, thanks AQA for potentially ruining my life with your ridiculous paper!'
>
> (*Guardian* 26 January 2010).

But interestingly there were no complaints from A-level biology students at Park View, who wondered what all the fuss was about! They had studied and prepared for the exam using BLP principles. They understood deeply the need to persist in the face of difficulty, to try another tack if their first one failed, to take time to reflect on their learning, and to stay calm and make best use of whatever they already knew. The biology staff at the school had ensured that their students were able to apply their subject knowledge and understanding to any possible set of exam questions.

The students acknowledged that the paper was challenging, with many unfamiliar elements, but they had made intelligent attempts at all the questions; demonstrating, according to their teachers, remarkable resilience and resourcefulness under difficult circumstances. When the exam results were published, the students found that they achieved among the highest marks of all schools in the country. 42% of Park View pupils obtained an A grade on this paper compared with 22% of students in similar schools and 27% of students nationally. Pupils achieving A to C Grades at Park View were 77% against 55% for similar schools and 60% for all schools. Interestingly, in the same paper in January 2011, 89% of Park View pupils achieved A to C grades against 53% in similar schools and 59% in all schools. This highlights success with a broader spread of ability ranges than just A grade students. The school's specific objective has been to improve the performance of middle-ability students using BLP.

2 Inspection reports

If BLP were jeopardising, or even damaging, pupils' levels of attainment, we would expect that to show up in Ofsted reports. So checking how BLP schools have fared in their inspection from before they introduced BLP to afterwards is useful. In the tables on page 253, we have listed these gradings for the BLP schools where the relevant data has been available. You will see that there is no evidence of decline or concern, in fact quite the reverse. The introduction of BLP is quite often associated with improved grading by the inspectors.

What does
Ofsted think?

But this is, again, a rather crude measure. It would be more interesting to see whether the inspectors, trained to be impartial and perceptive observers of schools, have seen anything noteworthy about the learning-related attitudes and habits of the pupils in BLP schools. If they are impressed enough to comment on these features of young people's engagement with learning, that would constitute strong evidence for the positive effects of BLP. To assess this, we have trawled the body of schools' Ofsted reports since they began their BLP journey. In the panel on page 254, we have added a few of the kinds of comments that recur and underpin our bullet list below.

A crude measure

Some inspection reports are happy to name BLP explicitly, and to attribute gains to the use of BLP. Others prefer to speak about the approach in more generic terms, but the thrust of their comments is the same. Overall, we have found no instances where inspectors comment critically on the introduction of 'learning to learn' initiatives such as BLP. On the contrary, it seems to be overwhelmingly the case that they value the kinds of changes in young people that BLP aims deliberately to cultivate. In reports, as illustrated in the quotations on page 254, inspectors have repeatedly commented positively upon several different kinds of impact of BLP on the students, including:

Naming BLP?

- The systematic, tangible development of long-lasting, transferable, learning-related habits of mind such as resilience, initiative, independence, concentration, collaboration and overall confidence as learners

- Students coming to see themselves as lifelong learners, and being prepared effectively for 'real life' as well as for examinations and further study

- Students' levels of engagement and enthusiasm for even quite challenging learning
- The positive effect of learning confidence on students' behaviour in school
- Students' levels of articulacy and maturity in thinking and talking about their own learning, and their understanding of the learning process itself
- The involvement of students in organising, planning, conducting and evaluation their own learning (and a concomitant reduction in formulaic, over-controlled or worksheet-based teaching)
- Students' ready ability to offer examples of how BLP-type teaching helps them learn more effectively both in and out of school
- Students' involvement in the development of whole-school approaches to more powerful learning
- A positive effect on staff planning, learning and collaboration, as well as on the students

A cautionary tale

As a footnote to this discussion of Ofsted inspections, we would like to remind you of the words of Michael Whitworth, Principal of Wren Academy in North London, which we quoted in Chapter 3. When the inspectors came to call, a number of teachers retreated into more conventional ways of teaching that did not accurately reflect the BLP ethos of the school. But the students gave the game away. Michael recalls that the inspectors said, in effect, 'Hang on a minute: there's a mismatch here. We're seeing predominantly quite defensive lessons, not much risk-taking. But your children are talking a completely different game! The teaching we are seeing can't be representative of what the children are getting!' And this discrepancy prompted the inspectors to take a deeper look at the culture of the school as a whole—and to improve their evaluation as a result.

Ofsted grades of secondary schools that participated in the BLP review

School	Year BLP introduced	Date of Ofsted Report	Pre-BLP Ofsted grade	Post-BLP Ofsted grade
George Pindar Community Sports College	2006	12/06 & 07/10	Satisfactory	Good
Park View Community School	2007	04/08	Good	Good
St Paul's Catholic School	2006	01/06 & 09/08	Outstanding	Outstanding
Park High School	2004	03/06 & 02/09	Good	Good and Outstanding
Walthamstow School for Girls	2005	04/07	Outstanding	Outstanding
Dr Challoner's Grammar School	2007	11/07	Outstanding	N/A
Bay House School	2006	04/08	Good	Good
Westcliff High School Girls	2008	09/08 & 11/10	Satisfactory	Outstanding
Landau Forte College	2009	10/08	Outstanding	N/A

Ofsted grades of primary and infant schools that participated in the BLP review

School	Year BLP introduced	Date of Ofsted Report	Pre-BLP Ofsted grade	Post-BLP Ofsted grade
Princeville Primary School	2007	07/07 & 09/09	Satisfactory	Good
Eastway Primary School	2008	03/07 & 07/10	Satisfactory	Good
Simpson School	2007	01/05 & 03/10	Special measures	Satisfactory
St Mary's CE Primary School	2007	01/07 & 12/09	Good	Good
Nayland Primary School	2006	10/05 & 01/09	Outstanding	Outstanding
Bushfield School	2009	03/08 & 11/10	Good	Good
Bransgore CofE Primary School	2009	01/08	Outstanding	N/A
Mosborough Primary School	2001	06/06 & 02/09	Good	Good

A selection of comments from Ofsted reports

'Pupils have a highly developed knowledge of themselves as learners, become confident and want to do well...'
Nayland Primary School (Outstanding, October 2008)

'In many lessons, careful attention is given to encouraging the development of independence, whether this be simply in collecting resources or in tackling problems.'
Christchurch Primary School, Bradford-on-Avon (Good, October 2001)

'Pupils display high levels of self-awareness and reflection... An emphasis on developing skills for learning promotes their independence and equips them very well for teamwork...'
Bushfield School, Milton Keynes (Good, June 2010)

'One pupil said, 'If it's easy, it will be boring', thus reflecting the school's ethos and the collective drive for continuing improvement...'
Cannon Lane First School (Outstanding, September 2008)

'Pupils share the vision of school leaders that education is about the development of wider skills and attributes as well as excellent academic.'
Wren Academy (Outstanding progress, March 2010)

'Parents report favourably on the growing confidence of their children, and the development of skills that prepare students for the world of work is exemplary... Students' enthusiasm for learning makes a major contribution... they work cooperatively with each other and achieve well.'
Park High School, Harrow (Outstanding, May 2009)

'Pupils with special educational needs and/or disabilities have particularly benefited from being trusted to learn more independently.'
Eastway Primary School, Wirral (Good, June 2010)

'Pupils are willing to take risks in their learning... various groups in the school take very active roles in leadership, for example the Eco-squad and the Student Leaders.'
Wren Academy (Outstanding progress, March 2010)

'Their insights into themselves as learners are quite extraordinary... Perhaps the most remarkable feature of pupils' achievement is that they have a very firm grasp of how to learn... Pupils have a wonderful preparation for life in the future.'
St Vigor and St John Primary, Somerset (Outstanding, February 2007)

3   External evaluations

Formal inspections are not the only source of external evaluation of the effects of BLP. Over the years, a number of schools, colleges, local authorities and 'education action zones' using the BLP framework have commissioned independent evaluations of the effectiveness of the approach. These have been extremely valuable to us, being both broadly reassuring and also very useful in helping us to develop the approach. To give a flavour of these evaluations, and the results they reported, we give summaries of five of them: the Bristol Education Action Zone, Solihull and Newport Local Authorities, Luton Sixth Form College, and St James School, Exeter. As you will see, several common messages and issues emerge.

Bristol Education Action Zone project (2005)

In 2003, several schools in Bristol Education Action Zone (BrEAZ) decided to adopt a BLP approach to raising pupils' attainment, attendance and attitude. Schools in BrEAZ had three times the national average of children on Free School Meals and high levels of unauthorised absence and of underachievement. The project ran from June 2003 to February 2005. Joint funding from the Esmée Fairbairn Foundation and the DfES Innovations Fund allowed teachers to be trained in BLP, and also supported an independent evaluation of the project by Professor Joan Whitehead and colleagues at the University of the West of England (UWE).[3] Using both qualitative and quantitative methods, they monitored perceptions of BLP by staff and students, factors affecting the success of implementation, and the effect of BLP on students' attendance, attitudes and achievement.

The most common reaction from classroom teachers was that BLP offered a congenial framework within which to bring together a range of approaches with which they were familiar—Emotional Literacy, Learning Styles, SEAL, Thinking Skills and so on. One said,

Brings a range of initiatives together

> 'It's put the icing on the cake. It's pulled all the strings together. It's not totally brand new but at the same time it's not old either. It's made it all clearer.'

The flexibility of the BLP framework was also attractive to many of the teachers. They appreciated the fact that they were encouraged to think about how to put it into practice and 'make it their own'. One of them summed it up like this:

> 'What I've learned from BLP is that it's not about having a strategy that you're going to use year in, year out. The whole point of BLP is that you evolve what is right for the children you are with...'

The effect of BLP on pupils' performance in test situations was noted by several teachers. Julian Swindale observed that BLP children were significantly more resourceful and resilient under examination conditions than those who were not used to BLP.

> 'The maths SATs paper this year had lots of reasoning. The class did brilliantly at those questions... even children who would not previously have attempted them. All the children who've been doing BLP attempted every question from all sorts of angles, even though they might not have got the right answer. The children were much freer, much more courageous. And if they don't find a solution one way they'll find another solution some other way'
>
> Julian Swindale, Ashley Down Infant School, Bristol

And he further commented

> 'I had a very able mathematician arrive in the class, but every time she saw a question she couldn't do she said "I can't do it; I've not been taught it in my last school," and put a line through the question.'

Only a few of the schools involved were able to gather statistically analysable self-report questionnaire data from their pupils. However, the data that was gathered showed a general increase in all of the four R's across the time course of the intervention, with reflectiveness (not surprisingly) showing the largest proportionate increase. Without properly constituted control groups, though, it is hard to show that this does not represent a general Hawthorne Effect rather than specific increase in self-reported learning power. There is a good deal of testimony from teacher interviews in the report (such as the quote above), however, to suggest that observable improvements have taken place in the intelligence and persistence with which pupils tackle problems, and the fluency with which they talk about their learning both to themselves and with each other.

Observable improvements in persistence and learning talk

St James School, Exeter (2006)

In September 2006, St James School in Exeter implemented a course called Learning for Life (L4L) for Year 7 students based closely on the BLP framework of capacities. During the second half of the following Spring Term, the school commissioned two researchers from the University of Exeter Graduate School of Education to evaluate the success of the programme, mainly through questionnaires and focus group interviews conducted with groups of students, staff and parents. Their overall conclusion was that

> 'there is strong evidence that the lessons are developing students' ability to learn and to reflect on that learning, and that their experience in L4L lessons is having a beneficial effect elsewhere in the curriculum and, for some, in their life outside school.'

Involve all teachers

Reflecting the lessons we have learned about leading the implementation of BLP, which we discussed in Chapter 8, the researchers noted that the impact of the stand-alone course would have been significantly greater if 'more members of staff had been included in the planning of L4L lessons to improve the general understanding of staff' and if 'other teachers reinforced the L4L vocabulary and learning approaches in their own subject areas'. We have consistently found that such stand-alone courses built on BLP principles can contribute to the effectiveness of a broader culture change programme, but cannot create that shift by themselves.

Newport (2006)

In Wales, Newport Council supported the development of BLP across the whole authority. A report to the Council in July 2006 notes:

> 'Building Learning Power is an initiative that is having a positive effect in 38 schools in Newport. It helps pupils become better learners in and out of school and there is evidence that it is improving resilience and teamwork in classrooms. It helps all children, especially those who used to lose heart when 'stuck'. BLP is an important new way of increasing pupil improvement and inclusion... The majority of the teachers who have taken part in the initiative so far have reported a significant change in pupils' attitudes and approach to learning in a relatively short time. Classrooms have been transformed and children as young as Reception are starting to take ownership of their own learning.... Several teachers comment that the different thing about BLP is that it has an effect on absolutely **all** the children leading to a more positive working environment.'

BLP works for all pupils

Solihull (2008)

After two years of working with BLP, twelve schools—ten primaries and two secondaries—in Solihull were subject in 2008 to an independent evaluation commissioned by the local authority. Overall, the initiative had been well-received. In every school 'it was clear that BLP engagement had made an observable difference to the learning environment, pupil confidence and attitudes towards learning'. Many of the schools said that 'their end of Key Stage outcomes had shown improvement since they had engaged with BLP', although hard evidence of a causal link was difficult to come by. The evaluation noted strong evidence for the following changes that were observable across schools:

Strong evidence for a range of changes

- Pupils' perseverance in the face of difficulty has improved markedly. They are more likely to see mistakes as a natural part of learning and not to worry if they get things wrong to start with. One secondary student remarked, 'If learning is hard, that means it's at your level'. A younger child said, 'I used to cry when I couldn't do my work. I don't any more.'

- Pupils show greater interest in the process of learning, and in how their BLP capacities can help them in out-of-school activities, and—especially in secondary schools—in their lives after they leave school. One said 'The 4 R's will help us when we leave school'. Another said: 'As we get older we'll depend on learning to learn more'.

- Students show greater collaboration and have learned naturally to coach each other.

- The lower-achieving students particularly have seemed to benefit in terms of confidence, perseverance and their interest in 'how to get better'.

- Classroom environments have changed to stimulate students' resourcefulness and independence. Resources are more available and pupils encouraged to make use of them as needed.

- Staff conversation and planning has shown a shift from 'teaching' and 'behaviour' to a greater focus on pupils' learning.

Overall messages

BLP knits together different initiatives

By and large, these evaluations speak for themselves. Though some are initially sceptical, teachers at all levels of education generally find the ideas behind BLP appealing, practical and effective. They see BLP not as a whole new way of doing things, but as an accessible and coherent framework that enables them to knit together a wide range of different initiatives. There is widespread agreement that talking to students about the way they learn, identifying the different 'learning muscles', and designing activities with these in mind, has a beneficial effect on their engagement, attitudes and attainment.

Pupils become highly articulate about their learning

From four-year-olds to sixth-formers, and from high-achievers to those with identified learning difficulties, many pupils themselves clearly welcome the opportunity to focus on the process of learning, and to strengthen the habits of mind that enable them to learn more effectively. Pupils can become highly articulate about their own learning, and are able to give examples, from inside school and out, of how a greater awareness of their own learning helps them learn more successfully. Some of the learning muscles are more obviously relevant and accessible than others, however. And some of the comments hint at gender differences which, if they are substantiated by further research, will clearly help us to target BLP more effectively.

4 Action research projects

Over the roughly ten years of BLP's life, we have been lucky enough to get support from several local authorities, including Cardiff and Oxfordshire,[4] for around 250 teachers to carry out action research projects in their classrooms and schools on many different aspects of the BLP framework. In addition, we have collected dozens of reports from teachers who have carried out BLP-type investigations for their masters' dissertations or BLP Foundation Courses, or who were simply keen to try out some new ideas in their own classrooms.

These teachers' willingness to help us test out our conjectures, and to develop practical tools and techniques to help pupils develop their learning-oriented habits of mind, have greatly enriched and strengthened the BLP framework.[5] Such small-scale, classroom-based projects enable us to explore the fine grain of BLP in a way that the larger-scale evaluations which we have just described often do not. Many of the 'seeds' and 'tools' that now make up the practical resource base of BLP began life in the classrooms of teachers who, having 'got the BLP bug', started to invent and trial new ways of building learning power for themselves. We have found that teachers who want to build their pupils' love of learning also tend to be imaginative, inquisitive and experimental in their own lives as well. We think it is no coincidence that John Hattie's review of research, which we outline in Chapter 1, links '*teachers who are learners about their own teaching*' with '*students who become their own teachers*'.

We have used a good many of these action research reports to illustrate particular points in earlier parts of the book. Here we describe a few more.

Cardiff (2001–2005)

Over the course of four years, the Cardiff School Service funded and supported a total of 168 action research projects on BLP across all phases of education.[6] Some of them gave rise to provenly successful tools for building the learning power of young children—such as Eleri Miles's now famous toy hamster Hattie. Hattie—introduced to the reception children at Caerau Infants as a 'powerful learner' in her own right—was also the guardian of a cupboard full of things the children might be able to make use of if they were stuck, or bored. Hattie helped a target group 'become more confident and independent', and they were also 'seen accessing toys independently... and working with other children with a new-found sense of self-worth and achievement.

Kevin Thomas's Year 6 pupils at Peter Lea Primary School benefited from direct tuition and conversation about their listening skills. Both independent observations of the children, and their self-report questionnaires, confirmed that, over the course of a few weeks, '*they have now created an atmosphere where their learning has become enhanced by their listening skills. The Headteacher, fellow teachers, supply teachers and myself have all noticed huge improvement in the children and the classroom climate.*'

Lorraine Smith worked with her very passive Year 6 pupils to build up their 'questioning muscles'. After some modelling and discussion about different types of question, the children in pairs had to prepare a presentation, and the rest of the class asked them questions about what they had presented. Lorraine rated their questions in terms of type and quality, and noted a significant improvement. Lorraine presented her findings to the rest of the staff, and as a result, 'all teachers are designing an action research project looking at enhancing students' questioning across the curriculum and across the Key Stages.'

Oxfordshire

In 2003–4, the Esmée Fairbairn Trust generously supported a project with Oxfordshire County Council called 'Playing for Life', in which some 70 early years teachers carried out action research investigations into how they could better support the development of the '4 R's' in young children. The settings varied from rural to urban and from centres for very young children with profound multiple learning difficulties to high-achieving primary schools. A variety of measuring tools were used to assess any change in the children, including the Positive Attitudes to Learning Scale (PALS) and the Child Involvement Scale from the Effective Early Learning (EEL) Project. The project was conceived and orchestrated by the Senior Adviser for Early Years, Julie Fisher, and overseen by two academics, Dr Alison Price from Oxford Brookes University and Dr Tony Eaude from Oxford University. The projects were written up and published by the National Primary Trust in 2006.[7]

Measuring tools

A number of findings emerged. Giving children language like 'stickability' or 'using your learning muscles' was shown to be effective in enhancing their resilience and resourcefulness. Designing opportunities where there were very clear expectations about, for example, how long they would have to stick with their chosen activity, helped them, as one child put it, to 'strengthen my learning stamina'. Adult modelling of the 4 R's also seemed to rub off on the children's own attitudes to learning. As a result of one study, Denise Walters and Laura Hockling at John Hampden Primary School in Thame concluded,

Modelling learning

> 'We must model resilience to our children. We need to think about how we react when things go wrong, and show elements of frustration and then triumph as we work through how to make it right.'

The opportunity to 'play' with more difficult materials like numbers and sums, before being taught how to 'do them right', resulted in children becoming more confident, resilient and imaginative mathematicians, according to Amanda Smith of Appleton Primary School. She changed her teaching to allow the Year 1 children extended periods of time to play with activities of their own choosing. Assessing the children after a half term of this new way of working, she found that 'all six of the target children

Exceeding expectations

showed increases in the area of concentration, curiosity and perseverance'. Parents reported children volunteering to do number work and additions at home, and also commented on their children 'who had been timid but now talked about, enjoyed, and wanted to do maths at home'. One of Amanda's main findings was that

> 'The children exceeded expectations by doing [choosing for themselves] work that would not have been set for this age group.'

And giving children more opportunities to plan and manage their own learning—provided there was enough adult support to ensure that things turned out encouragingly in the end—increased the children's perseverance and resourcefulness. Karen Braund, a Year 1 teacher at Barley Hill Primary School, also in Thame, for example, concluded:

> 'The children have become more able to be independent learners. They are able to stick at a task. I have seen them using skills that they have practised and transfer them to other areas. In the 'writing factory' they will [now] often come back to something that they have done before, either to finish it or to refine it in some way. The children are more confident. They will talk about their own learning and they are more able to help each other. They encourage each other and suggest improvements...'

Some of the project also highlighted adult behaviour that seemed *not* to enhance the 4 R's. Pat Bolton and Sue Vermes at Headington Nursery School, for example, observed that

> 'The least successful interventions were when adults involved themselves uninvited by trying to talk with children who were already demonstrating high involvement levels.'

Stay away

While Deborah Johnson at Aston and Cote C of E Primary School discovered that 'intervention in the form of "Why don't you try this?" seems to stop the children thinking and imagining [for themselves]'. In trying to be helpful, teachers can unintentionally disrupt children's existing powers of resilience and resourcefulness. BLP teachers often ask themselves, 'What's the *least* I can do to get this child's learning going again?' rather than 'How can I use this as an opportunity to teach them something I want them to know?'

Individual teacher research projects

To conclude these illustrations of the kinds of enquiries that BLP teachers carry out, and to balance the predominance of examples from primary schools in the two local authority projects, here are a couple of examples that illustrate how BLP ideas are being explored in different areas of the secondary school curriculum. Many projects that might have appeared in this section have already been described earlier in the book.

Some projects from secondary schools

Malcolm Lay is a highly-qualified football coach—Head Coach of the Milton Keynes Dons Football Academy for 15/16-year-olds—who teaches PE and sports at Denbigh School. He focused on a Year 12 group from the Football Academy programme who were aiming to get a BTEC Diploma in Sport. Malcolm homed in on the learning muscles of 'attentive noticing', 'reasoning', 'imitating' and 'distilling', to see if his students could boost their learning by watching and discussing video footage of their own training sessions and practice games. He was able to assess their progress by comparing the school's target grades for each student with the current 'working at' levels which they were displaying. Working with these older, but not necessarily academically oriented, students within the BLP framework, Malcolm found that most of the students far exceeded their target grades, with 'much of the work that was produced being at a good Level 3 standard'. Three students with poor GCSE grades, who were predicted to gain Merit at BTEC, were found to be working at Distinction level. Overall, Malcolm concludes his report:

> 'The most valuable part of the process [of the research] was witnessing learners develop their personal skills and qualities. As well as becoming increasingly adaptable, resourceful and resilient, the whole group were noticeably more self-confident in communicating their findings [in presentations]'.

Drama at Park High

Philippa Long teaches Drama at Park High School in Harrow. Her results are good, but quite a high proportion of her Year 8 students—especially those of Asian origin—have imbibed the strong belief that school is mainly about getting good grades in high-status subjects, and 'don't see the point' of drama. Philippa wondered whether this attitude would be affected if she made the BLP learning capacities more explicit and visible in her lessons. For example, she had them reflect on the learning capacities which they had been using in each lesson, and then discuss where, in out-of-school life, these skills would be of use. She monitored the students' achievement levels, and gave them an attitude questionnaire before and after her trial period (lasting half a term). She did the same with a control class who did not have the same emphasis on BLP, but who were otherwise taught in the same way.

Increasing progress

To her satisfaction, the BLP group showed significantly greater engagement with and valuing of Drama at the end of the half-term. But more to her surprise, they also made twice as much progress in terms of their achievement. 78% of the BLP group progressed by a least two sub-levels, whereas in the control group only 38% made the same degree of progress. Philippa's conclusion?

'Although this has been a relatively short-term study… clear differences can be seen between the attitudes of students at the start and the end of the Scheme. The inclusion and explicit use of BLP within Drama lessons has led to an increased interest on the part of the students, a greater respect and recognition for the subject in terms of skill development, and has had a real and noticeable effect on assessment grades.'

5   Students' perceptions

In the panel overleaf we show just a small selection of student comments that have been collected over the years.

6   Teachers' and other people's perceptions

Many of our sources of evidence—the Ofsted reports, the independent evaluations, and the action research studies—have made use of the impressions and perceptions of school teachers and leaders, and the students themselves. As part of our own commissioned evaluation, carried out by Dr Ian Millward, we also interviewed a large number of people about their impressions and experiences of BLP. Here we present a small sample of these impressions. They echo very strongly the perceptions that have emerged from the other data sources.

As BLP is a process of long-term culture change, many of our teachers were cautious about drawing conclusions about impact on their results. For many of them, it was simply 'too early to tell'. However, they are unequivocal in their view that BLP has had a positive impact on various aspects of students' attitudes and behaviour in school. The leadership team at Bushfield School in Milton Keynes, for example, noted a variety of shifts in the ways their children engage with learning.

'Lesson observations have recorded impact on learning, engagement and behaviour. For example, the way children learn together has been transformed. Real collaboration now takes place and children are increasingly articulate about what collaboration involves, and aware of the different roles they and their peers can take in groups. They can—and spontaneously do—reflect upon their group's effectiveness with increasing insight, and, as a result, stay more focused upon the task and are better at resolving conflict for themselves.

Transforming collaboration

'Their concentration has measurably improved. (Children self-assess regularly on their ability to stay focused, and this data is collated over the whole-school.) One day I (the headteacher) walked into a Year 3 classroom. The room was absolutely silent, except for some gentle background music. The children were engrossed in writing

Improving concentration

263

Students' perceptions

(Teacher: How do you learn best?) 'We learn from our brothers and we learn from our mistakes and we learn from each other.'

(Sara, 6)

'Before I was very independent, and much preferred working on my own. But now I've discovered the benefits of working with others as well. It's made me more of an all-rounder.'

(Hannah, 9)

'BLP is quite hard because you have to think about yourself. But it's not impossible—you really can change your habits!'

(Ellie, 8)

'BLP has helped me to see that when things change, it is mostly really interesting! I feel a lot more enthusiastic about going up to secondary school than I think I would have before.'

(Emma, 11)

'In my old school they just gave you harder and harder worksheets. But here they really stretch you to learn in different ways. You get lots of encouragement, so you learn to keep going and 'dig deep' when things get difficult. Now I always like to see if I can take things one step further.'

(Tom, 15)

'If something's hard you don't want to say 'Oh this is hard, this is hard, I'll just skip this.' You try because the best thing is, if you don't try what's the point? Because when you grow up you might come to some answer you'll still not know, so you can't skip it then.'

(Daneisha, 6)

'In football, you have to use your empathy muscles. It makes you more aware of other people, and makes you a better team player. And BLP has helped me stop and think what I'm going to do with the ball. I'm more tactical.'

(Alex, 10)

'It doesn't matter what my friend has done or got right, my effort is what is important.'

(Emma, 6)

'BLP has helped me be a better learner at home. Like if you've been focusing on one of the learning muscles in school, when I go home I think, 'How could I use that here?' When I go to swimming club, I think, maybe I could try harder, or ask more questions.'

(Madeleine, 12)

'I am a lot more resilient when working in my Big Write now—I used to give up quite easily, but now I really stick at it.'

(Ali, 8)

'I find it easier to describe how things work—BLP has made my mind clearer.'

(Oscar, 10)

independently and intently. No one stirred or even turned to look as I walked in, so I said "Hello, you all look busy. What are you doing?" One child turned slowly from his writing and said, most politely, "We are being absorbed, Miss Curtis, and you are being a distraction"!

'We have also noticed, in our conversations with children, that they are increasingly making links between their learning inside school and their learning outside.'

Several of our school leaders commented on the fact that, though the gains in pupils' confidence and sophistication as learners are hugely valuable, the journey is not without its difficulties. The headteacher of St Mary's Primary School in Swanley, Kent, for example, commented that, because approaches like BLP are not yet mainstream, it can take a degree of courage to adopt them wholeheartedly. She said:

It takes courage to adopt

'Although Ofsted recognise its [BLP's] value, it doesn't yet have the Secretary of State's seal of approval which, in my view, has made the last two years sometimes feel a bit risky. But we are fully sold on the big picture of BLP—learning should be a preparation for the challenges and opportunities of life—and so much of it isn't! BLP changes attitudes and has the potential to change lives. It empowers staff and pupils alike. It enthuses every professional who sees it 'live'.'

Again, the headteacher at Bushfield School emphasised the fact that BLP is asking teachers to change their habits, and this takes time and dedication. She said,

'BLP isn't quick or easy—it takes resilience! Teachers have to unlearn some of their old habits, and take time to consolidate new ones. BLP is actually as much a learning journey—one of individual and collective self-discovery—for teachers as it is for students.'

A journey of individual and collective self-discovery

She also pointed out a hazard with BLP that other schools should be ready for: once the pupils begin to discover and develop their learning power, and their ability to plan and manage their own learning, it can be impossible to go back.

'We have found that pupils, once they get a taste for BLP, become more demanding of quality learning experiences which really stretch them, and in which they have a say.'

Pupils become more demanding of quality learning experiences

Other schools, both primary and secondary, have noted the same hunger amongst the majority of students to take charge of their learning, and to take on more and more demanding challenges.

Gordon Hamilton, the headteacher of Mosborough Primary School in Sheffield, commented on the particular value of BLP for children who are starting from a low level of self-confidence as learners. In his words,

'We have found that BLP encompasses all areas of learning—academic, practical and social. We really do feel that "The 4 R's" can equip our children for life. Especially, children who regard themselves as poor learners can be helped to realise they are good at learning in other ways, which improves their confidence to "have a go" at things they would naturally shy away from.'

Perceptions from secondary schools

But what about secondary schools—especially those that are full of bright, articulate, high-achieving young people? Do they find any benefit of BLP, or do they agree with Gordon Hamilton, that its main value is to the lower-ability pupils? As the attainment graphs at the beginning of this chapter showed, such schools may have little room to show any improvement in their results. At Dr Challoner's Grammar School, for example, close to 100% of students gain five good GCSEs including English and Maths. So—confident that BLP has not *jeopardised* their levels of attainment—they must be looking for other kinds of benefits. This is how the headteacher puts it:

'As a high performing specialist school and a selective boys' grammar, the impact of BLP on results will be marginal and extremely difficult to measure with any certainty. However, we have seen a real impact of BLP on the 'qualitative' nature of our output, such as Year 13 UCAS personal statements, students' own reflections on their learning, and the involvement of students in key decision making in the school. Boys' confidence as learners has improved, especially in the younger year groups, as has the ability to discuss and reflect upon their learning and identify their own areas for development.'

Twin outcomes

The head of another high-achieving school, Wren Academy, puts it slightly differently. He sees the twin outcomes of good results on the one hand, and growing self-awareness and maturity on the other, not as separate and parallel, but as closely intertwined. He said:

'BLP is working. Ofsted judge the academic progress made by our students to be greater than that of students in like schools. Our students are achieving very highly and BLP has been a central part of their experience from the beginning. There is substantial evidence, from Ofsted and other visitors, that our students are exceptionally articulate and confident learners. They have a maturity and an understanding of their learning that is quite unusual. They're really quite exceptional. And BLP is largely to thank for that.'

Improvements in behaviour

Some schools have also noticed improvements in students' general behaviour since they began their BLP journey. As always, it is risky to conclude a causal relationship, but there are some grounds to suspect that students who feel more confident and capable learners might be less inclined to drift off task or 'muck about' when they face difficulty. Landau Forte College in Derby, for example, noted that:

> 'Behaviour has improved. Referrals to our Learning Support Centre are significantly down, freeing up time for LSAs to be in learning sessions.'

Other secondary leaders commented on the beneficial effects of BLP on their staff, and the way they learn and plan together, as much as the ultimate benefit to students.

> 'Overall impact of BLP in our school:
> - greater communication between teachers
> - better cooperation and learning through peer observation (with less fear of peer observation)
> - improved lesson planning sheet, emphasising the learning 'stretch' that students will experience
> - improved learning experience in the classroom'
> Dr Paul Hayman, headteacher, Westcliff High School for Girls

Reaction from parents

Overall, our schools have found that any initial scepticism on parents' part usually gives way to support and enthusiasm. In a focus group at Bransgore C of E Primary School, parents talked about the differences they had noticed in their children since joining the school. One said,

> 'Mollie lacked confidence in herself at her old school, but here she has become so much more happy and enthusiastic. She'll try things now that she wouldn't have dared to before.'

Another said,

> 'Here, there is a real focus on empowering the kids. They learn to handle degrees of freedom and responsibility that I would not have thought possible. They learn to enjoy stretching themselves, and they grow in their confidence and maturity—you can just see it.'

And again, the same kinds of development are also being observed, and valued, at Dr Challoner's. Their review stated that,

> 'Parental reaction, through information evenings, has been extremely positive, as has that of governors and other visitors to the school. Many are intrigued and enjoy visiting the school to see the ways in which the BLP message is communicated.'

The perceptions, small-scale enquiries, larger evaluations and Ofsted reports quoted above are drawn from across the ten years we have been working with schools. The beneficial and sometimes surprising results which they show are all due to the commitment, passion and interest of headteachers and teachers who are working to make the big ambition of BLP work.

Chapter 12

Taking stock and moving on

In this chapter we explore:

- our reflections on the BLP journey
- why BLP works
- the challenges ahead

In this final chapter we would like to offer some reflections on our journey with Building Learning Power so far, and a few thoughts about what the next steps might be.

We think we can say—and we hope, having got this far, you will agree with us—that BLP has been quite a success. Teachers and school leaders in a wide range of schools and colleges have found it to be practical and helpful in pursuing their own educational visions and values. It works in nurseries, primary and secondary schools, and in at least some sixth form and further education colleges. It seems to work with boys and girls, and with low, average and high-achieving pupils. It works in areas of considerable deprivation and in the 'leafy suburbs'. It works in Milton Keynes, Cardiff and the Isle of Man. And it works in Argentina and Chile, Australia and New Zealand, Thailand and Malaysia, and Abu Dhabi and Dubai. We have testimony from thousands of teachers in hundreds of schools that BLP has evolved into a set of ideas and practices that genuinely help them to provide what they consider to be the heart of twenty-first century education. But what is it about BLP, exactly, that has caught their attention—where other, superficially similar approaches, have not? What have we learned, from thousands of hours in schools, running workshops, and listening to teachers and their students, about what twenty-first century education can and should be, and how we can take practical steps—in the midst of all the real pressures and constraints—to move from 'here' to 'there'?

It works everywhere

The elements of BLP: why it works

BLP tries to be clear and precise in its aims. It has a well-articulated vision of education as a preparation for living in a turbulent world, where the major challenges are those of dealing with high levels of uncertainty, complexity, opportunity and responsibility. With our cultural emphases on the virtues of 'social mobility' and 'aspiration', with the choices and hazards afforded by digital technologies, with a daily plethora of conflicting images about how to live and what to value, and with the decline of traditional sources of stability and guidance: with all of this to cope with, young people need to be helped to learn how to think, imagine, persist, evaluate and collaborate. Where some other approaches are more broad and ambitious in the virtues they espouse, **BLP focuses on the life skills of learning.** We think that is the bit of the jigsaw puzzle that it is a school's business to concentrate on. Not everyone agrees with us, but many do; and at least we are clear about our goals.

Preparation for a turbulent world

But BLP is also about helping schools do what they are more used to doing: helping young people to gather information, understand concepts and do as well as possible in examinations. The trouble with more idealistic initiatives that don't address the 'standards agenda' is that they tend to be marginal.

They live *alongside* the mainstream concerns, either within a school, or as a separate 'alternative' school; they tend not to impact on the bulk of lessons, which continue to be seen as more 'important' or 'high status'. With its BOTH / AND philosophy, BLP tries to work new priorities into the mainstream thinking and functioning of a school. We believe that, unless that happens, initiatives about 'key competencies', 'character capabilities' or 'wider skills' are doomed to remain peripheral and ephemeral.

BLP tries to couch its messages in language that is congenial, accessible and appealing to students, parents and teachers. But we believe that the language is very important, and we have tried to make our vocabulary more vernacular, without losing its precision or rigour. Like us, some schools and local authorities have had to learn to be 'bilingual', using fancier or more formal language to persuade policy-makers of the seriousness and validity of the BLP approach, but translating that into a more accessible set of terms when talking to those on the ground whose understanding and support is crucial if the approach is going to take root. We have found that we are more likely to touch people's hearts and values, and thus get their buy-in, as well as their rational understanding, if we try to keep the language more straightforward. Some other people seem to think that you won't be taken seriously unless your publications look dull and your speech sounds pompous, but that is not our experience.

A congenial language

This brings us to another virtue of BLP: it is voluntary. It is not an 'initiative' that has been taken up by administrators and legislators and mandated. We mostly talk directly to schools—unless we find, as we sometimes do, an especially sympathetic local authority—because they can choose, in the light of their own values and priorities, whether BLP is for them. Schools decide for themselves whether they are going to buy the BLP books or go on some of the BLP courses, and we think that the fact that this puts them in the driving seat is a good thing. It is much harder to get the climate of curiosity and experimentation in a school—which is vital if deep change is to happen—if the school does not *like* and *own* the direction in which change is taking them. The history of educational innovation is littered with the withered remains of initiatives that were scattered abroad from 'on high', but which never took root.

It is voluntary

Many schools are attracted to BLP's blend of values, science and practicality—heart, head and hands, if you like. They respond to the passion and commitment of BLP, but also appreciate the hard-headed underpinnings from the learning sciences. Assuming we have read the research right, teachers and schools feel that BLP is underpinned by good, up-to-date thinking about the young mind, what it is capable of, and how it changes and develops. The thinking of the giants on whose shoulders BLP stands is of real interest to many schools, and they find that taking an interest in this research, and discussing its implications within the school, is a natural adjunct to the messages of BLP itself.

We think that one of BLP's attractions is the balance between the well-developed tools that we can offer schools, for designing and planning their own evolution, and the flexible and critical attitude which we encourage them to have towards those tools. We find that schools like to have their imaginations fired by practical illustrations and suggestions, and are grateful for the framework of the 'learning muscles', for example, that helps them think more clearly about the habits of mind they want their students to develop. But, once they have got their heads around the approach, they really welcome the encouragement to customise and adapt the tools and frameworks to their own situations. They like being treated as partners, with useful things to contribute, rather than as being simply told what to do. They have, many of them, had too much of that. So, more and more, we offer our experience to schools in 'could-be' rather than 'is' language. The risk is that schools may, inadvertently, use their discretion to introduce a 'lethal mutation'—a change that seems innocuous but is actually contrary to the spirit of BLP—and it does happen. But we think this risk is preferable to the complementary risk of trying to exercise too tight a control.

Schools often respond warmly to BLP's attempt to be comprehensive in its approach to learning, finding it a helpful umbrella under which they can gather a host of previously disparate initiatives such as SEAL, or the personal learning and thinking skills. It helps them develop a more coherent and sustainable model of their curriculum that integrates a range of different values and modifications. Instead of seeing the social and emotional aspects of learning as 'yet more things to be fitted in', BLP helps to weave such considerations into the daily life of lessons. When things are hived off or bolted on, their impact tends to be limited. The fact that BLP aims to be deep, coherent and sustained appeals to schools and teachers who have become fed up with approaches that they have come to see as piecemeal and superficial. And this reminds us of the point that many school leaders impressed on us about the importance of their *readiness* for something like BLP when they first met it. Consciously or unconsciously, they were already looking to go deeper. This means, inevitably, that BLP is not for everyone. Some schools, deep down, still only want a more efficient way of getting 'good results', or just like to collect badges and logos that they can put on their notepaper and home pages: these quickly tend to find BLP 'too hard', and move on. However, BLP is there for schools when they are ready to take widening their ambitions seriously, and make that jump into the twenty-first century.

Part of that deepening brings schools to the realisation that what is needed is not just a matter of changing teaching technique, or tinkering with the

Partners in the journey

An umbrella

timetable, but rather a change in culture at the level of the whole school, and habit change by everyone who works there. Part of what makes BLP appealing to schools who have reached this point is that it talks in those terms. Out of our years of working with schools, we have distilled useful things to say, not just about teaching methods, but about the way every aspect of a school can be adjusted to support those processes of habit and culture change. Small, concrete things like displaying more of pupils' work-in-progress, talking more about learning and less about work, re-thinking the nature of professional development and the role of learning assistants. Talking about all these facets of the life of a school (and many more) gives teachers and school leaders a host of ideas to try out that they might not have thought of on their own. We are able to tie many little adjustments, of many different kinds, into an overall vision of where a school is going, and how it is going to get there. And schools that are ready for the culture change approach are keen to collect these seeds of ideas, and go back and re-grow them in their own soil.

Seeds of ideas
to re-grow

Over the years, BLP has become something of a seed merchant, harvesting a broad range of examples and ideas from the innovating schools we work with, and helping to package and broadcast them more widely. Samples of these seeds have been scattered throughout this book, as you will have found. Many more can be found in our publications and online resources.

The final element of BLP that we should mention is the one that may provide our growth-point for the future. It is the attempt to connect what happens in school with the wider world in which young people live, and in which they will have to make their way as adults. About half will go on to college or university; about half will not. Some will make good use of the scholarly habits which their education cultivated in their working lives; a good many will benefit from their skill and pleasure in reading, their ability to write in different ways, and their real-world numeracy—but the niceties of essay-writing and equation-solving may not be of much use.

Connecting to
the wider world

Whatever their paths in life, however, their habits of determination, concentration, imagination and collaboration will certainly be of use. It is the job of twenty-first century schools not just to build those habits in the context of school, but to make sure they are transferred outside the school gates and used in the worlds of family, work and leisure. This means recruiting the interest of parents and employers in building learning power. We began to show how these relationships can be fostered in Chapter 10. But there is more researching and experimenting to do if we are to be sure that the skills of learning translate into real-life dispositions and attitudes. The job of building Building Learning Power continues. We would be very pleased if you were to join us in this most vital of explorations.

Transfer

Notes

Introduction

1. Guy Claxton (2002), *Building Learning Power: Helping Young People Become Better Learners,* TLO: Bristol.
2. Guy Claxton (2008), *What's the Point of School?: Rediscovering the Heart of Education,* OneWorld: Oxford.
3. Guy Claxton (1999), *Wise Up: The Challenge of Lifelong Learning,* Bloomsbury: London.
4. Bill Lucas and Guy Claxton (2010), *New Kinds of Smart: How the Science of Learnable Intelligence is Changing Education,* Open University Press: Maidenhead.
5. www.buildinglearningpower.com offers some routes in to the world of BLP schools.

Chapter 1

1. Bill Lucas and Guy Claxton (2009), *Wide Skills for Learning: What Are They, How Can They Be Cultivated, How Could They Be Measured, and Why Are They Important for Innovation?,* National Endowment for Science, Technology and the Arts: London.
2. Edexcel (2009), *Effective Education and Employment: A global perspective.* See http://www.eee-edexcel.com/Home
3. Signatories included Campbell Adamson, Lindsay Anderson, Ove Arup, Richard Attenborough, Peter Hall, Charles Handy, Jeremy Isaacs, Neil Kinnock, Claus Moser, and Lord and Lady Plowden—luminaries of the day from all walks of life.
4. Foresight Mental Capital and Well-being Project (2008), The Government Office for Science: London
5. Interestingly, the 'head learner' is more likely to be a girl in rural areas than in cities, where they seem more strongly socialised into deferring to the boys.
6. See http://www.ted.com/talks/sugata_mitra_shows_how_kids_teach_themselves.html
7. J.C. Chapman and G.S. Counts (1924), *Principles of Education,* Houghton Mifflin: Boston.
8. Originally: 'Any observed statistical regularity will tend to collapse once pressure is placed upon it for control purposes'.
9. Or, if 'number of visitors' becomes a museum's target, they start counting the couriers and electricians. A 2010 report by the Department for Education shows that, following the scrapping of Key Stage 2 Science tests, pupils' apparent levels of scientific understanding have dropped markedly. Alan Smithers, professor of education at Buckingham University, commented: 'When rewards and sanctions are attached to the test, teachers can [artificially] push up results simply by training children in the sorts of questions that will come up.' (*Daily Telegraph,* 11 August 2010; http://www.education.gov. uk/news/news/ks2-science-sample-test.) Duh!
10. Chart the emotional trajectory of Amy on August 19th as she (a) opens her envelope and discovers she has got the four A's she needed; (b) rings round her friends and discovers they have all got four A's; (c) goes down to school and finds that everyone in the school who sat four A-levels has got four A grades; (d) listens to the 6 o'clock news and finds that everyone in the country who sat four A-levels has got four A grades...
11. Andy Ross (2009), *Disengagement from education among 14–16 year olds,* National Centre for Social Research, DCSF Research Report RR187: London.
12. William Richardson (2010), in Bill Lucas, Guy Claxton and Rob Webster, *Mind the Gap: Research and Reality in Practical and Vocational Education,* Edge Foundation: London.
13. Ricky Gervais, interview with Bryan Appleyard, *Sunday Times,* 22 February 2009.
14. Carol Dweck (2006), *Mindset,* Ballantine: New York.
15. Telephone conversations with Guy Claxton, 2 July 2010. Both Alan and Mark were extremely generous with their time (for which I am most grateful) partly because they recognise what a serious and growing problem this is.
16. Robert Kegan (1994), *In Over Our Heads: The Mental Demands of Modern Life,* Harvard University Press: Cambridge, Massachusetts, and London.
17. Mihaly Csikszentmihalyi (2002), *Flow: The Psychology of Optimal Experience,* Rider: London.

Chapter 2

1. Guy Claxton (2002). See Note 1 to Introduction.
2. Guy Claxton (1999). See Note 3 to Introduction.

3. The phrase 'learning power' has now been taken up by a number of other authors and researchers who have put their own 'spin' on it: google 'learning power' to get an idea of the range of uses to which it has been put (not all of which we are comfortable with).

4. See Carol Dweck (2000), *Self-Theories: Their Role in Motivation, Personality and Development,* Psychology Press: New York; and the following.

5. Carol Dweck (2006), *Mindset: The New Psychology of Success,* Ballantine: New York.

6. Howard Gardner (1991), *The Unschooled Mind,* Basic Books: New York, p81. The 'seven' has become eight since this was written. See also Gardner (1983), *Frames of Mind,* Basic Books: New York.

7. John Hattie (2009), *Visible Learning: A Synthesis of Over 800 Meta-analyses Relating to Achievement,* Routledge: London.

8. David Perkins (1995), *Outsmarting IQ: The Emerging Science of Learnable Intelligence,* Free Press: New York.

9. David Perkins (2009), *Making Learning Whole: How Seven Principles of Teaching Can Transform Education,* Jossey-Bass: San Francisco.

10. Arthur L Costa and Bena Kallick, editors (2000), *Habits of Mind: A Developmental Series,* ACSD: Alexandria, Virginia. There are four titles in the series; Costa and Kallick are much more than just editors, being the joint authors of at least half of the total material. See also www.habits-of-mind.net

11. For more information on PEEL, see John Baird and Jeff Northfield (eds), (1992), *Learning from the PEEL Experience,* Monash University Press: Melbourne, Australia; and www.peelweb.org

12. We are drawing heavily in this section on three sources: Chris Watkins (2010), 'Learning, Performance and Improvement', International Network for School Improvement, *Research Matters,* 34; London; John Hattie, John Biggs and Nola Purdie (1996), 'Effects of learning skills interventions on student learning: a meta-analysis', *Review of Educational Research,* 66(2), 99–136; and John Hattie, op. cit.

13. Keith Topping (2006), 'PISA/PIRLS data on reading achievement: transfer into international policy and practice', *The Reading Teacher,* 59(6), 588–590.

14. Cheryl Flink, Ann Boggiano and Marty Barrett (1990), 'Controlling teaching strategies: undermining children's self-determination and performance', *Journal of Personality and Social Psychology,* 59(5), 916–924.

15. See Hattie, op. cit., p187.

16. A.R. McCrindle and C.A. Christiansen (1995), 'The impact of learning journals on metacognitive processes and cognitive processes and learning performances in science', *Learning and Instruction,* 5(3), 167–185. Quoted in Zoë Bonell's MEd dissertation, Institute of Education: London. We have also borrowed some of the children's quotes on page 264 from Zoë's dissertation. Many examples of the sophisticated use of such journals with primary children can be found at www.learninglogs.co.uk

Chapter 3

1. David Perkins (2009), op. cit.

2. See, for example, Diane Halpern (1998), 'Teaching critical thinking for transfer across domains', *American Psychologist,* 53, 449–455; Carol McGuinness (2006), 'Improving teaching and learning in schools', ESRC TLRP Bulletin.

Chapter 4

1. A preliminary overview of some of these factors was provided in Chapter 8 of Guy's 2008 book *What's the Point of School?* (see note 2 to Introduction). Chapter 5 here also draws on some of the same material.

2. Ellen Langer (1997), *The Power of Mindful Learning*, Addison-Wesley: Reading, Massachusetts.

3. These examples are adapted from Carol Dweck, *Mindset*, 177–8.

4. Neil Postman (1995), *The End of Education: Redefining the Value of School*, Alfred A Knopf: New York.

Chapter 5

1. John Hattie, op. cit.

2. Ron Ritchhart, Mark Church and Karin Morrison (2011), *Making Thinking Visible: How to Promote Engagement, Understanding and Independence for All Learners*, Jossey-Bass: San Francisco.

3. This study has been published. See Guy Claxton, Louise Edwards and Victoria Scale-Constantinou (2006), 'Cultivating creative mentalities: a framework for education', *Thinking Skills and Creativity*, 1(1), 57–61.

4. Raegan Delaney, Leanne Day and Maryl Chambers (2009), *Learning Power Heroes*, TLO: Bristol.

5. David Perkins (2009), op. cit.

6. Sarah Gornall, Maryl Chambers and Guy Claxton (2005), *Building Learning Power in Action*, TLO: Bristol.

7. Maryl Chambers, Graham Powell and Guy Claxton (2004), *Building 101 Ways to Learning Power*, TLO: Bristol.

Chapter 6

1. Independent Review of the Primary Curriculum: Final Report, April 2009, DCSF-00499-2009. Download from www.education.gov.uk/publications/standard/publicationdetail/page1/DCSF-00499-2009

2. Robin Alexander et al (2009), *Children, their World, their Education: Final Report and Recommendations of the Cambridge Primary Review*, Routledge: London

3. Michael Gove, Speech to the RSA, 30 June 2009. Download at http://www.thersa.org/__data/assets/pdf_file/0009/213021/Gove-speech-to-RSA.pdf

4. David Perkins (2009), op. cit.

5. Guy Claxton, Bill Lucas and Rob Webster (2010), *Bodies of Knowledge: How the learning sciences could transform practical and vocational education*, The Edge Foundation.

6. John Hattie, op. cit.

Chapter 7

1. BLP Activity Bank, Transition–KS2/3, TLO Limited: Bristol. Web-based resources.

2. *At a Glance* Series 2, TLO Limited: Bristol. Sets of five folded A3 cards, each encapsulating one BLP capacity, for teachers and classroom assistants..

3. BLP Activity Bank, Foundation/KS1, TLO Limited: Bristol. Web-based resources.

Chapter 8

1. Dr Dean Fink, 'How to grow a leader', *TES*, January, 2003

2. Michael Fullan (2001), *Leading in a Culture of Change*, Jossey-Bass: San Francisco.

3. NI Assembly Research and Library Service (2010), 'Qualities for effective school leadership: a briefing paper'

Chapter 9

1. M Eraut (1994), *Developing Professional Knowledge*, Falmer: London.

2. Marnie Thompson and Dylan Wiliam (2007), 'Tight but Loose: A conceptual framework for scaling up school reforms', presented at the annual meeting of the American Educational Research Association April 2007. Download at www. dylanwiliam.net

3. John Whitmore (2009), *Coaching for Performance*, 4th edition, Nicholas Brealey: London]

4. David L Cooperrider and Diana Whitney (2005), *Appreciative Inquiry: A Positive Revolution in Change*, Berrett-Koehler: San Francisco.

5. The '9 Thinks' model is a TLO lesson-planning tool for infusing learning power into everyday lessons.

Chapter 10

1. William Jeynes (2005) *Parent involvement and student achievement: a meta-analysis*, Harvard Family Research Project: Boston

2. Charles Desforges and Alberto Abouchar (2003) *The impact of parent involvement, parent support and family education on pupil achievements and adjustment: A literature review*, Department for Education and Skills (DfES): London.

3. Bill Lucas (2010), *The impact of parent engagement on learner success: A digest for teachers and parents*, Centre for Real-World Learning: Winchester.

4. Jen Lexmond and Richard Reeves (2009), *Building Character*, Demos: London.

Chapter 11

1. For a variety of reasons we were not able to collect this data for all the schools that were part of our original sample. Some of the primary schools, for example, did not enter their pupils for the SATs in 2010. We should emphasise that the research schools were selected in ignorance of their attainment data.

2. This in-built variation strengthens the case that change in pupil attainment is causally related to the introduction of BLP and not due to annual changes in other factors, or to more generic national trends.

3. Joan Whitehead, Amanda Edwards and Kim Diment (2005), *An Evaluation of Building Learning Power in the Bristol Education Action Zone*, Faculty of Education, University of the West of England: Bristol.

4. The Oxfordshire project was also generously funded by a grant from the Esmée Fairbairn Trust.

5. We are greatly indebted to Julie Fisher, Alison Price, Tony Eaude and Richard Howard in Oxfordshire, Ros Pollard, Bev Brown, Janet Clark and Hugh Knight in Cardiff, and Denise Bonnett and Greg Morris in Milton Keynes, as well as all the teachers, for their generous support and invaluable suggestions.

6. These appeared in four published reports entitled *Learning to Learn: Enquiries into Building Resourceful, Resilient and Reflective Learners*, 2001–2, 2002–3, 2003–4 and 2004–5. These reports are available from Cardiff Advisory Service for Education, County Hall, Atlantic Wharf, Cardiff CF10 4UW.

7. Julie Fisher, Guy Claxton and Alison Price (2006), *Playing for Life: The Oxfordshire / Guy Claxton Project*, National Primary Trust: Birmingham. Guy has written about one of these studies, with a two-year-old girl with severe hearing loss and autistic tendencies, in *What's the Point of School?*, 165–7.

Further reading...

Building Learning Power
by Guy Claxton

International research into how the mind works shows that we are all capable of becoming better learners. *Building Learning Power* applies this research directly to the work of teachers in classrooms, to provide a practical framework for fostering lifelong learning in all young people.

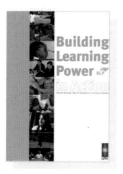

Building Learning Power in Action
by Sarah Gornall,
Maryl Chambers and Guy Claxton

Building Learning Power in Action shows how some schools have embraced BLP, and captures the exciting effects it is having in classrooms. It describes a range of real live examples where busy teachers have tried out some aspects of BLP, and been (to put it mildly) pleasantly surprised by the results.

You can find out more about these and other learning powered books, and buy them on-line, at:

www.buildinglearningpower.co.uk/books

www.tloltd.co.uk

TLO and BLP

Then ...

In 2001, TLO Limited started working closely with Professor Guy Claxton, as consultant and chief inspiration, on what was soon to become known as Building Learning Power™. Since then, we have worked with, and been further inspired by, many schools, teachers and young people, as we have sought to create a programme to translate Guy's ideas into successful, everyday practice.

.... and Now

For schools committed to expanding their students' powers as learners, we offer a growing range of publications, training and conferences to stimulate and extend practice in Building Learning Power.

You can find out much more from the websites:

www.buildinglearningpower.co.uk

www.learningqualityframework.co.uk

www.tloltd.co.uk

Or contact us to talk about how we could help you to help your students become better learners:

0117 937 8080

learningpower@tloltd.co.uk

TLO Limited, The Park Centre, Daventry Road, Bristol, BS4 1DQ